Business Filing and Records Control

FOURTH EDITION

ERNEST D. BASSETT

Analyst/Consultant, Records Systems
Santa Barbara, California

DAVID G. GOODMAN

Professor, Business Education
University of Wisconsin—Whitewater

Published by

K10   **SOUTH-WESTERN PUBLISHING CO.**

CINCINNATI   WEST CHICAGO, ILL.   DALLAS   PELHAM MANOR, N.Y.
PALO ALTO, CALIF.   BRIGHTON, ENGLAND

ISBN: 0-538-11100-3

Library of Congress Catalog Card Number: 73-80281

1 2 3 4 5 6 7 8 K 9 8 7 6 5 4

Printed in the United States of America

PREFACE

One of the more spectacular phenomena in the latter part of the 20th Century has been the attention given to the production and control of business records. This development was engendered by two elements—(1) the development of electronic means of producing certain types of records and (2) accelerated activity in the development of mechanical means for handling business records.

These factors have touched and changed many aspects of records control. For example, during the early period of electronic development, it was expected that all records would be produced and controlled by electronic means. It was also believed that the volume of records would decrease. However, as the electronics field progressed, it became evident that the volume of records was greatly increasing and that manual methods of records control were frequently needed in order to gain and to maintain command over certain types of electronically produced materials. Also, it developed that certain types of business papers would not be directly affected by electronic processes and would continue to require the application of manual methods.

The development of mechanical means for handling volumes of business records has greatly increased in the past decade and has included devices which assist in the moving of records from storage areas to working stations. These mechanical systems are valuable when they are used to speed the filing of very active papers, but such systems are not substitutes for the control to be gained by the manual processing of records before they are filed.

An analysis of the records management field indicates that it will be profitable for the student to understand all phases of filing and records control because job responsibilities frequently call for manual operations as well as for an *understanding* of mechanical and/or electronic processes.

The continuing importance of the area in filing and records control in which manual operations dominate is indicated by the recent introduction of new systems for alphabetic, numeric, and subject filing and by the production of new types of equipment for card and correspondence filing systems.

The Fourth Edition of BUSINESS FILING AND RECORDS CONTROL includes detailed descriptions of new filing systems and of new equipment. Every effort has been made to insure that students will become skillful in the fundamentals of records control and filing and knowledgeable in the mechanized and electronic phases of the art.

The new edition consists of 15 chapters organized into four parts. Part 1, "Filing and Finding Business Records," presents an overview of the scope of filing, the opportunities in the field, and gives the fundamentals of indexing for alphabetic card and correspondence filing purposes. Part 2, "Alphabetic Correspondence Filing," portrays the processes and procedures used in alphabetic correspondence systems; describes the procedures used in requisitioning and charging for file materials; presents the important matter of transferring papers from active files to storage areas; and, finally, presents four widely used commercial systems for alphabetic correspondence filing.

Part 3, "Other Filing Systems and Procedures," is designed to prepare students to understand and to work successfully with several types of filing systems: geographic, numeric, and subject. Each of these types of filing systems is illustrated, defined, and explained in detail.

In Part 4, "Records Management," four important chapters are presented. In Chapter 12, card records and systems are illustrated and described in their many forms. In Chapter 13, equipment and systems in records control are illustrated and described. In Chapter 14, the importance of data processing and microfilming is presented as these are applied to business records. In this chapter, equipment is shown and described; data processing and microfilming are described in relation to the production and control of business records. Examples are given of the way microfilming is used by various types of business organizations, and the advisability of using microfilming under various circumstances is considered. Finally, Chapter 15 presents ways and means of maintaining and improving filing systems. In this chapter, the use of procedural manuals is explained; standards for practice are recommended; a list of 14 concise indexing rules is given.

Accompanying BUSINESS FILING AND RECORDS CONTROL, Fourth Edition, are supporting materials titled FILING OFFICE PROCEDURES. These simulated filing systems consist of nine realistic jobs: Jobs 1-4, "Alphabetic Card Filing"; Job 5, "Alphabetic Correspondence Filing"; Job 6, "Requisition and Charge Procedures"; Job 7, "Geographic Correspondence Filing"; Job 8, "Numeric Correspondence Filing"; Job 9, "Subject Correspondence Filing."

The authors acknowledge with genuine appreciation the suggestions of the many teachers who have used the previous editions; the contributions and suggestions of many practicing records administrators; and especially the contributions of the late Dr. Peter L. Agnew whose coauthorship of the first three editions formed such a firm foundation for this publication.

Ernest D. Bassett/David G. Goodman

CONTENTS

PART 1   FILING AND FINDING BUSINESS RECORDS

Chapter   1 Nature and Scope of Alphabetic Filing **1**
Chapter   2 Alphabetic Indexing of Personal Names **9**
                Job 1, Card Filing—Names of Individuals **20**
Chapter   3 Alphabetic Indexing of Business and Geographic Names . . . **21**
                Job 2, Card Filing—Business Names **32**
Chapter   4 Alphabetic Indexing of Names of Organizations, Government
                Agencies, and Subjects **33**
                Job 3, Card Filing—Business and Institutional Names . . **46**
                Job 4, Card Filing—Indexing and Filing Review . . . **46**

PART 2   ALPHABETIC CORRESPONDENCE FILING

Chapter   5 Alphabetic Systems and Filing Procedures **47**
                Job 5, Alphabetic Correspondence Filing **69**
Chapter   6 Requisition, Charge, and Follow-up Controls **70**
                Job 6, Requisition and Charge Procedures **83**
Chapter   7 Transfer and Storage Controls **84**
Chapter   8 Types of Alphabetic Filing Systems **98**

PART 3   OTHER FILING SYSTEMS AND PROCEDURES

Chapter   9 Geographic Systems and Procedures **111**
                Job 7, Geographic Correspondence Filing **125**
Chapter 10 Numeric Systems and Procedures **126**
                Job 8, Numeric Correspondence Filing **139**
Chapter 11 Subject Systems and Procedures **140**
                Job 9, Subject Correspondence Filing **158**

PART 4   RECORDS MANAGEMENT

Chapter 12 Card Records and Systems **159**
Chapter 13 Equipment and Systems in Records Control **178**
Chapter 14 Data Processing and Microfilming **196**
Chapter 15 Maintaining and Improving Records Control Systems . . . **216**

                Index **231**

CHAPTER 1

NATURE AND SCOPE OF ALPHABETIC FILING

SECTION 1   FILING IN THE BUSINESS OFFICE

Why Study Filing

In offices throughout the country, information is needed to aid in keeping the business operating. "How much does George Andrews owe us now?" "What did Johnson Hardware say they would do about any paint we have to return to them? Our letters were written last year." "Do you have the proof of your fire loss last month? We need this for the income tax return." These questions and many others like them are asked countless times every day in business offices. The necessary records to answer these questions are examples of the records that offices place in their files for safekeeping.

Each year more records are created and handled. Increased numbers of workers are being employed in records control. In fact, studies have revealed that filing and records control ranks in the top ten of all office activities with over ninety percent of all clerical workers doing some filing work. Your knowing how to file and how to control records of one sort or another may be a key factor in your obtaining a job or keeping and advancing in a job you already have.

We store or file many records at home too—birth certificates, canceled checks, receipted bills, notices of dividend payments, acknowledgments of contributions, and many other items that we need to keep for future reference.

Considering all the attention that has been given to the preservation and control of records, we might wonder why so much concern with these matters is necessary. The reason lies in the fact that records of many kinds are invaluable to individuals and businesses. Some records are irreplaceable; others can be replaced only at great cost. These records must be preserved and controlled in such a way that they can be found when they are needed. The systems and procedures of filing are designed to perform this function for individuals as well as for business.

1

Filing is the process of arranging and storing materials safely and systematically so that they can be located easily and quickly when they are needed. Because a filing system provides a safe place for all materials related to the business affairs of a firm or an individual, the files are, in a sense, the "memory" of that firm or individual.

The main purposes of the various systems of filing are as follows:

1. To make records readily available when they are needed, whether for reference or evidence.
2. To keep all related materials together so that the history of the dealings with one firm or one individual will be available in one place. The materials may also be grouped so that those pertaining to one subject or geographical area are together.
3. To provide a permanent and safe place for business and personal records during the time they are not in use.

Filing Is Performed by Many

Filing is performed by many types of office workers. It is unusual if an office worker does not have occasion to do some filing work. Indeed, many supervisors, managers, and executives perform some filing activities themselves. Professional people, such as doctors, lawyers, teachers, and accountants, very frequently do a great deal of filing in addition to their regular activities.

In small organizations, secretaries and stenographers usually do the filing. As the business grows larger, clerks and typists supplement the staff of secretaries and stenographers; and any or all of these office workers will probably do some filing.

Large concerns frequently have a central filing department in which special *files operators*, sometimes called *records control clerks*, are employed under the direction of a *files supervisor* or *director*. Even in large firms where a special filing department is organized, a considerable amount of filing is done in departmental files by secretaries, stenographers, typists, and clerks. In an analysis of the duties of all office workers, filing was reported as one of the most frequently performed activities.

Qualifications for the Filing Job

Whether employed full time as a files operator or having some filing responsibility as only one part of an office position, the person performing this task must have certain capacities: He or she must know the rules for alphabetic indexing, alphabetic sequences, and common abbreviations. In addition, he or she must be able to read quickly and with good understanding.

A files operator must have all the personal qualifications of other office workers. The paramount qualification is a high loyalty to the firm because the files operator has in his possession the confidential records of the company—records that must be kept absolutely secret and secure.

In addition, a files operator should be accurate and should have a liking for detail. He or she should have manual dexterity, good eyesight, and a good memory.

While many office workers engage in filing considerably more than others, some of them find they especially like the work and undertake to study it in depth and make a career of it.

The Files Supervisor

The filing department is a service department. The supervisor of the filing department must be familiar with all systems, equipment, and routines. He or she must keep up to date on all new developments in the field of records management and control. The supervisor must train files operators and develop in them the prime requisites of accuracy, neatness, and orderliness. He or she must impart enthusiasm and interest in this important function of a company's work. There are great opportunities in this field, and it is well for the student of filing to recognize the importance of the work and the opportunities it provides. The alert files operator can look forward to promotions to records clerk, to supervisor, to manager, to executive in the records administration field.

Scope of Filing

The scope of filing is as broad as are the written records of modern business. Every written record that is of value should be filed. On the other hand, records that are no longer of value should be destroyed. The decision as to what should be filed and what should be destroyed requires a clear understanding of the business and its many phases. This aspect of filing will be covered in Chapter 7. Among the many types of records that are commonly filed in business are the following:

1. All types of correspondence related to business matters—incoming letters, interoffice communications, telegrams, cablegrams, and copies of outgoing communications.

2. Checks, statements, inventory lists, price lists, and statistical and accounting records.

3. Sales invoices, purchase orders, purchase requisitions, freight bills, bills of lading, and shipping receipts.

4. Legal documents, which are invaluable records of certain business agreements and transactions.

5. Blueprints and maps.
6. Catalogs and trade magazines, which must be held in readiness for immediate use.
7. Newspaper and magazine clippings.
8. Stock records, sales records, personnel records, library lists, and mailing lists.
9. Minutes of meetings, committee reports, and reports of the progress of the various business activities that may be of immediate value or definite historical value to the operation of the business.
10. Computer tapes, punched cards, magnetic discs, microfilmed records of all types, and computer print-outs.

SECTION 2   ALPHABETIC CARD FILING

Alphabetic card filing is a basic filing method that has many uses not only in business but also in personal filing situations. Since it is one of the simplest filing systems, a thorough understanding of this method makes the development of more complex systems easier. An alphabetic card file consists of a file tray or box or cabinet in which are kept, in alphabetic order, cards containing such information as the names and addresses of persons, businesses, and organizations.

Uses of Alphabetic Card Filing

An alphabetic card file has many uses. A few of the people who use card files, and some of the types of information they keep, are:

1. Secretaries: The names, addresses, and occupations of all frequent office callers. One card may contain the name of the caller, the name of the company he represents, the time he usually calls, and the length of time he spends in the office.
2. Office supervisors: The names of potential employees and their addresses, telephone numbers, and special abilities.
3. Stenographers: The names and addresses of frequent correspondents.
4. Typists: The names and addresses of persons who receive copies of company reports.

Illus. 1-1, **Card File**

A card file may be based on an alphabetic, geographic, numeric, or subject system. Card files ordinarily are used to store current records, but they may be used also to store seldom-used or less up-to-date records.

Ohio National Life Insurance Company

5. Club secretaries and treasurers: The name, address, and dues-payment status of each member of the organization.

6. Housewives: The names and addresses on a holiday card list; dates of birthdays, weddings, anniversaries; and recipes.

7. Salesmen: The names and addresses of potential prospects for the products they sell.

8. Supply clerks: The names and addresses of suppliers of various office items; the names and addresses of machine repairmen and other service suppliers.

Alphabetic Card Filing System

The cards in a card file are usually 5 inches wide by 3 inches high (5″ x 3″); other standard sizes are 6″ x 4″ and 8″ x 5″. These cards are usually white, but they may be of different colors in order to help find the right one rapidly. The cards may or may not be ruled. (See Illustration 1-2.) When the cards are ruled, the horizontal line provides for the same placement of the handwritten name on the card. When the cards are not ruled, the typist begins to type on the third line from the top of the card. The left margin is 3 or 4 spaces wide. This arrangement makes it easier to file as well as to find the desired card.

Guides. *Guides* are special cards or partitions that divide the file drawer into convenient alphabetic sections. The guides are usually made of material heavier than that of the cards so that they will help support the cards and also withstand the long use given them.

Tabs. A *tab* is a projection at the top of a guide. The tabs enable a person to see the guides above the other materials in the file. The tabs may be made of the same material as the guides, may be made of plastic, or may be made of metal with a plastic "window" through which information on the tabs can be read. Some tabs are bent slightly backward so that they can be read easily when the files operator is looking down on the drawer.

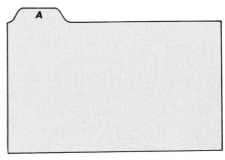

Abeling, John (Jr.)

Mr. John Abeling, Jr.
49 Broad Street
Newark, NJ 07134

A

Illus. 1-2, **File Card**   Illus. 1-3, **Card Guide**

Captions. *Captions* are titles or alphabetic divisions of the file that are written, typed, or printed on the tabs of card guides.

Illustration 1-4 shows not only a card guide with its tab and the tab caption, "A 1," but also the tabs on two other card guides farther back in the file drawer. In this illustration the tabs are cut one third the width of the guides with each tab the same size. Tabs of this width are called *one-third-cut tabs.* They vary in position at the top of the guides so that they are staggered across the file drawer from left to right. In this way three different positions are provided. This staggering of position enables the files operator to read the captions more easily. It is possible to obtain guides with tabs cut in different sizes. The most common, in addition to one-third-cut, are *one-fifth-cut* (five tab positions), *one-half cut* (two tab positions, each one half the width of the guide), or *full-cut* (each tab covering the entire width of the guide).

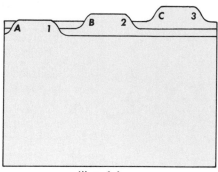

Illus. 1-4

One-Third-Cut Card Guides

Numbers are sometimes included in the captions to indicate the order for placing guides in the file drawer.

Organization. Cards are placed in a file tray or box or drawer so that the names are arranged in alphabetic order from front to back. Illustration 1-5 shows a drawer from a card file cabinet. In studying the illustration, notice the use of the guides with one-third-cut tabs on which names are printed as captions; and one-fifth-cut tabs on which letters of the alphabet are printed as captions. The guides (*Alf* to *Ap*) that appear in a row at the left are called *primary guides* and indicate the principal sections into which the drawer is divided. The guides (*Allen, Anderson,* and *Andrews*) that appear in a row at the center are called *auxiliary* or *secondary guides*; they divide the principal sections into subsections according to frequently used surnames. The guides appearing in a row at the right are *special auxiliary guides* that divide a single surname section into subsections according to the initial letters of the first names.

The cards are placed behind the appropriate identifying guides. The captions on two consecutive guides indicate the alphabetic range

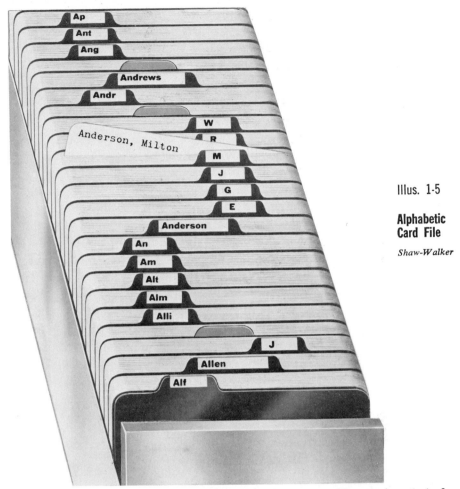

Illus. 1-5

**Alphabetic
Card File**

Shaw-Walker

of the names to be filed between the two guides. In Illustration 1-4, for example, the first guide is captioned *Alf*, and the second, *Allen*. Thus, cards bearing names from "Alf" to "Allen" would be filed between the first and second guides in this file drawer. A card bearing the name "American" would be found between the guides labeled *Am* and *An*.

For guides to be effective in an active file, one guide should be provided for about every twenty cards. For a less active file, one guide should be provided for about every half inch or inch of cards.

**Elements
of Filing
Control**

Filing control involves a series of related activities. These activities at first glance may not seem related, but they are all a part of a single large operation, or system, that involves the keeping of all records under control at all times. The cycle consists of the following work areas:

1. A filing system is formed by assembling a series of guides, folders, and containers.
2. Materials are received (or prepared), marked, sorted, and placed into the equipment according to a definite plan.
3. Materials are borrowed from the files, used, and then returned to the files under carefully developed procedures.
4. Materials or blocks of materials are removed from the active files and either destroyed or sent to storage files according to a systematic plan.

In order to work efficiently and effectively in records control, you must know the routines and procedures involved in each of the four work areas. You must understand something about the equipment and supplies needed; the procedures followed in processing papers for filing; the practices used in lending and charging for borrowed file materials; and, finally, the equipment and procedures followed in transferring material from active to destruction or storage files. This chapter and the next six chapters present these four parts of records control.

Need for Filing Rules

If cards in an alphabetic card file, or correspondence or other materials in other types of alphabetic files, are to be filed quickly and found easily, definite rules must be followed by the files operator in determining the order in which the materials are to be filed. These rules are known as *rules for alphabetic indexing.* Everyone who uses a file must be so familiar with these rules that he can apply them in any filing situation. Chapters 2-4 present these rules.

QUESTIONS FOR DISCUSSION

1. What is filing and what purposes does it serve?
2. Who does most of the filing (a) in small offices? (b) in medium-size offices? (c) in large offices?
3. What special capacities and personal qualifications are needed by a files operator?
4. What promotions are possible for the effective files operator?
5. What responsibilities does a files supervisor have?
6. What types of records and information are commonly filed?
7. What is an alphabetic card file?
8. What are some of the items kept in an alphabetic card file by (a) a secretary? (b) an office supervisor? (c) a stenographer? (d) a typist? (e) a club secretary? (f) a housewife? (g) a salesman? (h) a supply clerk?
9. What is a guide? a tab? a caption?
10. What is meant by a one-fifth-cut tab?
11. What are the most common cuts for tabs?
12. How close together should guides be placed in an alphabetic card file?
13. Why are filing rules necessary?

CHAPTER 2

ALPHABETIC INDEXING OF PERSONAL NAMES

Need for Systematic Procedures and Rules

Over the years, experience in the controlling of records has proved beyond a shadow of doubt that the only way to file papers is in a systematic manner. To do otherwise is folly since the whole purpose of filing is to be able to establish control over records so that papers can be found when they are needed—not an hour later—not a day later—but when requested.

In order to have the required control over records, the persons performing filing operations must be trained and required to follow certain established procedures and rules. If these are not followed, the chances of successful filing and, perhaps, the chances of improving or even keeping a job are placed in jeopardy.

Indexing Rules

The rules which must be followed if success in filing and finding records is to result are known as *indexing rules*. They can be generally explained in this manner: to "index" is to point out. Your "index" finger is aptly named since it is the one which "points out." In much the same manner, you will learn to file by using indexing rules so that each name under which something is to be filed will be "pointed out," because you have applied a rule to it. Thus, each indexed name will have a special place in the file that will make it distinct from all other names in the same filing system. So, when a record is requested from the file, you will be able to find it without undue delay.

Chapters 2, 3, and 4 present information about indexing rules that govern the filing of three general classes or types of names: (1) personal names, (2) business and geographic names, and (3) names of organizations, government agencies, and subjects.

Indexing rules are presented separately for each class of name because it is believed that to do so makes learning an easier process than it would be if a single set of rules were given for all classes of names.

**Indexing
Names for
Filing
Purposes**

The process of indexing is made up of two steps: (1) dividing names into units and (2) alphabetizing names. Since a name must be divided into units before it can be placed in alphabetic order, this procedure will be considered first in the explanation of indexing practice.

Dividing Names into Units. Two steps must be taken before a name can be placed in alphabetic order in relation to other names. First, the files operator must notice how many units a name contains and, second, he must determine which of the several units is the most important one to be used for filing purposes. This unit is the *key unit.*

An example of this process is as follows: If the name "Don Linsey" is to be indexed for filing, the operator would first notice that the name has two units—"Don" and "Linsey." Next, it must be determined which of these two units is the key unit—the one under which this name will be filed first. In this case, the key unit is the surname, "Linsey"; and the operator would mark it or rewrite it to point it out as the key unit.

If the name is to be rewritten on an index card, for example, the name will be written in this order—Linsey, Don; and the card upon which this name appears would be filed in the "L" section of the card filing system being used. If the name appears in a letter, on a printed or typed page, or as a signature, the name is not rewritten but is *coded*, that is, marked, to show the key unit and the second unit, thus:

2
Don/Linsey

This code marking indicates that the name is to be filed under the key unit, "Linsey," and that the given name, "Don," is to be used secondarily if it is needed in order to place the name in alphabetic order in relation to other names on cards or papers in the file.

Alphabetizing. If you wish to file alphabetically the two names "John Adams" and "James Bell," your procedure would be as follows: (1) Notice that "John Adams" is a two-unit name and determine that "Adams" is the key unit; (2) notice that "James Bell" is a two-unit name and determine that "Bell" is the key unit; (3) compare the key units in the two names; and (4) file the name "James Bell" after the name "John Adams" because "A" comes before "B" in the alphabet. The following tabulation illustrates the indexing of the two names.

Names	Index Order of Units	
	Key Unit	Unit 2
John Adams	Adams	John
James Bell	Bell	James

How to Study Indexing Rules

The manner in which you study the indexing rules in Chapters 2, 3, and 4 is very important. First, read a rule twice to be sure that you understand it; second, study all the names in the list below the rule; finally, restudy the names in the list, comparing each name with the names above and below it. In this way, you will discover the reason for the order of the names, that is, the units or the letters that determine the alphabetic order. This last step is very important because the comparison of the names in the list shows how the rules are applied even when names vary from a standard pattern. *This is important to know because names are sometimes so complex and varied that scores of rules could not cover every possible way of indexing all types of names.* Therefore, example names are sometimes presented in a manner designed to show many ways of applying a single rule.

RULE 1 Order of Indexing Units

Each part of the name of an individual is considered to be a separate indexing unit. The units are considered to be important in the following order: (1) the surname, that is, the last name, (2) the given name or initial, (3) the middle name or initial.

Names	Index Order of Units		
	Key Unit	Unit 2	Unit 3
Henry Wills	Wills	Henry	
Carl Wilson	Wilson	Carl	
Charles Wilson	Wilson	Charles	
Charles Stephen Wilson	Wilson	Charles	Stephen
Alton Wilton	Wilton	Alton	
Alton B. Wilton	Wilton	Alton	B.

Note: In each example in the list given above, the letter of the unit that determines the alphabetic sequence is underlined.

RULE 2 Initials and Abbreviations

Initials are treated as separate indexing units; commonly known abbreviations are indexed as though they were written in full; nicknames or brief forms of given names are indexed as written.

An example of a name with a commonly known abbreviation and an initial is Wm. L. Joyce. This name is coded as follows:

$$\underset{\text{William/L.}}{2} \underset{\text{/Joyce}}{3}$$

Examples of nicknames and of brief given names are Don; Viki; Ron; Pam; Dick; Billy. The name Clif R. Huycheck is coded as follows:

$$\overset{2}{\text{Clif}}/\overset{3}{\text{R.}}/\underline{\text{Huycheck}}$$

Note: *Coding* (marking of the units in a name) consists of (1) separating the units by diagonal lines; (2) underlining the key unit; and (3) writing above the remaining units numbers to indicate their rank in the filing order.

Names	Index Order of Units		
	Key Unit	**Unit 2**	**Unit 3**
Wm. R. Aames	Aames	William	R.
Wilmot T. Aames	Aames	Wilmot	T.
Jan Ames	Ames	Jan	
Janette Ames	Ames	Janette	
Janice Ames	Ames	Janice	
C. Richard Benton	Benton	C.	Richard
Chas. R. Benton	Benton	Charles	R.
Charlotte Benton	Benton	Charlotte	
T. Carlson	Carlson	T.	
Thos. L. Carlson	Carlson	Thomas	L.
Thor C. Carlson	Carlson	Thor	C.
Tom B. Carlson	Carlson	Tom	B.

RULE 3   Particles and Articles

A foreign particle (sometimes called a *prefix*) or a foreign article in a personal name is combined with the part of the name following it to form a single indexing unit.

Note: Examples of particles and articles are D', Da, De, Del, De la, Della, Den, Des, Di, Du, Fritz, L', La, Le, Les, Lo, Mac, Mc, O', Te, Ten, Ter, Van, Van de, Van der, Von, Von der.

Names	Index Order of Units		
	Key Unit	**Unit 2**	**Unit 3**
M. Richard Dacosa	Dacosa	M.	Richard
Chas. Da Costa	Da Costa	Charles	
Jon DaCosta	DaCosta	Jon	
Rona De la Rosa	De la Rosa	Rona	
Rose Della Rosa	Della Rosa	Rose	
Louis Lasada	Lasada	Louis	
LaVerne Lassalle	Lassalle	LaVerne	
Edward La Verne	La Verne	Edward	
Wm. Royal Mack	Mack	William	Royal
Louise Mac Kay	Mac Kay	Louise	
Florence McNeil	McNeil	Florence	
LeRoy N. Smith	Smith	LeRoy	N.
Derk Ter Bush	Ter Bush	Derk	
Hal L. Van Zant	Van Zant	Hal	L.

RULE 4   Titles and Degrees

A personal or professional title (such as *Mr., Mrs., Ms., Miss, Dr., Father, Mayor, Professor, Rabbi, Reverend, Senator*) or a degree (such as *D.D., Ph.D., D.V.M., M.D.*) is usually not considered in determining alphabetic order. A name consisting of a title followed by *only one name* is indexed in the order in which it is written.

Note: A title or degree not considered in indexing is written in parentheses at the end of the name for identification purposes.

Names	Index Order of Units		
	Key Unit	**Unit 2**	**Unit 3**
Brother John	Brother	John	
Brother Harold R. Fleming	Fleming	Harold	R. (Brother)
Miss Dale Macario	Macario	Dale (Miss)	
Joseph McKinney, M.D.	McKinney	Joseph (M.D.)	
Allen W. Murdock, D.D.	Murdock	Allen	W. (D.D.)
Rev. Walter John Murphy	Murphy	Walter	John (Rev.)
Sister Claire	Sister	Claire	
Sister Regina Smith	Smith	Regina (Sister)	
Senator Clinton K. Somes	Somes	Clinton	K. (Senator)
Professor Arnold Storr	Storr	Arnold (Professor)	
General Philip O. Storrer	Storrer	Philip	O. (General)
Mrs. Edna C. Storrs	Storrs	Edna	C. (Mrs.)
Judge H. R. Story	Story	H.	R. (Judge)

RULE 5   Seniority Titles in Identical Names

Seniority titles used to identify what would otherwise be identical names are not considered to be indexing units but as identifying elements in determining filing order. The seniority titles are considered before addresses or other means are consulted. The titles "Junior" (Jr.) and "Senior" (Sr.) are used in alphabetic sequence. The titles "I," "II," "III," and "IV" are used in numeric sequence.

Names	Index Order of Units			
	Key Unit	**Unit 2**	**Unit 3**	**Identifying Element**
Walter McDougal, Jr.	McDougal	Walter		(Junior)
Walter McDougal, Sr.	McDougal	Walter		(Senior)
Walter L. McDougal	McDougal	Walter	L.	
Donald Morris	Morris	Donald		
Donald Morris, II	Morris	Donald		(II)
Donald Morris, III	Morris	Donald		(III)
Donald Morris, IV	Morris	Donald		(IV)
Donald C. Morris	Morris	Donald	C.	
Donald W. Morris	Morris	Donald	W.	

RULE 6 Identical Names

When the full names of two or more individuals are identical (including seniority designations), addresses are used to determine filing order. Addresses are not considered as indexing units but as secondary means of determining filing order. Filing order is determined by using as many parts of an address as needed.

> **Note:** Usually, the order in which the parts of an address are considered is as follows: (1) city names, (2) state or province names when city names are identical, (3) street names, (4) house or building numbers.

Names	Index Order of Units			
	Key Unit	Unit 2	Unit 3	Address
(City Names Used to Determine Indexing Order)				
Helen Nelson 412 Argus Street Bangor, Maine	Nelson	Helen		Bangor
Helen Nelson 249 West Street Dallas, Texas	Nelson	Helen		<u>Dallas</u>
Helen D. Nelson	Nelson	Helen	<u>D</u>.	
(State or Province Names Used to Determine Indexing Order)				
Robt. Pryor 96 Empire Street Vancouver, B.C.	<u>Pryor</u>	Robert		British Columbia
Robert Pryor 465 A Street Vancouver, Washington	Pryor	Robert		<u>Washington</u>
(Street Names and House Numbers Used to Determine Filing Order)				
Jack Rowe 246 - 12 Street Toledo, Ohio	<u>Rowe</u>	Jack		246 - Twelfth Street
Reverend Jack Rowe 121 Twelve Oaks St. Toledo, Ohio	Rowe	Jack (Rev.)		121 Twel<u>ve</u> Oaks St.
Dr. Jack Rowe 409 - 23 Street Toledo, Ohio	Rowe	Jack (Dr.)		409 Twe<u>nt</u>y-Third St.
Jack Rowe 512 - 23 Street Toledo, Ohio	Rowe	Jack		<u>512</u> Twenty-Third St.
Jack A. Rowe 1016 C Street Toledo, Ohio	Rowe	Jack	<u>A</u>.	1016 C Street
Jack A. Rowe 2620 D Street Toledo, Ohio	Rowe	Jack	A.	2620 <u>D</u> Street

> **Note:** Numbered street names are considered in spelled-out **form**; house numbers are listed in ascending order.

RULE 7   Compound and Hyphenated Names

The separate parts of a compound name or of a hyphenated name are treated as separate indexing units. Hyphens are disregarded in indexing such names.

Note: Examples of compound and hyphenated names are Alice Bentley-Adams (3 units), Galen Lim-Lee (3 units), M. R. St. John (4 units), and Frank A. San Marco (4 units).

Names	Index Order of Units			
	Key Unit	**Unit 2**	**Unit 3**	**Unit 4**
Wm. B. Saddler-Wilson	Saddler-	Wilson	William	B.
Jim Sae-Kow	Sae-	Kow	Jim	
Dean E. Saeger	Saeger	Dean	E.	
Martin L. SaFranek	SaFranek	Martin	L.	
Mia Saint-Armand	Saint-	Armand	Mia	
William R. St. Charles	Saint	Charles	William	R.
Mme. Jean Ste.-Marie	Sainte-	Marie	Jean (Mme.)	
James John San Martin	San	Martin	James	John
Alvino Santa-Maria	Santa-	Maria	Alvino	
Jeanne-Marie Towns	Towns	Jeanne-	Marie	
Jo-Ann Young	Young	Jo-	Ann	
Joann Young	Young	Joann		
John K. Young-Wood	Young-	Wood	John	K.

Note: Foreign equivalents of the English word "Saint" are Sainte, San, Santa, Santo, and São. They follow the rule governing the English word "Saint."

RULE 8   Names of Married Women

A married woman's legal name, *when known*, is used for filing purposes. The legal name is either her first name and her maiden surname with her husband's surname, or her first and middle names with her husband's surname. The title "Mrs." is not used as an indexing unit, but it may be written in parentheses after a name to help identify it.

Names	Index Order of Units		
	Key Unit	**Unit 2**	**Unit 3**
Mrs. Andrew C. Hill (Mary Jones)	Hill (Mrs. Andrew C. Hill)	Mary	Jones (Mrs.)
Mrs. John A. Kramer (Anne Helen)	Kramer (Mrs. John A. Kramer)	Anne	Helen (Mrs.)
Mrs. Ceil A. Long	Long	Ceil	A. (Mrs.)
Mrs. Ella R. Mays	Mays	Ella	R. (Mrs.)

Note: Names of married women may be cross-referenced if necessary so that they will show in two places in a filing system. Cross-referencing procedure is explained in this chapter on pages 17 and 18.

RULE 9   Unusual Names

When it is difficult to decide which unit of a person's name is the surname, the last unit of the name as it appears in written form should be considered to be the surname.

Names	Key Unit	Unit 2	Unit 3	Unit 4
		Index Order of Units		
Frank Albert	Albert	Frank		
Dror Ben-Nun	Ben-	Nun	Dror	
Shunji Miyake	Miyake	Shunji		
Jean-Paul Ste. Marie	Sainte	Marie	Jean-	Paul
Tufo Sychoff	Sychoff	Tufo		
Benjamin Thomas	Thomas	Benjamin		
Song-Kuk Yi	Yi	Song-	Kuk	

Note: Unusual names may be cross-referenced if necessary so that both surnames and given names are shown in the filing system. Cross-referencing is explained on pages 17 and 18 of this chapter.

Typing Index Cards

The rules you have just studied have been illustrated by lists of names; but, in actual filing, such names usually are typed on index cards or on folder labels. Since your first filing job will involve the use of index cards, the following explanation and illustration will show how index cards are prepared and arranged.

As shown in Illustration 2-1, an index card includes (1) the name typed or written in indexed form on the second or third line from the top edge of the card and 3 or 4 spaces from the left edge and (2) the name and address typed or written 3 or 4 lines below the name. Carefully read each card in Illustration 2-1; observe how names and titles are typed and how they are spaced on cards.

Either all capital letters or capital and lowercase letters may be used for the name. Some filing supervisors prefer to have the first indexing unit typed in all capital letters and the other indexing units typed in capital and lowercase letters.

If the name contains a title, such as "Doctor," that is to be disregarded in filing, type the title in parentheses after the last indexing unit on the card. If the name includes another element, such as a seniority designation or the name of a city, type it in parentheses at the end of the name.

If the file card is to be filed according to a numeric system, the name is given a code number according to the rules of one of the numeric systems. The code number is then typed in the upper right-hand corner of the file card.

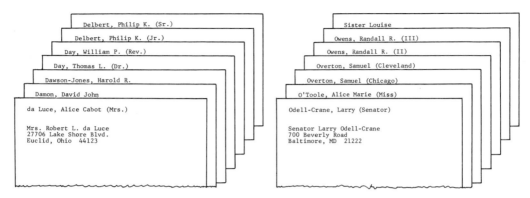

Illus. 2-1, **File Cards Typed in Index Form**

Cross-Referencing

When names are properly indexed and arranged aphabetically in a card file, there is usually little difficulty in locating a card bearing a particular name. In some cases, however, difficulties are encountered because (1) the unit in the name that was given second position for filing purposes is not known to the person looking for the card, as sometimes happens in the case of the name of a married woman, or (2) the name that is thought of by the person looking for the card is not the name under which the card is filed, even though the two names may be related—for example, *Fortune,* published by Time, Inc.

Such difficulties are overcome in filing practice in one of two ways:

1. The index form of a name is used as the basis for filing the original card; another form or arrangement of the name is used as the basis for the preparation of a second card, known as a *cross-reference card.* (Examples of this method of cross-referencing are given on page 18.)
2. The index form of the most important name in a given situation is used as the basis for filing the original card; the index forms of other names that are of secondary importance but that are associated with the original name are used on cross-reference cards. (An example of this method of cross-referencing is given in Chapter 4, page 42, under the heading "Periodicals.")

Cross-Referencing Names of Married Women. The legal name of a married woman is written in index form on the original card in a card file. Her husband's name, followed by the title "Mrs.," is used on a cross-reference card so that both names will be on file for reference purposes. For example, if the legal name of Mrs. Joseph L. Adams is Mrs. Mary Burr Adams, the original card and the cross-reference card for her name would be written as shown on page 18.

```
┌─────────────────────────────┐   ┌─────────────────────────────┐
│ Adams, Mary Burr (Mrs.)     │   │ Adams, Joseph L. (Mrs.)     │
│                             │   │                             │
│ Mrs. Joseph L. Adams        │   │ See Adams, Mary Burr (Mrs.) │
│ 1369 Forest Avenue          │   │                             │
│ Denver, CO  80206           │   │                             │
│                             │   │                             │
│                             │   │                             │
│                             │   │                             │
│                             │   │                             │
│                             │   │                             │
└─────────────────────────────┘   └─────────────────────────────┘
```

Illus. 2-2

Original Card   **Cross-Reference Card**

Cross-Referencing Unusual Names. Even though the last part of an unusual name of an individual is considered to be the surname, it is wise to prepare a cross-reference card for the name to show the name in the way in which it is written. This procedure insures that if the name is referred to by either of the two units, the card can be readily found. For example, if the name on the original card is shown in index form as *Lee, Wong*, the cross-reference card for the name would be written as follows:

```
Wong Lee
See Lee, Wong
```

QUESTIONS FOR DISCUSSION

1. Why must filing be a systematic process?
2. What does the term "indexing" mean?
3. How does the indexing of names help filing and finding?
4. What are the two steps in the indexing process?
5. Give an example of a name that has been divided into units.
6. If names are not rewritten in transposed form, how are the units in these names marked (coded) for filing purposes?
7. How is alphabetic order determined between two names?
8. What is the *key* unit in each of the following names?

   a. C. R. Bertone   **f.** Lin Toy Wah
   b. Jan Da Costa   **g.** Sasha Oliver
   c. Dr. C. James Hachiya   **h.** Sean O'Hare
   d. Sister Celia   **i.** W. Earl Noren, II
   e. Don Carter-Jones   **j.** William McWilliams, Jr.

9. What is the *second* indexing unit in each of the following names?

   a. Dan M. St. Martin   **f.** Arnold Den Besten
   b. R. Norman Sokol   **g.** Mrs. C. J. (Pam Cross) Jones
   c. D. F. Wiler, Jr.   **h.** A. Albert FitzGerald
   d. Reverend Stephens Johnson   **i.** Rene Dell'Aqua
   e. Viki Sue Van Del   **j.** Rabbi Philip Weinstein

10. Is the order of the two names in each of the following pairs **correct or** is the order incorrect?

a. Anne Greger
Larry Greer

b. Hans Gronowski
Al Gronfeldt

c. W. M. Haight
Allen R. Hiafing

d. B. R. Santa-Maria
Sister Evelyn

e. Pete Carr, IV
Pete Carr, III

f. Ron Le Vieux
Fred Leview

g. Tom Ten Eyck
Tim Te Roller

h. Harold Jung, Jr.
Harold Jung, Sr.

i. Rose Dela Santa
Robert Della Santa

j. Tom S. Sarto
Thomas S. Sarto

k. Miles Harvey
Harvey Miles

l. Morton Jones
Morton A. Jones

m. Dick Slone
Richard Sloan

n. M. Miles La Shelle
Mrs. Mildred Lashino

o. J. L. Dalton
J. L. Dalton, II

p. D. K. Damato
Dan D'Amato

q. Hal Downes, Sr.
Harold Downes, Jr.

r. Perkins Wan
Wan Kwan

s. Xenophone Kourkoutakis
Denis Kourkoumelis

t. Danny Mac Intosh
Angus McIntosh

FILING PROBLEMS

1. A. Type or write each of the following names in transposed indexing order on a 5″ by 3″ index card or on a slip of paper cut to that size. Place in the upper right-hand corner of the card the letter that identifies the name.

B. When you have typed all the cards, arrange them in alphabetic order.

C. Prepare an answer sheet similar to the one illustrated at the right; type or write the numbers 1 to 10 in a column. After the numbers list the letters representing the names in the order in which you have them arranged.

Name
Problem ____ / ____ Date _____
1. *i*
2.
3.
4.
5.
6.
7.
8.
9.
10.

Sample Answer Sheet

a. Thomas Takahashi
b. Joseph J. Taylor
c. Maryanne Van Tassel
d. Mac C. Tabb
e. Tom Takahashi

f. Mary Ann Van Tassel
g. Josie Taylor
h. Van J. Tassel
i. Mervin Taba
j. Jos. H. Taylor

2. A. Type or write each of the following names in transposed indexing order on a 5″ by 3″ index card or on a slip of paper cut to that size. Place in the upper right-hand corner of the card the letter that identifies the name.

   B. When you have typed all the cards, arrange them in alphabetic order.

   C. Prepare an answer sheet: Type or write the numbers 1 to 10 in a column. After the numbers list the letters representing the names in the order in which you have them arranged.

   a. Jules Le Valdo
   b. P. L'Esperance, Jr.
   c. Mme. Nellie Lessere
   d. Miss Janette Lett
   e. Kin Kung Leung

   f. Herman Levaro, M.C.
   g. Nina Lesperance
   h. Mr. Roy Let
   i. Mrs. Mary Lessa
   j. M. Leung, M.D.

3. A. Type or write each of the following names in transposed indexing order on a 5″ by 3″ index card or on a slip of paper cut to that size. Then, three or four lines below, type the name in address order. Place in the upper right-hand corner of the card the letter that identifies the name.

   B. When you have typed all the cards, arrange them in alphabetic order.

   C. Prepare an answer sheet: Type or write the numbers 1 to 20 in a column. After the numbers list the letters representing the names in the order in which you have them arranged.

   a. A. Bruce Dickson, 563 N. Park Street, Philadelphia, PA 19116
   b. Shirley Dietzen, 8765 Shoreline Avenue, Chicago, IL 60605
   c. Hon. Ronald Dietz, 897 Dowling Street, Miami, FL 33103
   d. Dan Dilbert, III, 5050 Main Street, Lomita, CA 90717
   e. Karen Dickinson, R.N., 900 Bush Avenue, Reading, PA 19602
   f. Ron Dietz, 477 West 30 Street, Houston, TX 77009
   g. Jos. Di Benedetti, 48 Indiana Avenue, New York, NY 10013
   h. Ted Didio, 1397 Las Vegas Blvd., Chandler, AZ 85224
   i. Lawson Dickey, Sr., 2102 Main Street, Columbus, OH 43216
   j. Al B. Dickson, 1459 Vine Street, Cincinnati, OH 45212
   k. Victoria Diba, 588 Central Avenue, Chicago, IL 60634
   l. Paul Dieffenderfer, 1007 Westlake Blvd., Los Angeles, CA 90012
   m. Don Dilbert, II, 111 W. Washington Street, Brownville, NY 13615
   n. Jean Dicochea, 121 North Broadway, Pittsburgh, PA 15213
   o. Lino Di Benedetto, 1015 Meredith Drive, Cincinnati, OH 45212
   p. Sam Di Dio, 496 Columbus Avenue, San Francisco, CA 94116
   q. Lawson Dickey, Jr., 355 North Baker Street, Richmond, VA 23208
   r. Warren Diefenthaeler, 3182 Ridge Avenue, Cincinnati, OH 45213
   s. Theodore DiDio, 9004 Tenth Avenue, Topeka, KS 66609
   t. Milton Dickstein, D.D.S., 457 Brown Street, Denver, CO 80211

JOB 1   Card Filing—Names of Individuals

At this time complete Job 1 in OFFICE FILING PROCEDURES, Fourth Edition. The instructions and supplies for this job and the following jobs are included in the practice set.

CHAPTER 3

ALPHABETIC INDEXING OF BUSINESS AND GEOGRAPHIC NAMES

Complexity of Business and Geographic Names

Although there are many unusual and complex personal names, personal names as a whole cannot compare in complexity with the types of names given to business and industrial organizations. Many business names are devised so that they reflect the name of a product or a service and thus bring added attention to the business enterprise. This practice, of course, is an asset to the business organization; but it is apt to be a problem to those who process names for filing purposes.

The more complex names are, the more difficult it becomes to index them properly, and the more necessary it becomes to know and use definite rules for indexing. Therefore, this chapter presents a series of rules which have been developed for indexing business and geographic names. As you study this chapter, follow the same study procedure suggested in Chapter 2: Read a rule twice; study the list of examples; then restudy the examples in detail, comparing each name with the names above and below it.

RULE 10 Order of Indexing Units

The units in a business or geographic name are usually indexed in the order in which they appear and are read unless they include personal names. Personal names are indexed in this order: (1) by surname, (2) by given name or initial, (3) by middle name or initial.

Names	Key Unit	Unit 2	Unit 3
General Supply Corporation	General	Supply	Corporation
Ben F. Guyman	Guyman	Ben	F.
Guyman Carbon Company	Guyman	Carbon	Company
Guyton Appliance Center	Guyton	Appliance	Center
Albert Guzman Company	Guzman	Albert	Company
Albert S. Guzman	Guzman	Albert	S.
Guzman Printing Corporation	Guzman	Printing	Corporation
Arthur A. Gwinn	Gwinn	Arthur	A.
Gwinn Associates	Gwinn	Associates	
Gynafoil Company	Gynafoil	Company	

(column headers: Names / Index Order of Units — Key Unit, Unit 2, Unit 3)

RULE 11   Minor Words

Some minor words in business and geographic names do not add meaning to the names and generally are not used as indexing units. Such words are *and, the, of, by, to, for*. Minor words that appear as *meaningful first units* in names are taken as key units. Such words are *at, on, in*.

Note: Minor words disregarded as units may be enclosed in parentheses to avoid confusing them with units considered in indexing.

Names	Index Order of Units		
	Key Unit	Unit 2	Unit 3
The Ames and Lane Company	Ames (and)	Lane	Company (The)
Anne of Paris Salon	Anne (of)	Paris	Salon
Arnett & Horn, Attorneys	Arnett (&)	Horn	Attorneys
At Home Shops	At	Home	Shops
In Town Markets	In	Town	Markets
The Inland Company	Inland	Company (The)	
On Guard Locksmiths	On	Guard	Locksmiths
The On Time Service	On	Time	Service (The)
Wabash at State Building	Wabash (at)	State	Building
Westwood on the Bay Hotel	Westwood (on the)	Bay	Hotel

RULE 12   Abbreviations

Abbreviations of *commonly known* words (such as *Co., Corp., N.Y., U.S.*) are considered as if they were written in full.

Names	Index Order of Units			
	Key Unit	Unit 2	Unit 3	Unit 4
Alaben Bros. Limited	Alaben	Brothers	Limited	
Wm. Alamar & Sons	Alamar	William (&)	Sons	
America Travel Assn.	America	Travel	Association	
Thos. Black & Co.	Black	Thomas (&)	Company	
Ft. Worth Steel Co.	Fort	Worth	Steel	Company
Frontier Corp.	Frontier	Corporation		
Mt. Washington Inn, Inc.	Mount	Washington	Inn	Incorporated
Mountain View Realtors	Mountain	View	Realtors	
St. Lawrence Tours	Saint	Lawrence	Tours	
George E. St. Louis	Saint	Louis	George	E
Ste. Croix Ltd.	Sainte	Croix	Limited	
Salem Mdse. Co., Inc.	Salem	Merchandise	Company	Incorporated

RULE 13   Single Letters

A single letter in a business name, including an abbreviation of a word that is unknown and cannot be ascertained, is treated as a separate indexing unit; the letter is placed before all names in the same unit beginning with that same letter. Hyphens are disregarded in single-letter and combination names. Spacing between single letters is of no significance.

Names	Key Unit	Index Order of Units		
		Unit 2	Unit 3	Unit 4
A-B-C Company	A-	B-	C	Company
ABC Corporation	A	B	C	Corporation
A.B.C. Metals	A.	B.	C.	Metals
A-Bell Answering Service	A-	Bell	Answering	Service
Jack T. Ames Co.	Ames	Jack ·	T.	Company
C B O Radio	C	B	O	Radio
C-B Title Co.	C-	B	Title	Company
C B C	Canadian	Broadcasting	Corporation	
Chrysler Corporation	Chrysler	Corporation		
C B S, Inc.	Columbia	Broadcasting	System	Incorporated

Note: Names such as *Canadian Broadcasting Corporation* and *Columbia Broadcasting System, Incorporated,* are usually filed under the full names and then cross-referenced under their well-known abbreviations.

RULE 14 Compound Names

Actual or coined names, words, or word substitutes in compound business names and compound geographic names are indexed as they are written. Hyphenated parts of such names are treated as separate indexing units.

The following names are examples of *coined* compound business names (note that the key unit of each name is underlined):

C-Thru Ruler Company	(a 4-unit name)
Pepsi-Cola Bottling Company	(a 4-unit name)
Sunkist Growers Association	(a 3-unit name)

Examples of *actual* compound business and geographic names are:

Georgia-Pacific Corporation	(a 3-unit name)
New Haven Insurance Company	(a 4-unit name)
News-Press Publications	(a 3-unit name)
Santa Barbara Research, Inc.	(a 4-unit name)

Names	Key Unit	Index Order of Units		
		Unit 2	Unit 3	Unit 4
New Castle Lock Co.	New	Castle	Lock	Company
Newcastle-Arden Corp.	Newcastle-	Arden	Corporation	
Nik-Nak Stores	Nik-	Nak	Stores	

(Continued on page 24)

| Names | Index Order of Units | | | |
	Key Unit	Unit 2	Unit 3	Unit 4
Nikko Electric Corp.	Nikko	Electric	Corporation	
Nivens Sun-Ray Co.	Nivens	Sun-	Ray	Company
Northport, Nova Scotia	Northport	Nova	Scotia	
Nu-Matic International	Nu-	Matic	International	
Numan-Morton, Inc.	Numan-	Morton	Incorporated	
Numan-Plasticote Co.	Numan-	Plasticote	Company	
Porto Nuovo Cia.	Porto	Nuovo	Cia.	
St. Cloud, Minn.	Saint	Cloud	Minnesota	
San Antonio, Texas	San	Antonio	Texas	
Santa Fe Historical Society	Santa	Fe	Historical	Society
Santa Rosa Resort	Santa	Rosa	Resort	
Sir John's Portraits	Sir	John('s)	Portraits	
Sister Marie's Cakes	Sister	Marie('s)	Cakes	

Note: Names such as *Newcastle-Arden Corp., Nivens Sun-Ray Co., Numan-Morton, Inc.,* and *Numan-Plasticote Co.* usually require cross-referencing under the second units.

RULE 15 Titles

Titles in business names are used as indexing units and are indexed in the order in which they appear in the names.

| Names | Index Order of Units | | | |
	Key Unit	Unit 2	Unit 3	Unit 4
Dr. Pepper Bottling Co.	Doctor	Pepper	Bottling	Company
D. D. Du Pont, M.D.	Du Pont	D.	D. (M.D.)	
Jr. C of C	Junior	Chamber (of)	Commerce	
The Jr. House, Inc.	Junior	House	Incorporated (The)	
Mister Ed Farms	Mister	Ed	Farms	
Mr. E. A. Morton	Morton	E.	A. (Mr.)	
Mr. Martin Shoe Store	Mr.	Martin	Shoe	Store
Mrs. Adams Shops	Mrs.	Adams	Shops	
St. Louis Gas Co.	Saint	Louis	Gas	Company
San Luis Gas Company	San	Luis	Gas	Company
Sr. Citizens, Incorporated	Senior	Citizens	Incorporated	

Note: When the titles *Mr., Mrs.,* and *Ms.* are used in business names, they are indexed as written. Other titles, such as *Dr.* and *Prof.,* are indexed as though they were spelled in full.

RULE 16 Possessives

When "apostrophe s" ('s) is added to a name to form a possessive, such as *Bowen's,* the added "s" is not considered in alphabetizing. When the ending is "s apostrophe" (s'), the "s" is considered part of the word.

Names	Index Order of Units		
	Key Unit	**Unit 2**	**Unit 3**
Lew's Driver School	Lew('s)	Driver	School
Lewin's Art Gallery	Lewin('s)	Art	Gallery
C. P. Lewin, M.D.	Lewin	C.	P. (M.D.)
Lewis' Office Service	Lewis'	Office	Service
Lewis Petrol Ltd.	Lewis	Petrol	Limited
Lewison & Lawler	Lewison (&)	Lawler	
Lewison's Trading Post	Lewison('s)	Trading	Post
Little Joe's Pizzas	Little	Joe('s)	Pizzas
Joe Thos. Little	Little	Joe	Thomas
Lt. M. S. Lopez	Lopez	M.	S. (Lt.)
M's Records Service	M('s)	Records	Service

RULE 17 Separated Single Words

When a single word is separated into two or more parts in a business name, the parts are considered to be one indexing unit. When a word is separated from its prefix, the prefix and the word are considered to be one indexing unit. Hyphens are disregarded in such names.

Note: Examples of words that are sometimes separated into two words are *airport, carload, crossroads, downtown, eastside, goodwill, halfway, railroad;* points of the compass words such as *northeast, northwest, southeast,* and *southwestern.*

Note: Examples of words that are sometimes separated from their prefixes are *antiacid, biannual, midlands,* and *noncorrosive.*

Names	Index Order of Units		
	Key Unit	**Unit 2**	**Unit 3**
Air Port Rentals	Air Port	Rentals	
Airport Restaurant	Airport	Restaurant	
Air-Port Transit Co.	Air-Port	Transit	Company
The Antia-Holshoy Co.	Antia-	Holshoy	Company (The)
Anti-Defamation League	Anti-Defamation	League	
Bi-Rite Drug Stores	Bi-	Rite	Drug Stores
Bi-Monthly News Service	Bi-Monthly	News	Service
Code-A-Fone	Code-	A-	Fone
Co-operative Products	Co-operative	Products	
Cross Roads Market	Cross Roads	Market	
Di-Line Company	Di-	Line	Company
Don E. Di Maggio	Di Maggio	Don	E
Down Town Clothiers	Down Town	Clothiers	
East-West Club	East-	West	Club
Eastern Air Lines	Eastern	Air Lines	

RULE 18 Numbers

For indexing purposes, numbers appearing in digit form are considered to be written out. Despite the length of a number, the number is considered to be *one* indexing unit.

Note: Four-digit numbers usually are written out in hundreds for indexing purposes so that coding uniformity will be assured. Thus, such a number as "1040" is indexed as "Ten hundred forty."

Names	Key Unit	Index Order of Units Unit 2	Unit 3
K - 9 Kennels	K-	Nine	Kennels
9 Hour Cleaners	Nine	Hour	Cleaners
The 950 Restaurant	Nine hundred fifty	Restau- rant (The)	
19th & Doan Market	Nineteenth (&)	Doan	Market
Nineteenth & Lake Hotel	Nineteenth (&)	Lake	Hotel
Nine-Thousand Club	Nine-Thousand	Club	
9500 Front Bldg.	Ninety-five hundred	Front	Building
92d St. Apartments	Ninety-second	Street	Apartments
The 12,000 Wilton Bldg.	Twelve thousand	Wilton	Building (The)

RULE 19 Particles and Articles

A foreign particle (sometimes called a *prefix*) or a foreign article in a business or geographic name is combined with the part of the name following it to form a single indexing unit.

Names	Key Unit	Index Order of Units Unit 2	Unit 3
Della Rosa Bros.	Della Rosa	Brothers	
Del Monte Brands	Del Monte	Brands	
De Lux Trailers	De Lux	Trailers	
Des Moines REGISTER	Des Moines	REGISTER	
Elman & Associates	Elman (&)	Associates	
El Mirage Hotel	El Mirage	Hotel	
El Paso Freight Lines	El Paso	Freight	Lines
Lang & Morse Co.	Lang (&)	Morse	Company
La Strada Restaurant	La Strada	Restaurant	
Mac Tavish and Sontag	Mac Tavish (and)	Sontag	
McTavish & Sons	McTavish (&)	Sons	
Pan-American Imports	Pan-American	Imports	
Teneco Builders	Teneco	Builders	
Ten Eyck & Jones	Ten Eyck (&)	Jones	

RULE 20 Identical Names

When the full names of two or more business organizations are identical, addresses are used to determine filing order. Addresses are not considered as indexing units but as secondary means of determining filing order. Filing order is determined by using as many parts of an address as needed.

Note: Usually, the order in which the parts of an address are considered is as follows: (1) city names, (2) state and province names if the city names are alike, (3) street names, (4) house or building numbers.

Names	Index Order of Units		
	Key Unit	**Unit 2**	**Address**
	(City Names Used to Determine Filing Order)		
Devox Corporation 96 Kings Row London, England	Devox	Corporation	London
Devox Corporation 12 Rue de Richelieu Paris, France	Devox	Corporation	Paris
Devox Corporation Av. Paula 1009 São Paulo, Brazil	Devox	Corporation	São Paulo
	(State Names Used to Determine Filing Order)		
Monarch Shoes 201 Main Street Newark, New Jersey	Monarch	Shoes	New Jersey
Monarch Shoes 51 Front Street Newark, Ohio	Monarch	Shoes	Ohio
	(Street Names and Building Numbers Used to Determine Filing Order)		
VARO, Inc. 320 Seneca St. Seattle, Wash.	VARO	Incorporated	320 Seneca St.
VARO, Inc. 1149 Tenth St. Seattle, Wash.	VARO	Incorporated	1149 Tenth St.
VARO, Inc. 5512 Tenth St. Seattle, Wash.	VARO	Incorporated	5512 Tenth St.
VARO, Inc. 2420 Third St. Seattle, Wash.	VARO	Incorporated	2420 Third St.

RULE 21 Obscure Domestic and Foreign Names

Unusual or obscure business and geographic names are usually indexed as written, and standard rules are used for indexing such names. Hyphens are disregarded in dividing unusual names into units.

Names	Index Order of Units			
	Key Unit	**Unit 2**	**Unit 3**	**Unit 4**
Alta Vista Company	Alta	Vista	Company	
Ask Mr. Foster	Ask	Mr.	Foster	
J. Avery & D. Cresti	Avery	J. (&)	Cresti	D.

(Continued on page 28)

Names	Index Order of Units			
	Key Unit	Unit 2	Unit 3	Unit 4
BWM Autozentrum	B	W	M	Autozentrum
C O^2 Equipment	C	O	two	Equipment
The 5's Club	Five ('s)	Club (The)		
Albert Frank Co.	Frank	Albert	Company	
InfoMetrics	InfoMetrics			
K's TV Service	K ('s)	Television	Service	
Ljusne-Woxna AB.	Ljusne-	Woxna	AB.	
Pan-Pacific Imports	Pan-Pacific	Imports		
Santa Fe, N.M.	Santa	Fe	New	Mexico
7 - 11 Food Stores	Seven-	Eleven	Food	Stores
U-Jim Cia.	U-	Jim	Cia.	
Zora Gilbert Co.	Zora	Gilbert	Company	

Note: Names like *J. Avery & D. Cresti, Albert Frank Co.,* and *Zora Gilbert Co.* are usually cross-referenced.

Cross-Referencing

Business names, like individuals' names, sometimes present difficulties in filing because someone requesting information about a certain company may not remember the exact name of the company or may remember only part of it. For this reason it is good practice to cross-reference certain types of business names.

Combined Surnames in a Business Name. (See Rule 14.) When a business name includes two or more individual surnames, it is often desirable to prepare a cross-reference card for each surname other than the first. Examples are as follows:

If an original card is made out for Carew-Evers, Incorporated, a cross-reference card for the name should be prepared. The two cards will appear as follows:

```
Carew-Evers, Incorporated

Carew-Evers, Incorporated
317 East Fourth Street
Cincinnati, OH  45202
```

```
Evers-Carew, Incorporated

See Carew-Evers, Incorporated
```

If an original card is made out for Davis, Banks, and Alston Hardware Store, the two cross-reference cards should show the following information:

```
Banks, Alston, and Davis Hardware Store
See Davis, Banks, and Alston Hardware Store

Alston, Davis, and Banks Hardware Store
See Davis, Banks, and Alston Hardware Store
```

If an original card is made out for Ron Strong & Paul Kite, Associates, the original card and the cross-reference card should be made out to show the following information:

```
Strong, Ron (&) Kite, Paul, Associates

Ron Strong & Paul Kite, Associates
8942 Maple Avenue
Spokane, WA  99212
```

```
Kite, Paul (&) Strong, Ron, Associates

See Strong, Ron & Kite, Paul, Associates
```

Combined Surname and Coined Name in a Business Name. When a business name such as Reynolds-Visaview Company (a surname and a coined name) occurs in a filing system, materials may be requested by the name "Visaview" only as well as by the complete company name. In such a situation, if the original card is made out for Reynolds-Visaview Company, the cross-reference card should be made out to show the following information:

```
Visaview-Reynolds Company
See Reynolds-Visaview Company
```

Abbreviations and Single Letters. (See Rules 12 and 13.) Many companies and associations are referred to by titles in abbreviated form or by letters rather than by full titles. Cross-references should be prepared for all names or titles of this type.

```
ARMA
See American Records Management Association
CBS
See Columbia Broadcasting System
C G & E
See Cincinnati Gas and Electric Company
P & G
See Procter and Gamble
RCA
See Radio Corporation of America
```

QUESTIONS FOR DISCUSSION

1. Why are business names apt to be more complex than personal names?

2. Are business names always indexed as they are written? Why?

3. Why are minor words in business names not usually taken as indexing units?

4. What do you believe might happen if all types of abbreviations (not just commonly known ones) were written out by all who use a filing system?

5. What is the difference between the indexing of two words separated by a hyphen and a single word separated into two parts?

6. Why do you believe that there is a difference between indexing personal titles and indexing titles in business names?

7. An "s" added to a name to form a possessive is not considered when names are being alphabetized. Why is this done?

8. When the names of two or more businesses are identical, is the state name or the city name considered first as the location unit for indexing purposes? Why?

9. What is the difference between the indexing of compound geographic names containing two English words and the indexing of compound geographic names written as one word?

10. Compare the rule governing the indexing of an individual's name containing a particle and the rule governing the indexing of a business name containing a foreign article or particle.

11. Discuss three types of business names that require cross-referencing.

12. What is the *key unit* in each of the following names?

    a. Mr. & Mrs. Apparel Store
    b. The In Crowd Restaurant
    c. The Sea Side Company
    d. Car-U-Drive Co.
    e. Chi-Can Freight, Ltd.
    f. 10-20 Mart
    g. 1020 Cafe
    h. Du Mond & Baker Co.
    i. TenBrook Brothers, Inc.
    j. Les the Sign Man
    k. N. H. Te'o & Sons
    l. Double-Eagle Brands

13. What is the *second* indexing unit in each of the following names?

    a. The Bi-Yearly Audit Bureau
    b. San Antonio Credit Bureau
    c. Santa Claus Industries
    d. The Y-Not Shop
    e. Fai-Yee Company
    f. At Cross Roads Inn
    g. The Neuro-Psychiatric Clinic
    h. Silver Mt. Mining Co.
    i. IML Optics, Inc.
    j. North-Western Land Co.
    k. The 1595 Building
    l. T-Vee Specialists

14. Is the order of the two names in each of the following pairs correct or incorrect?

    a. Art Fashions, Inc.
       Art's Fashion Fabrics
    b. One Hundred & One Products, Inc.
       101 Brands, Incorporated

    c. The Bob Onley Company
       On-Line Systems, Incorporated

    d. MD—LF Company
       M & D Transfer Co.

    e. Blue Bell, Inc.
       Bluebell Farms, Inc.

    f. Mister New Yorker Stores
       Mr. Dino's

    g. Mitchell & Co. (Boston, Massachusetts)
       Mitchell & Co. (New Haven, Connecticut)

    h. Jean-Alan, Ltd.
       Jean Alan and Company

    i. G A R Auto Parts
       G. W. Furth Associates

    j. Utah Auto Ins. Co.
       Utah Automobile Club

FILING PROBLEMS

1. A. Type or write each of the following names in indexing order on a 5″ by 3″ index card or on a slip of paper cut to that size. Then, a triple space below, type the name in address order. Place in the upper right corner of the card the letter that identifies the name.

   B. When you have typed all the cards, arrange them in alphabetic order.

   C. Prepare an answer sheet similar to the one illustrated on page 19. Type or write the numbers 1-11 in a column. After the numbers, list the letters representing the names in the order in which you have them arranged.

    a. Lakeside Bus Lines, 149 Carter Road, Philadelphia, PA 19116
    b. L-A Rubber Products, 98 Central Avenue, Chicago, IL 60644
    c. La Rue's Salon, 164 Dowling Street, Miami, FL 33103
    d. L'Artisan, 27 Broomfield Street, Lomita, CA 90717
    e. Lake Side Trailers, 900 Bush Avenue, Reading, PA 19602
    f. La-Ru Rentals, 264 West 40th Street, Houston, TX 77009
    g. Lasala, Trent & Lynch, 48 Indiana Avenue, New York, NY 10013
    h. Lasco-Ohio Corp., 2102 Manning Street, Columbus, OH 43216
    i. L A R Drugs, Inc., 1306 Vine Street, Cincinnati, OH 45212
    j. LaRue Travel Club, 1208 Regent Avenue, Tucson, AZ 85742
    k. La Salle Theater, 231 West Lake Street, Los Angeles, CA 90012

2. Type or write in alphabetic order the three names in each of the following groups. Include the number of each name as you list each one.

    1a. J. A. Davis, Portland, Oregon
    1b. J. A. Davis, Portland, Maine
    1c. J. A. Davis, Portland, Pennsylvania

    2a. Bell Aire Apartments
    2b. Belair Cleaners
    2c. Bel-Vue Paint Co.

    3a. Twentieth Century Plastics
    3b. 12th & Grant Store
    3c. 28th St. Market

4a. Southern Gas Stations
      1099 E. Spring St., Atlanta, Ga.
4b. Southern Gas Stations
      114 W. Spring St., Atlanta, Ga.
4c. Southern Gas Stations
      2864 E. Spring St., Atlanta, Ga.
5a. In-And-Out Photo Service
5b. In-VAL-Co
5c. H. I. Ina Heating Co.
6a. J. M. MacDodson, II
6b. John Mac Donald, Sr.
6c. John Mac Donald, Jr.
7a. Ed's Discount Stores
7b. Edward's Marine Service
7c. Edwards & Carlin
8a. Jay Auto Products
8b. J-M Auto Parts
8c. JMA Truck Terminal

3. On 5″ x 3″ cards or on slips of paper cut to that size, type or write cross-reference cards *when needed* for the following names. When, in your opinion, a cross-reference is not needed, omit a card for that name.

   a. UTA-French Airlines
   b. Rodin, Ritter & Rouse, Attys.
   c. A. O. Fisher & Sons
   d. Rod Dana & E. M. Hart, Associates
   e. Illinois International
   f. Acme-Weston Group
   g. DeWalt Trailers, Inc.
         Penfield & White, Agents
   h. E & R Products Corp.
   i. Colorado Mines, Inc.
   j. Fusilier Odessa, Inc.
   k. Hi-Fi Equipment Co.
   l. FTD Speed-A-Gift
   m. CSE Bus Lines
   n. Carlin-Dahl Associates
   o. Gordon, Grant & Gray

JOB 2   Card Filing—Business Names

At this time complete Job 2 in OFFICE FILING PROCEDURES, Fourth Edition. The instructions and supplies for this job are included in the practice set.

CHAPTER 4

ALPHABETIC INDEXING OF NAMES OF ORGANIZATIONS, GOVERNMENT AGENCIES, AND SUBJECTS

The types of names to be considered in this chapter are unusual in the sense that they require special attention during the indexing process. For example, a name such as National Association of Investment Clubs can be correctly indexed in either of two ways:

$$\overset{3}{\underline{\text{National}}}/\overset{4}{\text{Association (of)}}/\overset{2}{\underline{\text{Investment}}}/\text{Clubs}$$

or

$$\overset{2}{\underline{\text{National}}}/\overset{3}{\text{Association (of)}}/\overset{4}{\text{Investment}}/\text{Clubs}$$

Since this is true, the indexing method used by a person depends either upon his experience and training, or upon the indexing policy that has been established by the company for which the person is working. If no company policy exists, each person might use a different method of indexing and thus create confusion in the records system.

Selective Indexing

The way out of this dual indexing problem is, first, to know that there are two possible ways of indexing certain types of names and, second, to select one of the methods and use it to the exclusion of the other.

If this is not done, one person will index a name like "The Bank of Toronto" first under "Bank," while another person will index it first under "Toronto." In this situation, papers concerning this bank will be lost or made difficult to find for one or the other person.

Because there are many types of names in the general category of organizations and agencies, the indexing problem cited is critical and must be resolved before accurate, dependable records control can exist.

Solving the Indexing Problem

The two types or methods of indexing identified above are known as (1) the descriptive method of indexing and (2) the as-written method of indexing. The differences between these two methods are explained on page 34.

Descriptive Method of Indexing. In this method, the most definitive unit in a name is used as the key unit. For example, in the name "National Association of Investment Clubs," the term "Investment Clubs" most accurately defines this organization. Thus, in the descriptive method of indexing, the word "Investment" is used as the key unit, and the word "Clubs" is used as the second unit. Names of other organizations and agencies are indexed in this same manner. Of course, all previously learned rules for indexing are followed when names of organizations and agencies are being indexed. The descriptive method only assists in determining the key unit to be used.

As-Written Method of Indexing. In this method, names of organizations and agencies are considered, for indexing purposes, in the form in which they are written and are read. Thus, the name "National Association of Investment Clubs" is coded with "National" as the key unit, "Association" as the second unit, "Investment" as the third unit, and "Clubs" as the fourth unit. Again, other indexing rules that are presented in Chapters 2 and 3 apply to the indexing of names of organizations and agencies. The as-written method is used as an assist in determining the key unit to be selected for filing purposes.

Selecting the Indexing Method

The decision about which indexing method to use, the descriptive or the as-written, must be made by the records manager or supervisor in each office. Once such a decision is made, all records personnel must follow it so that confusion will not result because two methods are being used in the same office.

The basis for deciding to use one or the other method is usually governed by the nature and extent of operations in a given company. If, for example, the operations of a business organization involved only limited contact with organizations and agencies, the as-written method of indexing would prove adequate. On the other hand, if business contacts included many organizations and agencies, the descriptive method of indexing would provide better control over records because this method is the more comprehensive and accurate of the two. *It is for these reasons that the descriptive method of indexing will be used in showing examples and in presenting rules for study in this textbook.* Also, all practice materials will be based upon the descriptive method.

Rules for Descriptive Indexing

Rules are given for using the descriptive method of indexing in relation to the following types of organizations and agencies: associations, clubs, and service organizations; financial organizations; religious institutions; educational institutions; publications; broadcasting stations; and hotels, motels, and related service units.

RULE 22 Associations, Clubs, and Service Organizations

The name of an association, a club, or a service organization is indexed according to the most descriptive unit in the name. If the name begins with such general words as "Association of," "American Association of," "Society of," the name is transposed and the most descriptive unit is used.

When a location is included in the name, the location name is treated as an indexing unit wherever it appears. Names composed of more than one descriptive unit can be cross-referenced.

Names	Descriptive Index Form		
	Key Unit	Unit 2	Unit 3
Albany Chamber of Commerce	Albany	Chamber (of)	Commerce
American Broadcasting Company	American	Broadcasting	Company
The American Legion	American	Legion (The)	
Fraternal Order of Eagles	Eagles	Fraternal	Order (of)
Association of Engineers	Engineers	Association (of)	
Foundation for Legal Service	Legal	Service	Foundation (for)
Rotary Club, Akron	Rotary	Club (Akron)	
Rotary Club, Ashland	Rotary	Club (Ashland)	
Society of Utah Pioneers	Utah	Pioneers	Society (of)
Welfare Board			
10th Street Office	Welfare	Board	Tenth
Welfare Board			
West Avenue Office	Welfare	Board	West

RULE 23 Financial Organizations

Locations are used as the most descriptive units in names of financial organizations because such names frequently are identical or similar in form. Branch names and/or district names are used as units or are added, when needed, as identifying units.

Names	Descriptive Index Form				
	Key Unit	Unit 2	Unit 3	Unit 4	Unit 5
First National Bank					
(Boston, Mass.)	Boston	First	National	Bank	
First National Bank					
(Denver, Colo.)	Denver	First	National	Bank	

(Continued on page 36)

Names	Descriptive Index Form				
	Key Unit	Unit 2	Unit 3	Unit 4	Unit 5
First National Bank (Providence, R.I.) (University Branch)	Providence (University)	First	National	Bank	
First National Bank (Providence, R.I.) (Water Street Branch)	Providence (Water)	First	National	Bank	
Raleigh Bank & Trust Co.	Raleigh	Bank (&)	Trust	Company	
City Savings & Loan Assn. (Springfield, Ill.)	Springfield (Illinois)	City	Savings (&)	Loan	Assn.
City Savings & Loan Assn. (Springfield, Mo.)	Springfield (Missouri)	City	Savings (&)	Loan	Assn.
City Savings & Loan Assn. (Springfield, Ohio)	Springfield (Ohio)	City	Savings (&)	Loan	Assn.

RULE 24   Religious Institutions

Denominational names of churches, if known, are used as the most descriptive units. The words "Church," "Temple," or "Cathedral" are not used as key units even though they appear as the first words in church names. Names of synagogues vary in form; because of this, local or regional custom should be observed when these names are being indexed.

Names	Descriptive Index Form	
	Key Unit	Unit 2	Unit 3
All Saints Church	All	Saints	Church
Calvary Baptist Church	Baptist	Church	Calvary
Temple Beth Israel	Beth	Israel	Temple
Christ Church	Christ	Church	
The Community Temple	Community	Temple (The)	
Grace Episcopal Church	Episcopal	Church	Grace
Holy Trinity Church	Holy	Trinity	Church
Faith Lutheran Church	Lutheran	Church	Faith
Church of the Nazarene	Nazarene	Church (of the)	
Norwood Community Church	Norwood	Community	Church
St. Mary's Church	Saint	Mary's	Church
Cathedral of St. Peter	Saint	Peter	Cathedral (of)

RULE 25   Educational Institutions

a. (1) Locations are used as the most descriptive units in names of elementary and secondary schools and (2) the most distinctive words in the names of schools are used as further indexing units. This procedure is followed in order to avoid confusing the names among the separate, independent school systems that usually operate in metropolitan areas.

When the name of the city is the first word of the school name, the city name is used only once in indexing. State names are not considered unless city names in two or more states are alike, in which case state names are considered second as identifying elements.

Names	Descriptive Index Form			
	Key Unit	Unit 2	Unit 3	Unit 4
Country Day School				
Boston, Mass.	Boston	Country	Day	School
Nativity School				
Boston, Mass.	Boston	Nativity	School	
William Taft High School				
Boston, Mass.	Boston	Taft	William	High
East High School				
Cleveland, Ohio	Cleveland	East	High	School
John Hay High School				
Cleveland, Ohio	Cleveland	Hay	John	High
St. Paul School				
Cleveland, Ohio	Cleveland	Saint	Paul	School
Granger High School	Columbus			
Columbus, Georgia	(Georgia)	Granger	High	School
Columbus Elementary School	Columbus			
Columbus, Ohio	(Ohio)	Elementary	School	
Columbus High School	Columbus			
Columbus, Ohio	(Ohio)	High	School	
High School				
Dayton, Ohio	Dayton	High	School	
Pilot School for the Deaf			(for	
Dayton, Ohio	Dayton	Pilot	School the)	Deaf

b. The most descriptive unit in the name of a college or university is used as the key unit. City names, unless they are part of the college names, are not considered except as identifying elements when identical college names are involved.

Names	Descriptive Index Form			
	Key Unit	Unit 2	Unit 3	Unit 4
Calumet Commercial School	Calumet	Commercial	School	
John Carroll University	Carroll	John	University	
Salmon P. Chase Law School	Chase	Salmon	P.	Law
University of Cincinnati	Cincinnati	University (of)		
Clarke Business College				
Erie	Clarke	Business	College (Erie)	
Clarke Business College				
Troy	Clarke	Business	College (Troy)	
Columbia University	Columbia	University		
University of Detroit	Detroit	University (of)		
Mount Hood Community				
College	Mount	Hood	Community	College
St. Catherine College	Saint	Catherine	College	

RULE 26 Publications

a. Locations are used as the most descriptive units in names of newspapers. If the location is not part of the name of a newspaper, it is written in as the key unit in the name.

Names	Key Unit	Unit 2	Unit 3	Unit 4	Unit 5
		Descriptive Index Form			
New York Journal-American	New	York	Journal-	American	
Long Island Press (New York)	New	York	Long	Island	Press
New York Times	New	York	Times		
Oregon Journal (Portland)	Portland	Oregon	Journal		
Portland Oregonian	Portland	Oregonian			
Richmond News Leader	Richmond	News	Leader		
Salt Lake City Tribune	Salt	Lake	City	Tribune	

b. Units in the names of periodicals, like those in business names, are considered in the order in which they appear. (A cross-reference may be made for the name of the publisher of a periodical so that this information will be available if and when needed.)

Names	Key Unit	Unit 2	Unit 3	Unit 4	Unit 5
		Descriptive Index Form			
Better Homes & Gardens	Better	Homes (&)	Gardens		
Changing Times	Changing	Times			
Federal Reserve Bulletin	Federal	Reserve	Bulletin		
Managerial Planning	Managerial	Planning			
Newsweek	Newsweek				
Time	Time				
U.S. News & World Report	United	States	News (&)	World	Report

RULE 27 Broadcasting Stations

When correspondence with radio and television stations is limited, the names of these stations are indexed by call letters, as indicated in the illustrative examples following Rule 13, page 23. When there is correspondence with a number of such stations, however, the call letters are generally filed under the subject titles "Radio Stations" and "Television Stations."

Names	Key Unit	Unit 2	Unit 3	Unit 4	Unit 5	Unit 6
		Descriptive Index Form				
KOMO Radio Station	Radio	Station	K	O	M	O
WFBM Radio Station	Radio	Station	W	F	B	M
WLW Radio Station	Radio	Station	W	L	W	
KNX--TV	Television	Station	K	N	X	
WCPO--TV	Television	Station	W	C	P	O

RULE 28   ## Hotels, Motels, and Related Service Units

The most descriptive unit in a hotel or motel name is used as the key unit. If the word "Hotel" or "Motel" appears first in the name, it is transposed to follow the more clearly identifying word. This rule also applies to related service units using the hotel or motel name.

Names	Descriptive Index Form			
	Key Unit	**Unit 2**	**Unit 3**	**Unit 4**
Hotel Geneve	Geneve	Hotel		
Hotel Geneve Restaurant	Geneve	Hotel	Restaurant	
The Sheraton-Gibson Hotel	Sheraton-	Gibson	Hotel (The)	
Hotel Sherman	Sherman	Hotel		
Hotel Sherman Beauty Shop	Sherman	Hotel	Beauty	Shop
Hotel Sherman Restaurant	Sherman	Hotel	Restaurant	
Hotel Sherman Travel Service	Sherman	Hotel	Travel	Service
The Statler Hilton Hotel	Statler	Hilton	Hotel (The)	
Roy Strong's Motel	Strong('s)	Roy	Motel	

Government Names

In general, the processing methods for controlling government materials are directed primarily toward preventing confusion among the many types of names at the national, state, regional, and local levels of government. To attain this end, the files operator identifies government names according to their most distinctive and descriptive parts.

RULE 29   ## Federal Government Names

The parts of the name of a federal government office are considered in the following order: (a) United States Government—three indexing units, (b) the principal word or words in the name of the executive department, (c) the principal words in the name of the bureau, and (d) the principal words in the name of the division.

Names	Index Form
Population Division U. S. Bureau of the Census	United States Government Commerce Department Census Bureau Population Division
Bureau of Mines U. S. Department of the Interior	United States Government Interior Department Mines Bureau
Bureau of Labor Standards U. S. Department of Labor	United States Government Labor Department Labor Standards Bureau

Note: If the key name, United States Government, does not appear on the material as part of the name, it is written in for filing purposes.

RULE 30 Political Subdivisions

The parts of the name of an office in a state, county, city, or other political subdivision are considered in this order: (a) the principal word or words in the name of the political subdivision, followed by its classification such as "State," "County," or "City," and (b) the principal word or words in the name of the department, board, or office.

Names	Index Form

Purchasing Department
State of Indiana
Indianapolis, Indiana
	Indiana, State
	  Purchasing Department
	  Indianapolis, Indiana

City Purchasing Department
Indianapolis, Indiana
	Indianapolis, City
	  Purchasing Department
	  Indianapolis, Indiana

Market Enforcement Office of Oregon
Salem, Oregon
	Oregon, State
	  Market Enforcement Office
	  Salem, Oregon

State Bureau of Markets
Salem, Oregon
	Oregon, State
	  Markets Bureau
	  Salem, Oregon

Office of the Assessor
San Diego, California
	San Diego, City
	  Assessor, Office
	  San Diego, California

County Assessor
San Diego, California
	San Diego, County
	  Assessor, County
	  San Diego, California

Notes: (1) Two titles are usually sufficient for identifying state, county, and city names because these names are usually less complex than those in the federal government. (2) If the key name does not appear on the material as a part of the name, it is written in for filing purposes.

RULE 31 Foreign Government Names

a. Names of agencies or offices of foreign governments are indexed in a manner similar to that for American government offices: (a) the name of the country, (b) the name of the executive department, (c) the name of the office, bureau, or agency.

Names	Index Form
Minister of Trade Australia	Australia, Commonwealth Trade, Minister of

Agricultural Research Council
Ministry of Agriculture
Great Britain
	Great Britain, Kingdom
	  Agriculture, Ministry
	  Agricultural Research Council

b. When foreign language names are to be processed for filing, company policy will probably dictate that such names be translated and adequately cross-referenced. This procedure involves filing names primarily under translated titles and making cross-references to the foreign language names.

Names	Processed Names—Index Form
Estados Unidos Mexicanos	Mexico, Republic
Secretaria de Industria y	Industry and Commerce,
Commercio	Secretary
Mexico, D. F.	Mexico, Federal District
Koninkrijk der Nederlanden	Netherlands, Kingdom of
Centrale Dienst voor Innen	Import and Export Office,
Vitvoer	Central

Note: National names used as key titles can be made as informal as distinctive identification will permit. For example, the shorter title "Kingdom of Great Britain" may serve in place of the exact title "Kingdom of Great Britain and Northern Ireland." The title "Republic of Mexico" may be used in place of the formal title "United States of Mexico (Estados Unidos Mexicanos)."

Subjects as Primary Titles

When it is evident that the use of a certain subject title would be preferable to the use of names as titles for indexing purposes, such a subject title is authorized for use. This subject title then can be used as a key unit, and personal or business names can be used as secondary and subsequent indexing units. If the subject title does not appear on material being coded, it should be written in.

Applications for employment and bids on construction, as examples, are usually filed according to the subject titles rather than by correspondents' names. In such a subject breakdown, names of correspondents are arranged alphabetically within the subject classification.

Names	Descriptive Index Form			
	Key Unit	Unit 2	Unit 3	Unit 4
John Cramer	Applications (Employment)	Cramer	John	
Harold Eagen	Applications (Employment)	Eagen	Harold	
E. F. Adams	Bids (Construction)	Adams	E.	F.
Thompson-Walters Corp.	Bids (Construction)	Thompson-	Walters	Corp.

Cross-Referencing Special Names

Like personal names, business names sometimes present problems in indexing that require the preparation of cross-reference cards. The extent of cross-referencing is determined primarily by the needs of the office or business which the card file serves. If it is probable that more than one name will be associated with the same information or material, cross-reference cards should be used. Unnecessary cross-referencing should be avoided because it may create confusion and it is a time- and space-consuming operation.

Newspapers. If the city of publication of a newspaper is not the first word or words in the name of the newspaper, a cross-reference should be prepared under the newspaper name.

Original Card	Cross-Reference Card
New York: Long Island Press	Long Island Press See New York: Long Island Press
New York Times	(No cross-reference necessary)
New York: Wall Street Journal (The)	Wall Street Journal (The) See New York: Wall Street Journal (The)
Newark News	(No cross-reference necessary)

Periodicals. Since a file card is prepared for the name of a periodical, a second card may be prepared for the name of the publisher and, if necessary, for any other name closely associated with the name. For example, *Farm-Home Magazine,* published by the Rahe and Dawson Magazine Publishers, may have been printed formerly under the name *Rural Home.* A new card prepared for a card file would show the name "Farm-Home Magazine" and the date or approximate date the change was made. In addition, two cross-reference cards would be prepared: one for the name of the publishing company and another for the former name of the magazine. This system of cross-referencing makes it possible to locate the desired information easily and rapidly regardless of the name that first comes to mind, for each cross-reference card refers to the original file card.

```
Farm-Home Magazine

Farm-Home Magazine
Rahe and Dawson Magazine Publishers
1225 Euclid Avenue
Cleveland, OH  44102


Until 10/10/-- published under the name
   Rural Home
```

```
Rahe (and) Dawson Magazine Publishers

Rahe and Dawson Magazine Publishers
1225 Euclid Avenue
Cleveland, OH  44102


See Farm-Home Magazine
```

```
Rural Home

See Farm-Home Magazine
```

Similar Names. When several surnames are identical or similar in pronunciation but different in spelling, permanent cross-references should be made to each of the various spellings of the name as shown below.

```
Schneider, See also Schnieder, Shneider,      Schnieder, See also Schneider, Shneider,
Snider, Snyder, Synider                       Snider, Snyder, Synider
```

Businesses Known by More Than One Name. There are several circumstances under which a business may be known by more than one name: (1) A business operating under a long name may be popularly referred to by a shortened name, such as "Clark's" for "Clark Specialty and Department Store." (2) A business may have its own name, but it may actually be a subsidiary of another company. For example, a firm with the name "Gardley Company" may be a subsidiary of the firm "Consolidated Manufacturers, Inc." (3) A store (for example, "Youngstown Suppliers") may be a branch of a large organization ("Metropolitan Wholesale Suppliers"), which gives to each branch the name of the city in which the branch is located. The name used on the original card should be either (1) the better known or more commonly used name or (2) the name appearing on the letterhead.

Original Card	Cross-Reference Card
Clark's	Clark Specialty and Department Store See Clark's
Gardley Company	Consolidated Manufacturers, Inc. See Gardley Company
Youngstown Suppliers	Metropolitan Wholesale Suppliers See Youngstown Suppliers
Zenia Suppliers	Zenia Suppliers

Foreign Language Names of Companies and Foreign Government Agencies. When a translation is given for a foreign language business or a foreign language government name, the original card is prepared under the translated name, and the cross-reference card is prepared under the foreign name. Otherwise index the name as shown.

Original Card	Cross-Reference Card

Uruguay, Republic of
  Public Education, Secretary
  of
	Republica Oriental del Uruguay
	Secretaria de Education Publica
	See Uruguay, Republic of
	    Public Education, Secretary of

Aluminum Corporation of Belgium
  (The)
	L'Aluminium Belge Societe Anonyme
	See Aluminum Corporation of
	    Belgium (The)

QUESTIONS FOR DISCUSSION

1. What names are given to the two methods of indexing names of organizations and agencies?

2. Why might the name "Calvary Baptist Church" be indexed in either of two ways?

3. Why might the name of a newspaper be indexed correctly in either of two ways?

4. If your filing system included materials about schools located in several different states, would you be *more apt* to use the descriptive or the as-written method of indexing?

5. If your filing operations were concerned with papers from local businesses, institutions, and organizations in a city of less than 50,000 population, would your indexing system *probably* be in the descriptive or in the as-written manner? Why?

6. Why would it not be advisable to use both the "as-written" and the "descriptive" methods of indexing in one filing system?

7. Give two examples of subject titles that would probably be used as key units instead of names of businesses or of persons.

8. Give four examples of names that probably should be cross-referenced.

9. What is the *key unit* in each of the following names when the descriptive manner of indexing is used?

    a. University of Hawaii
    b. Cathedral of St. Paul
    c. Dorsey High School, Los Angeles, Calif.
    d. The Barristers Club
    e. Free Methodist Church
    f. Hotel Arlington
    g. Des Moines <u>Register</u>
    h. National Association of Secretaries
    i. Hotel Riviera Galleries
    j. Computer Training College, Miami, Fla.

10. What is the *second indexing unit* in each of the following names when the as-written manner of indexing is used?

    a. <u>Family Health Magazine</u>, New York, N.Y.
    b. Andrew Jackson High School, Atlanta, Ga.
    c. Hotel Los Arcos
    d. Temple Beth Am
    e. CFTO-TV
    f. Foundation for Cooperative Housing
    g. <u>Records Management Quarterly</u>, Chicago, Ill.
    h. Motel Mobile
    i. 20-30 Club
    j. American Federation of the Arts

11. Each of the following groups of names contains three names in correct alphabetic order. A fourth name is given in italics below each group. Where in each group should the fourth name be placed?

a. H I S Sportwear
H and J Publishing Co.
H & S Soul Food

H I D O International

b. Bar Association of Burbank
Bowling Assn. of Boston
Butchers' Trust Fund

Society of Botanists

c. UNA-USA
United Nations Center
United States Bank

U.S. Chamber of Commerce

d. Wilson High School, Denver
C. R. Wilson & Drury Associates
Wilson-DuBois & Co.

Wilson's Drug Stores, Inc.

**FILING
PROBLEMS**

1. Type or write the following names and addresses in correct descriptive indexing order. If a name or an address is incomplete, add the words required to complete it.

a. Department of Health,
Education & Welfare
Office of Education
b. U.S. Commerce Department
Bureau of International
Commerce
c. Canadian Travel Bureau
600 Market St.
San Francisco, CA 94108
d. National Park Service
Department of the Interior

e. Mexican Govt. Tourism Dept.
National Tourism Council
Republic of Mexico
Mexico D.F.
f. Landsvirkjun
Sudurlandsbraut 14
Reykjavik, Iceland
g. Trainees Exchange Office (IAESTE)
Ministry of Communications
and Public Works
Republic of Finland

2. A. Type or write each of the following names in descriptive indexing order on a 5″ by 3″ index card or on a slip of paper cut to that size. Place in the upper right corner of the card the letter that identifies the name.

B. When you have typed all the cards, arrange them in alphabetic order.

C. Prepare an answer sheet similar to the one illustrated on page 19. Type or write the numbers 1 to 10 in a column. After the numbers, list the letters representing the names in the order in which you have them arranged.

a. Thos. Reeder Elementary School
Rochester, NY 14609
b. Rachel's Club Unique
Durham, NC 27709
c. Readers' Review Magazine
Racine, WI 53404
d. RTA Products
Burlington, VT 05403
e. Revere High School
Rochester, NY 14611

f. Raab, Radcliffe & Simonetti
Charleston, WV 25307
g. Reader's Processing Co.
Bangor, ME 04402
h. R-Tistic Decorators
Kansas City, KS 66112
i. Ramsey County Recorder
St. Paul, MN 55121
j. Association of Retailers
St. Louis, MO 63126

3. A. Type or write each of the following names in descriptive indexing order on a 5″ by 3″ index card or on a slip of paper cut to that size. Place in the upper right corner of the card the letter that identifies the name.

B. When you have typed all the cards, arrange them in alphabetic order.

C. Prepare an answer sheet similar to the one illustrated on page 19. Type or write the numbers 1 to 20 in a column. After the numbers, list the letters representing the names in the order in which you have them arranged.

a. Air Ways Freight Service
b. The Assurance Co. of Canada
c. Association of Industrial
   Consultants
d. Antigua Iron Imports
e. At Your Service, Inc.
f. The Associates Leasing
   Corporation
g. Amsco Corp.
h. Associated Travel Services, Ltd.
i. Aircraft Welding Company
j. Alitalia Airlines
k. Astro-Arc, Incorporated

l. Automotive Exchange Co.
m. The Anti-Acid Products Co.
n. Allison & J. B. Curtis
o. Aerolinea Argentinas
p. Associated Steel Co.
q. American University,
   Amsterdam
r. Assured Business
   Consultants
s. Arkansas Gazette,
   Little Rock, Arkansas
t. Airports Department
   Allegheny County
   Pittsburgh, PA 15221

4. On 5" x 3" cards or on slips of paper cut to that size, type or write cross-reference cards *when needed* for names given in the list below. Do not prepare a cross-reference card if, in your opinion, a cross-reference card need not be made for a certain name. Follow the example of the first name in the list.

1. APSA Peruvian Airlines
1x. Peruvian Airlines
    See APSA Peruvian Airlines
2. Association of Trial Lawyers
3. J. C. Barbour & W. L. Reed
4. New York Times
5. Mrs. Katherine Wicks
   (Mrs. Arnold Wicks)
6. Byron Williamson, Agent
   Southern Insurance Co.
7. Charles Mason Van Den Berg
8. Dan Blackburn and Associates
9. Administrative Management Magazine
   Geyer-McAllister Publications, Inc.
10. Rawlins-Templa Corporation
11. Acme Visible Records, Inc.
12. The HON Company
13. Ames Color-File Corporation
14. Harpers of Oklahoma
15. Remington Rand
    Office Systems Division
    Sperry Rand Corporation

JOB 3 Card Filing—Business and Institutional Names

JOB 4 Card Filing—Indexing and Filing Review (Optional)

At this time complete Job 3, and Job 4 if desired, in OFFICE FILING PROCEDURES, Fourth Edition. The instructions and supplies for these jobs are included in the practice set.

CHAPTER 5

ALPHABETIC SYSTEMS AND FILING PROCEDURES

In this chapter, three very important aspects of filing are examined: (1) the principal ways of organizing a filing system, (2) the elements of an alphabetic correspondence filing system, and (3) the procedures followed as papers are being processed for filing.

These three important aspects of filing are given detailed attention later in the chapter; but first, you must know why a filing system is a necessary part of a business office and why filing and the control of records are important.

Every business organization must communicate with those it serves as well as with those who serve it. Thus, in the ordinary course of business activity, many letters, memorandums, telegrams, purchase orders, invoices, and many other kinds of messages are sent and received. These evidences of business activity must be filed for future reference.

The volume of such correspondence in any given organization depends upon the type of operation being pursued. For example, in some companies that contact customers as well as suppliers of goods and services primarily by letter, the volume of mail is very heavy. In other types of businesses that make contacts largely in an over-the-counter manner, correspondence is light. Regardless of the volume of correspondence, however, success in the operation of any business depends in part upon maintaining a filing system that is adequate for the control of communication materials as well as for the control of all other types of records.

Not every piece of correspondence is valuable for future reference; thus, not all material is retained and filed. Almost all correspondence, however, is held for a certain length of time as an active record of a business transaction, at least until a satisfactory conclusion has been reached. Beyond that point certain records may be destroyed, while others may be preserved to provide evidence of action taken on a particular matter or to be used as a guide to future action.

Incoming materials and copies of outgoing materials that relate to the same individual, company, or subject are, in most instances, filed together so that the record on that individual, company, or subject will be complete. For example, when a purchase order is received from a customer, the purchase order, a copy of the letter acknowledging the order, and a copy of the invoice covering the shipment are all filed together. Later, a copy of the letter acknowledging payment and all other related papers are added to the material in the file. Thus, a complete history of the transaction is available in one place.

Interoffice memorandums or copies thereof are filed under the name of the individual or the department, office, or subject to or about which the memorandums were written, or from which they were received. If desired, copies may be filed in a place separate from the general incoming and outgoing correspondence of a firm.

In all the circumstances mentioned above, it is the purpose of filing, and of records control in general, to keep related materials together and to hold them in readiness for withdrawal at the request of persons desiring to use them. In order to hold records in a state of control, a system of filing must be used; and careful, systematic procedures must be followed in all phases of the filing operation.

SECTION 1   ORGANIZATION OF A FILING SYSTEM

In very broad terms, a filing system is made up of all the elements and items that are essential to the filing, retrieval, and use of information, including (1) the equipment used, (2) the guiding plan used, and (3) the procedures followed in processing file material. Each of these factors will be explained in this chapter, beginning with a consideration of the basic equipment used not only in alphabetic filing but also in all other types of filing systems.

Equipment and Supplies

Folders. Basically, all papers are held in containers called *folders,* because, by themselves, sheets of paper sag, tear, and become unmanageable when placed unsupported in a file drawer or on a file shelf. To avoid this problem, folders to hold papers in an upright position are made of a heavy paper known as manila or kraft paper or, sometimes, of plastic material. A sheet of this material is folded into a "V" shape, with the front part about one-half inch shorter than the back part to form

Illus. 5-1, **File Folder**

   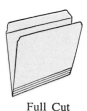

One-Fifth Cut   One-Third Cut   One-Half Cut   Full Cut

Illus. 5-2, **Standard Tabbing on Folders**

a pocket into which papers can be placed. Several score marks are usually made at the bottom of the "V" so that the bottom can be refolded into an expanded position to permit storage of more papers than would otherwise be possible.

Along the top of the back part of a folder, there is a projecting piece, known as a *tab*, about one-half inch in height. It serves as the signboard of the folder, for on it is written or typed the title or *caption* that indicates the type of material filed in the folder. (See Illustration 5-1.) Since it is desirable to have the folder tabs as useful and visible as possible in the file drawer, tabs are cut in different positions so that the folders can be arranged to show the tabs in various positions across the width of a file drawer. When tabs are cut to such a width that five show across the width of a file drawer, the cuts are known as *fifth-cut;* and folders prepared in this way are known as *fifth-cut folders*. The tabs most commonly used are *fifth-cut, third-cut, half-cut,* and *full-cut*.

Captions on Folders. The caption on a folder usually is typed on a gummed label, which is then affixed over the folder tab. When you type a caption on a label, follow the steps given below. These suggestions, when followed consistently, will assure uniformity in style, correct alignment, and easy visibility in the file drawer.

1. Type the caption before you tear the label off the strip of perforated, gummed labels. (See Illustration 5-6, page 51.)
2. Type the first line of the caption on the second line from the top edge or score line of the label so the caption will be clearly visible.
3. Type the caption at the third space from the left edge of the label.
4. Use a uniform style in typing captions. A combination of capital letters and lowercase letters is the preferred style.
5. Type the caption in index form.

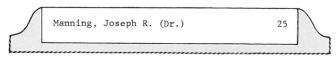

Manning, Joseph R. (Dr.)   25

Illus. 5-3, **Folder Caption**

Guides. Although each folder is given a caption, this identification by itself is not sufficient to provide for ease in filing or retrieving papers in a filing system. A "signpost" is required to guide the eye and the hand to the place in the file drawer where the desired folder is held. For this purpose, *guides* were devised and are used in all types of filing systems.

Correspondence filing systems are equipped with letter-size pressboard guides, which serve to divide each file drawer or shelf into alphabetic compartments. Thus, guides make filing and finding of folders an easier process than would be the case if only folders were used to mark the alphabetic sections of a filing system. Guides are therefore the signposts in a filing system. They call attention to the major sections as well as the minor sections of the file and are, in fact, an indexing outline for any type of filing system.

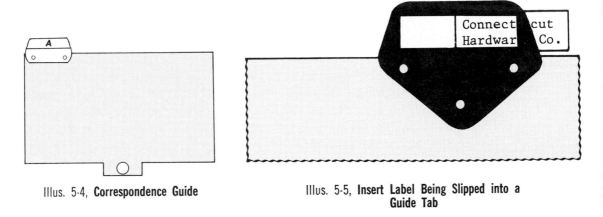

Illus. 5-4, **Correspondence Guide**   Illus. 5-5, **Insert Label Being Slipped into a Guide Tab**

Inserts and Labels on Guides and Folders. As stated in Chapter 1, the *tabs* (projections) on card guides are sometimes made of a plastic material, or of metal with a plastic "window" through which the captions (titles) on the tabs can be read. This is true also of guides and sometimes of folders that are used in correspondence filing systems. (See Illustrations 5-4 and 5-5.)

A widely used guide tab, made of clear plastic, has a front and a back with a space between them into which a slip of paper bearing a caption can be inserted. This is convenient when supervisors wish to construct their own filing systems, that is, systems suited to the needs of their own particular business organizations.

A common way to prepare a file folder is to use a gummed label, upon which the notation may be typed or printed, and to affix the label to the tab of the folder. (See Illustration 5-6.) The combination of guides with insert slips and folders with gummed labels is widely used in forming and in extending filing systems.

Cabinets and Shelves. A total system of filing is made up of not only guides and folders but also of cabinets (or other types of units) that consist of drawers or shelves that "hold" or "store" the guides and folders. Generally, there are three types of holding or storing units: (1) vertical or "standard" cabinets with pull-out type drawers, (2) lateral cabinets with pull-out shelves, and (3) stationary shelves with a variety of special equipment for holding folders and papers. (See page 52 for illustrations of these three types of cabinets.)

An open-faced frame is attached to the front of every drawer in a file cabinet. This frame provides space for the insertion of the *drawer label,* which is a small card or tab, about three inches by one and three-quarter inches. The caption on a label shows the alphabetic range of materials held within one file drawer. Thus, the labels guide the files operator to the particular drawer that contains the alphabetic section in which he desires to file or to find materials.

In Illustration 5-10, page 55, the label on the front of the drawer is captioned *A-BAN* to show that materials within this alphabetic range are filed in this drawer. This caption is read "from A *through* Ban."

Smead Manufacturing Co.

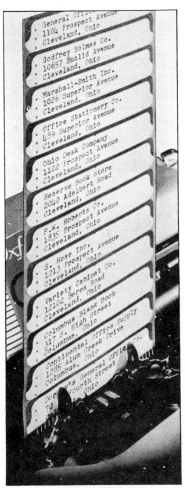

Oxford Filing Supply Co.
Oxford Pendaflex Corp.

Illus. 5-6, **Gummed Labels for Folder Tabs**

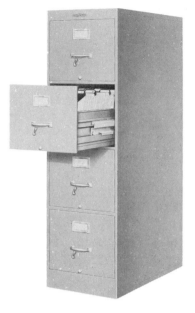

Shaw-Walker
Illus. 5-7, **Vertical Cabinet**

Shaw-Walker
Illus. 5-8, **Lateral Cabinet**

TAB Products Co.
Illus. 5-9, **Shelf-Filing Unit**

SECTION 2   ELEMENTS OF A FILING SYSTEM

The need for a well-planned filing system and the importance of using systematic procedures in its operation make it necessary for all office workers who are concerned with filing or records control to understand what a "system" is and how it must be used. This is true because a system is effective only when it is used properly and intelligently.

What is a filing system? It is not just a random assembly of guides and folders held in a cabinet. It takes much more than just pieces of equipment to form a system that holds records in a controlled manner.

In the first place, a system can be constructed only after definite and careful planning has been undertaken to determine the best possible use of equipment and procedures. Files that "just grow" are not systems; systems are planned. In addition, more than use of equipment is involved in a system, for it is also essential that procedures be planned and followed by all who are concerned with filing and with records control. In very broad terms, a filing system is made up of all the elements and items that are essential to its existence and effective use: the plan of the system, the equipment used, and the procedures followed.

Use of Guides and Folders

Guides. The first requirement in an alphabetic filing system is a master guiding plan that will show the primary alphabetic divisions in the system. For this purpose, a series of markers called *primary guides* is used to set off these alphabetic divisions. A primary guide always precedes all other materials in a section, including special guides, special folders, and miscellaneous folders, that fall within the alphabetic range of the primary guide.

Folders. The second requirement in an alphabetic filing system is a set of containers called *folders* to hold file materials in such a way that they can be found in the easiest manner possible. Provision must be made for several types of folders in which to house several kinds of correspondence since correspondence varies in importance as well as in volume and purpose.

The importance of filed material is judged by its activity, that is, by the number of times it is requested for use as well as by the number of related pieces that accumulate over a relatively short period of time. It is neither advisable nor necessary to prepare an *individual folder* for correspondence to, from, and about one correspondent if that correspondence is not referred to frequently, or if it is limited to a very few pieces. Such correspondence as this is housed in a folder known as a *miscellaneous folder*. In the alphabetic method, there is one miscellaneous folder for every primary guide; and each miscellaneous folder is given exactly the same *caption* (title) as the primary guide that heads the section of which the miscellaneous folder is a part. All papers to, from, and about correspondents who do not have individual folders, and whose names fall into the alphabetic range indicated by the caption on the folder, are arranged in the miscellaneous folder first in alphabetic order by name and next by date with the most recent date in front of each name group. When correspondence with one individual or one company is requested frequently and/or accumulates rapidly, this correspondence is usually removed from a miscellaneous folder; and an individual folder is prepared for it by typing the name of the company or the individual on the tab of the new folder.

Arrangement of Guides and Folders. There are many ways of arranging guides and folders in file drawers. Usually the various parts of an alphabetic system are arranged to conform to the types of materials being filed so that there will be a maximum of efficiency in the filing process. Efficiency requires arranging guides and folders in a manner that will give the greatest possible access to folders and, at the same time, will make all guide and folder tabs as visible as possible.

Illustration and Description of One Alphabetic System

The file drawer in Illustration 5-10 contains items arranged in five positions, as follows:

1. Primary guides (the signposts) are shown in first position. There are three primary guides: *A-Al 1, Am-Az 2, B-Ban 3.* The numbers are used to indicate the order in which the guides should appear in the drawer.
2. Miscellaneous folders are shown in second position. There are three miscellaneous folders—one for each of the primary alphabetic sections in the file. A miscellaneous folder bears the same caption as the primary guide that opens the section; it is always the last item in the section.
3. Two special guides are shown in third position. These mark two special sections—one for *Applications* and one for names beginning with *Bailey.* Two special folders—one to hold special section materials for Applications and one to hold all materials bearing the name "Bailey"—are also in third position.
4–5. Individual folders (cut two positions wide) occupy fourth and fifth positions in the file drawer.

This file drawer contains all materials in the alphabetic range *A* through *Ban.* A description of each of the items will help you to understand the various positions and purposes of the guides and folders.

1. The first item in the file drawer is the primary guide *A-Al 1,* which heads the first alphabetic section and calls attention to the alphabetic range within this section.
2. The second item is an individual folder in fourth and fifth positions for A & K Mart. This folder has been prepared because the correspondence with A & K Mart is too voluminous and important to be held along with materials from other companies in the miscellaneous folder in this alphabetic section of the system.
3. The third item is an individual folder for the Adrian Shoppe. This folder was prepared for the same reasons as those given for the preparation of the individual folder for A & K Mart.
4. The miscellaneous folder for the alphabetic section *A-Al 1* is the fourth item and the final one in this section of the system. In this folder are filed all papers not otherwise provided for by individual folders in this section. Within the miscellaneous

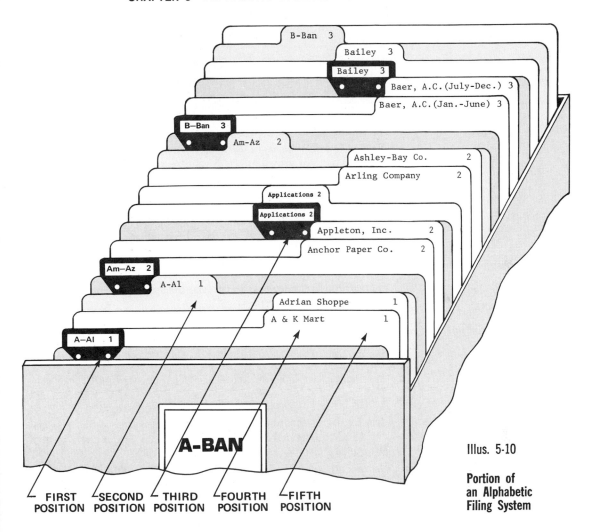

Illus. 5-10

Portion of an Alphabetic Filing System

folder, papers in the alphabetic range *A-Al* are filed according to the alphabetic order of the names found on the papers. When two or more papers bear the same name, they are filed as a group and thus form a unit within the miscellaneous folder. Papers that form an identical name group are placed according to the dates of writing, with the most recently dated paper placed in front position ahead of all other papers in the group.

5. The second of the primary guides, captioned *Am-Az 2*, is next in order. It shows the alphabetic range of the second section in the file drawer.

6–7. Two individual folders in alphabetic order are the next items. These were prepared for active and important correspondents whose papers were too numerous to be held in the miscellaneous folder for this alphabetic section of the system.

8–9. The eighth and ninth items in the file drawer are a special guide (in third position) and a special folder (in third position). The guide marks the location of the special section for the filing of all letters concerning applications for work. The special folder, labeled *Applications*, has been placed in the file in order to hold all papers relating to this subject. Letters within this folder are filed according to the alphabetic sequence of the names of the individuals who have applied for work.

10–11. These two items are individual folders: one for the Arling Company; the other for the Ashley-Bay Co.

12. The miscellaneous folder, *Am-Az 2*, in second position holds all miscellaneous materials in this alphabetic section and closes this division of the file drawer.

13. The primary guide, *B-Ban 3*, shows the alphabetic range of the next section.

14–15. These items are individual folders for the same correspondent— A. C. Baer. Originally there was only one folder for this individual; but as more materials concerning him accumulated during the year, it was evident that the single folder was not sufficient to hold the material being accumulated. Thus it became necessary to open a second folder. This was done by keeping in the original folder all material that had gathered prior to July of the current year. Then, the second folder was labeled to show that it was to hold all his papers for the remaining months of the year (July through December).

16–17. A special guide and a special folder are used to form a special section to house all papers from persons and companies whose names begin with the name "Bailey." This special section was prepared because it was found that materials concerning several persons and companies with this surname were accumulating in and crowding the miscellaneous folder for this section of the file. It was also determined that there was not enough material from any one of these persons or firms to justify the preparation of an individual folder.

18. The miscellaneous folder captioned *B-Ban 3* is the last item in this section. It houses all papers for which no other provision has been made in this alphabetic section of the file.

Expansion in a Filing System

In actual business operations, a small system can be started by using only the following basic equipment: a set of primary guides, a limited number of individual folders, and a set of miscellaneous folders. Space should be left in the file drawer so that as the system expands, there will be room to add the extra guides and folders needed to hold additional correspondence.

In a small system, only a few primary divisions are needed; therefore, only a few primary guides are used along with a corresponding number of miscellaneous folders. For example, a small system might be started with 25 primary guides and 25 miscellaneous folders. Added to these would be enough individual folders to handle important and voluminous correspondence with persons or companies. This amount of equipment would make the equivalent of a one-drawer filing system.

As time passes and as correspondence increases in this small system, however, some miscellaneous folders may hold so many papers that the finding of a single paper becomes a difficult task. When this condition becomes evident, it is necessary to divide the contents of some of the overcrowded miscellaneous folders in order to decrease the volume of accumulated materials in them. Since miscellaneous folders hold papers from several different individuals or companies, the papers concerning one "important" correspondent may be removed from the miscellaneous folder, and an individual folder may be opened for him. This individual folder is labeled with the correspondent's name. From this time on, materials to, from, and about him will be filed in his individual folder and not in the miscellaneous folder. This makes his papers easier to find and relieves congestion in the miscellaneous folder.

A second method of relieving overcrowding in miscellaneous folders is to prepare and use special title sections and special subject sections as a regular part of an alphabetic filing system. Illustration 5-10 shows the use of two types of special sections in third position. The first one, *Applications,* is a subject section. The second one, *Bailey,* is a special name section. Each of these special sections is prepared for a different reason and is handled in a different manner, but both serve to bring related materials into one part of the system and also to relieve overcrowded conditions in miscellaneous folders.

A special subject section is started when it becomes evident that the search for papers would be made easier and surer if all materials about one topic or subject could be found in one folder placed behind a guide that would direct the searcher to that section of the file.

An example of how a special subject section is used to advantage is when a subject folder is used to house all letters of application for employment. This is a case in which it is probable that no one in an organization would be apt to remember the name of an individual applicant and thus there would seldom be a call for his correspondence by using his name. A request for such file material would come in terms of the applicant's only contact with the firm—his application for employment. Thus, if his letter were filed under his own name, the letter would probably not be found when needed because no one would be likely to remember his name.

Special name sections are set up in a system for much the same reason as that used for establishing subject sections, but special name sections may include many kinds of titles that can be used to form useful divisions which make filing and finding easier and safer. Such a section for the name "Bailey" is shown in third position in Illustration 5-10.

Another way to bring related materials together in a system is to provide special sections for commonly found geographic names. This type of special section is especially useful when papers are received from firms in metropolitan areas because the name of a city or an area is frequently used by companies as the first unit in the company name. Under such circumstances it is sometimes desirable to open a special geographic title section in which the city name is given as the caption on a special guide. This guide can be followed by a series of both individual and miscellaneous folders, depending upon the volume of material to be handled. For a city with the area and population of Chicago, the special guide could show the city name; and a series of individual folders might follow this guide. These folders would be for names of companies having "Chicago" as the first unit; for example, Chicago Airlines, Chicago Business Association, Chicago Business Machines Co. At the end of the group of individual folders, there might be one miscellaneous folder for all other correspondence with firms using the name "Chicago." Or, it might be necessary to have a series of miscellaneous folders if the volume of material is large enough. If so, folders of this type could be divided into segments of the alphabet, as: *Chicago, A-F*; *Chicago, G-L*; *Chicago, M-Z*.

This same pattern for using special sections to gather related materials into one section of the system and to relieve crowded conditions in miscellaneous folders is commonly used for names having as first units such common terms as National, American, Eastern, Western, Northern, Southern, and United.

SECTION 3 PROCESSING OF PAPERS IN ALPHABETIC FILING

In the preceding section of this chapter, the organization of an alphabetic filing system was presented because an understanding of how a system works is necessary if there is to be accuracy in filing.

Illus. 5-11

Dictation of a Letter

Dictation of a letter is the first step in a process that ends with the filing of a copy of the letter.

In this section, an equally important matter is considered—the exact method for handling and processing papers that are to be filed in an alphabetic system.

Filing is sometimes considered to be only a matter of arranging materials in alphabetic order and putting them into filing cabinets. There is, however, much more than this involved in the processing of papers for filing. Some important steps in processing papers take place before the papers reach the filing department for storage.

Processing of Papers Before Transmission to Filing Department

Before an *incoming letter* reaches the filing department of a large organization, it has passed through at least two other departments—the mailing department and the department to which the letter was routed. (In a smaller organization, an incoming letter is usually opened by one person authorized to handle and distribute incoming mail.) As a result of action taken in these departments (the mailing department and the department to which the letter was routed), the letter should show two marks when it is received by the filing department: (1) a time stamp placed on it when the mail was opened and (2) a release mark placed on it by the department that handled the letter. (See page 61.)

Time Stamp. When incoming mail is received, the mail clerk opens it and stamps each piece with a rubber stamp or by machine with a mark known as a *time stamp*. This mark records the date and, sometimes, the time of receipt of each piece of correspondence; and it serves as a check on the time that elapses before a reply is sent.

Release Mark. After the mail is stamped by the mail clerk, it is sorted according to the names of the individuals and departments concerned and is delivered to them. The person to whom a letter is addressed, or someone designated by him, answers the letter. After the reply has been typed, two items of correspondence are sent to the filing department—the original incoming letter and a copy of the outgoing reply. Before the original letter is sent, however, the initials of the secretary or those of the employer are marked in the upper left-hand corner to indicate to the filing department that the letter has been released for filing. These initials, or other mark if a rubber stamp is used, are known as a *release mark* (M.A. in Illustration 5-12). The release mark gives the files operator the authority to file the letter.

The copy of an outgoing letter does not require a release mark because it may always be assumed that the copy is ready to be filed.

Processing of Papers in Filing Department

Inspection. In processing correspondence received by the filing department, the files operator should first inspect each incoming letter to see that it bears a release mark as authorization for filing. As mentioned before, this inspection is not necessary for copies of outgoing letters.

Reading Correspondence. The next step taken by the files operator in processing materials to be filed is to read and analyze each piece of correspondence in order to determine the title under which it should be filed. Sometimes before correspondence is sent to the filing department, it has been marked to show the key title under which it should be filed. If this key title is not shown, the files operator must read the letter in order to select the name or title in it that should be used for filing purposes. To prevent having materials filed under the wrong names or titles, therefore, careful reading of correspondence is a vital part of good filing practice.

Making Key Title Decisions. There is a difference in procedure between processing names on index cards or on lists and processing names appearing in letters. In index card and list processing, only one name appears at a time so the files operator can proceed directly to process this name. In correspondence material, however, several names or subjects may appear in each letter; and, because of this, a decision must be made regarding which of several possible names or subjects is to be used as the key name, or *key title,* under which the paper will be filed.

Rules for Selecting Key Titles. In general, correspondence is filed under the most important name appearing in it; and, for filing purposes, the most important name is the one likely to be used by persons who will be calling for a given piece of correspondence. In selecting the

$\mathcal{M}.\mathcal{A}.$

                                April 5, 19--

Mr. Arthur R. Channing, President
Astrolite, Incorporated
412 Westways Boulevard
Phoenix, Arizona 85004
U.S.A.

APR 9 19-- A.M.

Dear Mr. Channing:

    Subject: Financial Arrangements for New Plant

    Our division office in Montreal has informed us
that you are interested in securing financing in Canada
for a new production unit to be located near Windsor,
Ontario.

    This company will consider it a privilege to assist
your organization with this matter. So that we may begin
immediately, please fill out the enclosed set of papers
and return them directly to me.

    Your Vice-President in charge of Canadian Astrolite
Ltd. has met several times with our Montreal representatives. From the information he has presented, we are
impressed with your product. We feel that your company
has great growth potential in Canada, and we will give
you every possible assistance with your development program.

                Sincerely yours,

                I. A. Wilson

                I. A. Wilson, President

ds

Enclosures 2

Illus. 5-12

Incoming Letter Coded, Time-Stamped, and Released for Filing

most important name as the key title, it is necessary for the files operator to be familiar with definite rules concerning the selection of key titles.

1. The name most likely to be used by a person in calling for an original letter is the name that appears on the letterhead. This name is usually taken as the key title for filing original letters.

2. The name most likely to be used by a person in calling for the carbon copy of an outgoing letter is the name of the company that appears in the inside address. If no company name is given, the name of the individual on the address line is used.

3. When an incoming letter is written on paper without a letterhead, the name of the person who signs the letter is usually taken as the key title; or the name of his company is used if it appears in the body of the letter or is known by the files operator and is considered to be of greater importance than the person's name.

4. If a subject or a name that is given in the body of a letter is considered to be of greatest importance to filing and finding, it is used as the key title.

5. In an original letter of a personal nature, the key title is usually the name of the individual who signs the letter. In the carbon copy of an outgoing letter of a personal nature, the key title is the name of the person who is identified in the inside address.

6. If special sections are included in an alphabetic system, the titles of these sections are used as key titles for all letters relating to matters covered by special section titles. For example, in a letter pertaining to advertising rates, the key title used would be *Advertising,* and the letter would be filed in a folder especially prepared for holding letters pertaining to advertising.

   When names of special sections in the files are used as key titles, the files operator must write these titles in exact form on letters or other materials being processed. For example, in the case of a letter pertaining to advertising rates, the title *Advertising* would be written by the operator at the top of the letter; and this title would serve as the key title for that letter.

7. If there is reasonable doubt in the mind of the files operator concerning the name to be used as the key title, he or she should consult the supervisor. Or, if an office manual on filing procedure has been prepared, this should be used as a guide to the selection of the correct key title.

Coding. After it has been decided which name is to be used as the key title, a very definite procedure is followed in marking it so that the operator will not have to go through the process of determining the key title for this particular letter if it must be filed again at a later date. The marking of the key title is called *coding,* and these are the steps which are taken by an operator in the coding process:

J.A. **DATE:** May 30, 19--
TO: J. E. Amestoy, Astrolite, Phoenix
FROM: Logan C. Horton

JUN 1 19-- P.M.

SUBJECT: Business Show in New York City

The Business and Commerce Association of Greater New York is sponsoring a business show to be held in Madison Square Garden from October 2 to 15.

This will be one of the largest events of its kind ever held in the United States. It would seem advisable for us to enter an exhibit in this show.

Mr. L. M. Halverson is exhibit committee chairman. His address is 1290 Empire State Building.

ek

Illus. 5-13

**Incoming Interoffice Communication Form Coded,
Time-Stamped, and Released for Filing**

1. All units in the key title are marked off by diagonal lines; for example, if the name "Carter Home Products" were to be coded, the first step would be to mark off the units in the name as follows: Carter/Home/Products.

2. The primary unit is underlined: Carter/Home/Products.

3. The remaining units are coded by writing above them numbers to indicate their position or rank in the indexing order; an identifying element is indicated by a check mark beside or above the element.

$\overset{2}{\text{Carter}}/\overset{3}{\text{Home}}/\text{Products}$

(The)$\underset{}{\text{Kline}}/\overset{2}{\text{Realty}}/\overset{3}{\text{Co.}}$

$\overset{2}{\text{U.}}/\overset{3}{\text{S.}}/\overset{4}{\text{Copper}}/\overset{5}{\text{Company,}}/\text{Inc.}$

$\overset{2}{\text{R.}}/\overset{3}{\text{C.}}/\underset{}{\text{Wall}}\ (\&)/\overset{4}{\text{Company}}$

Society (of)/$\overset{2}{\underline{\text{Writers}}}$

$\underset{}{\text{Young}}/\overset{2}{\text{Merchandise}}/\overset{3}{\text{Mart}}$
√ Denver, Colorado

$\underset{}{\text{Young}}/\overset{2}{\text{Merchandise}}/\overset{3}{\text{Mart}}$
√ Lorain, Ohio

These coding and rating marks are very important because they clearly identify the key title and show exactly the units under which the name will be filed. Coding marks are made with a colored pencil so that the marks will stand out and not be confused with other markings that might appear on a paper.

Coding and rating key titles make the refiling of papers a much easier process than it would be if such marks were not used, because uncoded material would have to be processed each time it was removed from the file and then refiled. In some offices coding is done by underlining the whole name under which a piece of correspondence is to be filed. This procedure, however, is not particularly effective because it does not show which of several units was used as the key unit. Thus, in refiling such material, the operator must again decide which unit to use as the key one. Also, a general code mark does not show how the secondary units in a name were considered, and this factor has vital bearing on the order in which a name is filed in relation to other names.

Cross-Referencing. When the files operator reads a letter and codes it, the operator must decide whether it should be cross-referenced. To cross-reference means to prepare a form which shows another title under which a paper might be requested from the files. Just how much cross-referencing should be done is a matter for decision in each office, for, although cross-referencing is a far safer practice than risking the loss of an important paper, the practice can be carried to extremes.

June 22, 19--

Mr. L. A. Meenan
(The) East Side Corporation
1060 De Kalb Street
De Kalb, IL 60115

Dear Mr. Meenan

We have wired our representative in Chicago to contact
your office. You may have talked with Mr. E. L. Simmons
on previous occasions because he has been in the lighting
business in the Chicago area for many years.

Please call on Mr. Simmons at any time during the development of your home and shopping center building program.
He will have access to our staff at the Astrolite of New
York offices in Utica and thus will have and will make
available to you a wide variety of technical advisers on
cost, installation, transportation, and service.

We appreciate your call upon Astrolite, Incorporated. We
can assure you that Starlite units will prove to be inexpensive and will add greatly to the attractiveness and
buyer-appeal of your homes and shops.

Sincerely yours

James E. Amestoy, Manager
Advertising and Sales

ga

cc Mr. E. L. Simmons
   Mr. Logan C. Horton

Illus. 5-14

**Copy of Outgoing Letter with Key Title Coded
and Cross-Reference Marked**

CROSS-REFERENCE SHEET

Name or Subject *Simmons, E. L.*

Date of Item *June 22, 19--*

Regarding *Contact to be made with
The East Side Corporation in
Chicago*

SEE

Name or Subject *East Side Corporation*

Authorized by *Grace Anderson* Date *6/22/--*

Illus. 5-15

**Cross-Reference Sheet for Letter Shown in
Illustration 5-14**

When cross-referencing is overdone, it is expensive because of working time lost and materials wasted, for each cross-reference means double filing and also double the number of papers in a file drawer. Sometimes one or more extra copies of a letter are made so that each copy may be filed under a separate key title and thus serve the same purpose that a cross-reference sheet would serve. At other times a facsimile copy of a letter is made so that it may be filed under a separate title from that used on the original letter and thus serve as a cross-reference.

When there is a possibility that a letter may be called for by a name other than the one selected as the key title, two steps are taken in preparing a cross-reference. First, a wavy line is drawn under the cross-reference name if it appears in the letter, or the cross-reference name is written in the margin of the original letter if the name does not appear in the letter. In the former case, the name to be cross-referenced is indicated by an "x" in the margin opposite the name; the wavy line under the cross-reference name distinguishes it from the straight line used to code the key title. Second, a *cross-reference sheet* is prepared, which will be filed under the name selected as the cross-reference one.

An example of the use of a cross-reference sheet is to be found when a company name is composed of two personal names and either one might be used in calling for the correspondence of that company. If a company name is Jones, Lang & Co., correspondence would be filed under the name with "Jones" as the first indexing unit. But it might be found necessary to make a cross-reference sheet for the name "Lang," because someone might request papers from the company by using this name. Thus, a cross-reference sheet filed under "Lang" would tell the files operator that all papers about this company would be found under the key name "Jones."

If a permanent cross-reference to a number of pieces of correspondence in the files is desired, it is better to use a *visible cross-reference guide*. This is a manila card of the same size as a guide, with a tab in the same position as that used for the tabs of individual folders. A situation in which this type of cross-reference is used is as follows: The name of the correspondent is changed from Wright & Huber to the Norwood Hardware Center. A new folder is therefore opened for the new name of the company, and all the correspondence is transferred from the old folder to the new one. The old folder is removed from the file, and in its place is inserted a visible cross-reference card with a tab on which appears the information shown in typewriter type on page 67.

Wright & Huber
<u>See</u> Norwood Hardware Center

Sorting. After key titles have been coded and cross-reference sheets prepared, the materials must be sorted. *Sorting* is the process of making a preliminary alphabetic arrangement of materials before placing them in folders. Sorting serves two purposes: (1) It saves time in filing. If materials were not sorted, the operator would have to move unsystematically from one file drawer to another. (2) If papers are needed before they have been filed, the papers can be found more easily in a sorted order than in a random arrangement.

Correspondence and cross-reference sheets may be sorted by means of such specially made equipment as sorting trays or compartments. (See Illustration 5-16.) Equipment of this kind provides spaces, labeled alphabetically or otherwise to fit the filing system in use, into which papers may be placed in a preliminary alphabetic arrangement and held in this arrangement until they are filed.

If special sorting equipment is not available, materials may be sorted into alphabetic units in the following manner:

1. Materials are divided into stacks of alphabetic units according to the first letters of the primary units in names; for example, five alphabetic stacks: A-D, E-H, I-M, N-S, T-Z.
2. In each of these five stacks, papers may then be sorted into single alphabetic units; for example, papers taken from the A-D stack may be sorted into separate stacks for A, B, C, and D. This procedure may be followed for all the remaining groups.
3. Finally, papers in each stack may be sorted alphabetically.

Illus. 5-16

Using a Correspondence Sorter to Get Coded Papers into Alphabetic Order

Yawman & Erbe of Calif. Corp.

Steps 1 and 2 are known as *rough sorting;* Step 3, *fine sorting.*

Procedure for Placing Processed Papers in the Filing System. After correspondence has been sorted, it is taken, either as a unit or in alphabetic sections, to the filing area. Then, depending upon the type of storage equipment being used in a given office, the files operator should:

1. Locate the desired file drawer or the shelf section by examining labels on drawers or markers on shelf sections.
2. Scan the primary guides in a file drawer or a shelf section in order to locate the major alphabetic division needed.
3. Check the alphabetic section to see if there is an individual folder or a special folder for the material being filed; and if there is such a folder, file the letter in it.
4. If there is no individual or special folder for the material, file the letter in the miscellaneous folder for the section.

Placing Correspondence in Folders. All correspondence is placed in folders with the letterhead or the inside address at the left side and the writing facing forward.

In an individual folder, correspondence is arranged according to date of writing, with the most recent communication at the front.

In a special folder, such as an Applications folder, correspondence is placed in alphabetic order according to the units in the names of individuals and companies concerned. When two or more pieces of correspondence are for the same individual or company, letters are arranged according to date of writing, with the latest letter being placed in front of the ones bearing earlier dates.

In a miscellaneous folder, the correspondence is placed in alphabetic order according to the units in the names concerned, and then according to date of writing in each name group, with the most recent correspondence at the front of the group. An example of this order is given below. In a miscellaneous folder marked *A-Am 1,* letters would be filed in the following order (reading from front to back):

Order of Letters		Correspondents' Names	Dates on Letters
	(Back)		
5	↑	American Supply Co.	February 12, 19--
4		American Supply Co.	April 16, 19--
3		Aker-Johnson Co.	June 21, 19--
2		Adams & Brooks Co.	May 20, 19--
1		Adams & Brooks Co.	May 26, 19--
	(Front)		

In the foregoing illustration, the Adams & Brooks Co. letter of May 26 is first in the folder because (1) "Adams" precedes "Aker" and "American" in alphabetic order and (2) of the two letters concerning Adams & Brooks Co., the one dated May 26 is the more recent.

QUESTIONS FOR DISCUSSION

1. Why is it necessary to keep some correspondence for a period of time instead of destroying it immediately?
2. What are the three major elements that are essential to a filing system?
3. Why are guides needed in a filing system?
4. In what way are insert slips and gummed labels used in a filing system?
5. What three types of storing units are used to hold file materials?
6. What is the difference between an individual folder and a miscellaneous folder?
7. For what reasons would a section entitled "Applications" be added to an alphabetic filing system?
8. Why is it more efficient to use some individual folders rather than to use only miscellaneous folders in a system?
9. Why would a special name section be added to an alphabetic system?
10. If a special name folder is very active and papers in it accumulate quickly, how can such a folder be extended in order to prevent overcrowding?
11. What is meant by the term "coding"? Why must correspondence be coded before it is filed?
12. Why is it sometimes advisable to cross-reference a piece of correspondence?
13. How are papers arranged in a miscellaneous folder?
14. Why does sorting papers before filing them save time?
15. What does the term "rough sorting" mean?

FILING PROBLEM

Using Illustration 5-10, page 55, as a model, make a similar outline of guides and folders which could be used by a company with which you are familiar. Use the alphabetic sections *C-Ce 15, Cf-Ci 16, Cj-Co 17,* and *Cp-Cz 18.* Include the following items in your system: at least 1 special section for a subject; at least 12 individual folders; at least 1 special name section. Suggestions for the subject are as follows: Car Rental, Caterers, Contracts, Conventions, and Credit Agencies. You may prefer to use others to fit the filing needs of the company you choose.

JOB 5 Alphabetic Correspondence Filing

At this time complete Job 5 in OFFICE FILING PROCEDURES, Fourth Edition. The instructions and supplies for this job are included in the practice set.

CHAPTER 6

REQUISITION, CHARGE, AND FOLLOW-UP CONTROLS

The principal reason for holding papers and other materials in a filing system is to make them available for reference purposes by all departments within an organization. Thus, one of the primary responsibilities in a records department is that of being able to deliver materials from the files when they are requested by other departments. This means that when papers are requested, they must be located quickly, removed from the files, and sent to the requesting party.

In performing this vital service, those who work in the records department and those who borrow papers from it must follow systematic procedures so that order will be maintained throughout all phases of the borrowing and charging processes. In order to achieve this goal, procedures must be used that will control all charge-out activities, from the requisitioning (requesting) of papers through all actions leading to their final replacement in the files.

The total system for maintaining such control is sometimes referred to as the *charge-out system*. It includes the following phases:

1. Requisitioning materials from the files.
2. Removing requested materials from the files and making records of such removals.

Illus. 6-1, Files Supervisor

Requests for filed material may be made in person, through interoffice delivery, or by telephone. A form is then prepared to identify the material removed from the file.

Ohio National Life Insurance Co.

3. Charging borrowers for file materials that have been sent to them.
4. Tracing or accounting for borrowed or overdue file materials.
5. Releasing papers on dates specified in earlier requests.
6. Canceling charges for borrowed papers when the papers are returned to the files.

SECTION 1 REQUISITIONING MATERIAL FROM THE FILES

Material from the files may be requested in several ways: by calling in person at the filing department, by sending the request through interoffice delivery, or by telephoning the request. However, regardless of the way a request is made, a form must be prepared that describes and identifies the file materials desired. Such a form, known as a *requisition,* may be in the form of a 5- by 3-inch slip, or it may be in the form of a 6- by 9½-inch sheet of paper. Whether slips or sheets (Illustrations 6-2 and 6-3) are used, the information printed on requisition forms is standard; it includes spaces for filling in a description of the file material wanted, the name of the borrower, and the date of the request. Other information that is often recorded on a requisition form includes the date on which the requested material is delivered to the borrower and the date by which the borrowed material is to be returned to the filing department.

Name or subject	Return date
Wright Supply Co.	*10/13/--*
Re:	Date of letter
Adjustment in invoice	*9/30/--*
Taken by	Date taken
Alice Swanson	*10/6/--*
Signed	Dept.
R. F. L.	*Credit*

REQUISITION

OUT

To File Dept.

REQUEST FOR PAPERS

Papers Wanted on _*6/9/--*_
(date)

Description of Papers

Date _*5/21/--*_

Name _*W. R. Gibson*_
*and Co.*

Address _*Baltimore, Md.*_

Subject _*Request for*_
*catalog*

Wanted by _*C. R. Avery*_

Department _*Sales*_

For File Dept. Use

Return Date _*6/16/--*_

Illus. 6-3, **Requisition Sheet, 6″ x 9½″**

Illus. 6-4, Out Card with a Requisition Slip

Illus. 6-5, Out Card with Printed Lines

Requisitions may or may not be filled out by records department personnel; this depends upon how requests for papers are received. When a request is made in person, the descriptive sections of the requisition form are usually prepared by the requester, and the charge sections of the form are completed by records department personnel. When requests are telephoned or sent through office delivery systems, the entire requisition form is completed in the records department. Requisition forms usually are prepared in duplicate.

SECTION 2 CHARGING FOR MATERIALS BORROWED FROM THE FILES

The procedure followed in charging a borrower for a single piece from a folder or for selected pieces from a folder is necessarily different from the procedure followed in charging a borrower who requests an entire folder from the files. In the former case, the folder remains in the files; in the latter case, the entire folder (or its contents) is removed from the filing department and sent to the borrower.

Requests for Selected Papers from File Folders

When a request is made for only one piece of file material or for a few related papers from a single file folder, these papers are removed from the folder and a marker is placed in it. The marker is used as a substitute for the borrowed papers. The type of marker used for this purpose depends upon the type of requisition form used by the records department.

Out-Card Method. If a requisition slip (see Illustration 6-2), is used, the marker that is placed in the folder is an *out card,* which is cut to hold one copy of the requisition slip. Such an out card is shown in Illustration 6-4.

The files operator places the out card holding the requisition slip in the file folder from which the paper has been taken. When placed here, the out card serves as a substitute for the borrowed paper as well as a marker to show that a paper has been taken from a particular folder. Also, the notation on the requisition slip serves as a charge against the person who requested and received the borrowed paper.

Another style of out card, instead of having cuts to hold a requisition slip, is ruled and printed to provide a form on which the charge information may be written. When this form of out card is used (see Illustration 6-5), only one copy of the requisition slip is prepared, and information from the requisition slip is written on the out card. The out card is then placed in the file folder as a substitute for the borrowed paper. The requisition slip is then placed in the departmental follow-up file (see Illustration 6-10, page 78).

Out-Sheet Method. If requisition sheets (see Illustration 6-3) are used, two copies are prepared. One sheet is placed in the folder from which a paper has been taken. This sheet, which is 6 by 9½ inches, serves as a substitute for the paper which has been removed from the folder. The other copy of the requisition sheet is placed in the departmental follow-up file.

If out cards which are lined and printed are being used in conjunction with requisition sheets, only one copy of the requisition sheet is made. This is taken to the files, and data from it are written on the face of the outcard which remains in the file folder. The requisition sheet is placed in the departmental follow-up file.

Use of Second Copies of Requisition Forms

When an out card with cuts to hold a requisition slip is used (see Illustration 6-4), two copies of the slip are made, either by the requester or by records department personnel. One copy of the slip is inserted into the out card, which is then taken to the main files and used as a replacement for the paper or papers removed from a file folder. A second copy of the requisition slip is placed in a card-size follow-up file. This file is used by the records department to trace borrowed material taken from the main files. (See page 78.)

When requisition sheets are the only markers used by a records department, one copy is taken to the files and left as a marker and a charge. A second copy is placed in the departmental follow-up file.

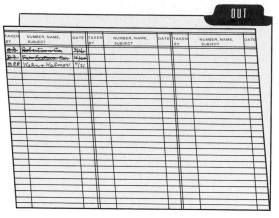

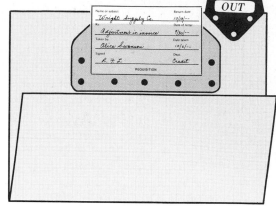

Illus. 6-6, **Out Folder with Printed Sections**

Illus. 6-7, **Out Folder with Requisition Slip**

Request for an Entire Folder

Out-Folder Method. When an entire folder is removed from the files, some firms use an out folder that is placed in the file drawer as a substitute for the folder removed. *Out folders* are of two types: (1) a folder with a ruled form printed on the front (see Illustration 6-6) and (2) a folder on the inside back flap of which is a pocket to hold a requisition slip (see Illustration 6-7).

When the ruled and printed out folder is used, the information on the requisition slip is transferred to the face of the out folder; and the requisition slip is placed in the follow-up file where it serves as a guide to locate the borrowed folder if that folder is requested while it is out on loan.

When the pocket-type out folder is used, the requisition slip must be prepared in duplicate. One copy is placed in the follow-up file.

Regardless of the type of out folder used, the out folder is substituted in the file drawer for the folder that is removed; and it is used to hold materials filed during the time the borrowed folder is out of the file drawer. When the regular folder is returned, material accumulated in the out folder is filed in proper order in it. The charge information on the out folder is then crossed out, or the requisition card is removed from the pocket, and the out folder is available for reuse.

Out-Guide Method. When a folder is sent to the person requesting it, a form known as an out guide may be placed in the files as a substitute for the borrowed folder. An *out guide* is a pressboard guide with the word "OUT" printed on the tab so that it can be readily seen in the files. One type of out guide has a pocket in the upper right corner

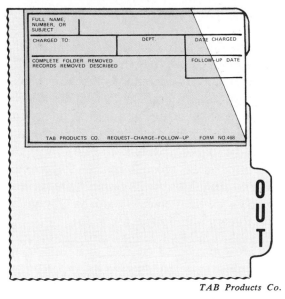

TAB Products Co.

Illus. 6-8, **Requisition Slip in Portion of an Out Guide for a Shelf File**

OUT								
TAKEN BY	NUMBER, NAME, SUBJECT	DATE	TAKEN BY	NUMBER, NAME, SUBJECT	DATE	TAKEN BY	NUMBER, NAME, SUBJECT	DATE

Illus. 6-9, **Lined and Printed Out Guide**

to hold a 5- by 3-inch requisition slip (see Illustration 6-8). Two copies of the requisition are prepared. One copy is placed in the pocket of the out guide; the other copy is placed in the follow-up file. The out guide is put in the space formerly occupied by the borrowed folder. Thus, the out guide serves as a marker for the missing folder, and the requisition card in the out guide pocket serves to identify and charge the borrower. The guide remains in the file until the borrowed folder is returned. (See Illustration 5-9, page 52.)

Out guides, though frequently used, do not permit the regular filing of incoming papers in the main files while folders are out on loan. For this reason, out folders are preferable to out guides as replacements for borrowed folders.

In some filing systems, out guides that are ruled on both sides are used. The charge-out information is recorded on one of the lines by the files operator, and then the guide is placed in the file drawer in the space originally occupied by the folder.

Both forms of out guides are reusable after the folder is returned by the borrower and replaced in the files. If the pocket-type out guide is used, the guide is removed from the file and the requisition card is removed from the pocket. When the ruled form of out guide is used, the information regarding the borrowed material is crossed off, and the guide is ready for use again with new charge information written on the next line.

Carrier-Folder Method. When the entire contents of a folder are borrowed, it is sometimes advantageous to put the borrowed papers into a *carrier folder* and send this folder and its contents to the borrower.

Using carrier folders has several advantages: (1) Such folders usually are made of heavy manila stock and thus are able to take wear much better than thinner file folders; (2) carrier folders ordinarily are of a distinguishing color and may be marked "Return to Files"; (3) incoming papers can be filed as usual since the regular file folders are left in place when carrier folders are used. As a result there is less disruption of normal filing procedures than there would be if regular folders were removed and out folders substituted for them.

Canceling Charges for Borrowed File Materials

When borrowed materials are returned to the files, it is important that the return is properly recorded and the charge-out records are adjusted. The procedure used is governed by the charge method used. For example, if the out-card method is used, the card is immediately removed when the borrowed materials are returned and refiled. If the charge information is written on the out card itself, this information is crossed out before the card is stored for reuse. If a requisition slip is part of the system, the requisition slip is removed from the pocket and disposed of. The out card with the pocket empty is then stored for future use. The copy of the requisition slip is removed from the follow-up file and is destroyed.

A similar procedure is followed when the out sheet method is used. The files operator must be certain that the duplicate copy of the sheet is removed from the follow-up file immediately.

When an entire folder that has been borrowed is returned, the out guide, the out folder, or the carrier folder is promptly corrected to show the return of materials, and the follow-up file is cleared. (See page 79.)

SECTION 3   FOLLOW-UP METHODS AND PROCEDURES IN THE RECORDS DEPARTMENT

Control over the procedures used to secure the return of borrowed material is a major function of the records department, for without such control it is impossible to maintain order within the filing system.

In order to establish control over the return of file material, it is necessary first to establish limits of time for the return of borrowed items. Such limits vary from one firm to another, largely because of differences in the value of items being held in different filing systems.

Some papers held in files are very valuable, and company rules usually determine that these may not be borrowed for a period of time greater than one day, or less. Other less valuable papers may be borrowed over a period of a week, or ten days, or two weeks. In general, it is better to allow relatively short periods of time for the return of papers. The longer the time permitted, the less chance there is of having materials returned on time unless checking and follow-up work by the records department is accelerated. However, it is necessary to make provision for extending a set time for returning borrowed papers when it is evident that they are still needed by the borrower. This can be done either by rewriting the "due date" on the original requisition and/or on other charge-out forms, or by preparing a new requisition and noting a change of date on all out forms held in the files.

Follow-up Methods to Trace Borrowed Materials

If all borrowed materials were returned on time and if there were no requests for papers which were out on loan, there would be no need for following-up or tracing overdue papers. However, such is not the case and probably never will be in any filing operation involving more than one person. Therefore the records department must have a system for checking on out-of-files materials.

In checking on the due dates for the return of borrowed papers and folders, any one of three basic procedures may be used: (1) the main files may be scanned; (2) a master control sheet may be used; (3) a follow-up filing system may be set up.

Scanning the Files. When the filing department is relatively small (for example, when approximately 5 cabinets or sections comprise the filing area), the files operator can check the due dates of borrowed materials by going through the files and reading the due dates written on requisition forms, out cards, out guides, or out folders.

Master Control Sheet. If the filing department has 6 to 15 cabinets or sections, follow-up work can be handled by using a master control sheet or a simple follow-up system. A *master control sheet* is a running record of borrowed file materials and is kept by the files operator at the desk. As requisitions are written or received in the department, data from these are posted to the master control sheet. When borrowed materials are returned, the corresponding charges written on the master control sheet are crossed out.

Follow-Up System. If the filing department is large, a follow-up system simplifies the procedures in charging for papers and folders taken from the department and in tracing them at later dates.

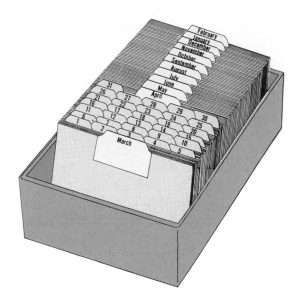

Illus. 6-10, **Follow-Up File with Requisition Slips**

A *follow-up file* is one into which copies of requisitions are filed. Such a file is sometimes known as a *tickler file*, presumably because its function is to tickle or jog the memory.

The card follow-up file shown in Illustration 6-10 consists of 12 primary monthly guides in central position and 31 secondary guides captioned for the days in the month. Usually only one set of daily guides is needed for a follow-up file. As the operator checks and processes the requisitions held behind the guide each day, he moves the guide for that day out of the current month section and places it behind the guide for the next month. Thus, the system is self-perpetuating; and, unless a large volume of requisitions must be handled, a single set of daily guides is sufficient.

If requisition sheets are used instead of requisition slips, a follow-up file may consist of 12 monthly guides and 31 folders captioned for the days in the month.

Follow-Up Procedures

When a follow-up file of the type shown in Illustration 6-10 is used as the record of borrowed materials, the file is used in the following manner.

1. Requisitions are the only materials placed in the file.
2. Each requisition is placed in the follow-up file according to the date on which the borrowed materials are to be returned. If that date

is in the current month, the requisition is placed behind the day-of-the-month guide that corresponds to that date. If the date of return is in the following month, the requisition is placed behind the guide for that month. Then at the beginning of the next month, the guide for that month is placed in the front of the file and the requisitions for that month are placed behind the day guides.

3. Each day the operator of the follow-up system checks to see which borrowed materials are due on that day and notifies the borrower in each case. If materials are still needed by a borrower, the due date may be extended by changing the due date on the existing requisition and on the out card in the main files. The changed requisition is then refiled in the follow-up file according to the later date. If the time is not extended, the borrowed materials should be returned to the records department and refiled.

4. When the borrowed papers are returned, the charge against the borrower is canceled by removing the requisition from the follow-up file and destroying it. If an out card or folder or guide which holds a requisition is used, the requisition is destroyed when papers are returned. If a lined and printed out card or folder or guide is used, notations are crossed out, and the out card or folder or guide is brought back to the operator's work station for future use.

Avoiding Follow-Up on Borrowed Materials

No matter how careful the files operator is in charge and follow-up methods, important papers may be lost or destroyed. To guard against this possibility, many companies avoid transmitting certain types of original material from the files except when such removal is absolutely imperative. Two methods of accomplishing this are: (1) making exact copies and (2) microfilming materials.

When copies of materials need to be delivered a distance of many miles from the file room, electronic facsimile transmission equipment is used to send the copies. Facsimile is described in Chapter 14, page 214.

Exact Copies. The removal of material from the files is avoided in many concerns by sending the borrower an exact copy of the material requested rather than the material itself. There are on the market a large number of copymaking machines that produce exact copies in a matter of seconds. When this technique is used, the requested paper is removed from the folder only long enough to be put through the copying machine. The original is then refiled, and the exact copy is sent to the borrower with instructions to destroy it after use. This method is used most frequently when a single letter or a few related pieces are needed.

Some firms, in order to prevent the loss of an entire folder, have established rather rigid rules on who may borrow a folder. In some organizations, authorized persons are required to come to the filing department where they may examine the contents of the folder rather than have it sent to them. If selected pieces are needed for further study, exact copies can be made at that time.

Microfilmed Materials. Microfilming involves taking a small picture of a document. This picture is retained on a roll of film, in a special jacket, or on a small piece of film that is mounted on an *aperture card*, a card with a die-cut hole.

A great number of concerns now microfilm some of their materials; some firms destroy the originals as soon as the film has been inspected. If a microfilmed document stored on a roll of film is requested, the files operator locates the particular roll of film containing the needed item, runs it through a reader-printer machine until the requested document is found, and then prints out a readable copy. This copy is sent to the person requesting the document and is destroyed after use.

If the desired item is mounted on an aperture card, the card is found in the files and a readable copy is printed out by using a reader-printing machine.

Microfilming is discussed more completely in Chapter 14.

SECTION 4   FOLLOW-UP PROCEDURES FOR FUTURE-ORDER ITEMS

The records department frequently receives requests for file materials that are desired at a future date. Often, too, requests come for materials that are currently on loan to someone else. In each of these situations, follow-up procedures are needed that will assure the delivery of the requested papers on the date that they are needed or as soon as possible, as the case may be.

Requests for items to be delivered at some future time usually come from persons who receive and answer correspondence and thus are aware that at some future time further action will be necessary in connection with a given piece of correspondence. In such circumstances, the person or his secretary marks the correspondence before sending it to the records department so that it will be known that some future action is required. The records department is thus given notice by such marked correspondence that some sort of follow-up action will be required. Correspondence is marked by a note in the margin showing some such wording as "Wanted by MRB 3/15," or "Follow-up, MRB, 3/15," or "Date Ahead, MRB, 3/15."

Request for Future Delivery

On-Call Cards. When the files operator inspects and codes materials on which a notation about a future order appears, or when a request is received for the future delivery of material from the files, a requisition, called an *on-call* or *follow-up card,* is filled out for each item or for each folder so requested. The requisition generally used for follow-up filing calls for the same information as that appearing on a regular requisition card, but in addition it shows the date the requested materials are wanted. On such forms, the lines which read, "Papers Wanted On" or "Date of Request," can be applied to the future-order items.

Requisition forms for future orders (on-call or follow-up cards) may be filed in the regular follow-up file in the records department. (See Illustration 6-10.) However, when the volume of orders for future delivery of file materials justifies, a separate "future-orders" follow-up file should be installed in the records department. All requisitions for future delivery of filed papers or folders are placed in the "future-orders" follow-up file according to the date the papers will be needed or, in the case of papers currently on loan, according to the date that the requested papers will be returned to the files and become available for reloaning. Each day the files operator checks the on-call follow-up file and removes the requisitions from behind the guide (or the folder) for the current date to determine which papers and folders are requested for that particular day. Requests are then filled by taking all requisitions to the main files, locating the desired papers, and sending them to the requesters. Copies of requisition forms are then filled in with the charge-out dates and the due dates and are held in the follow-up file according to the due dates noted on the forms.

Dated Follow-up Folders. Folders especially printed for follow-up files sometimes are used not only in the filing department but in other departments as well. Such departments as Purchasing, Accounting, Shipping, and Sales are all concerned with matters which require future attention that make advisable the use of follow-up systems.

Printed follow-up folders are straight-cut with the left side of the tab reserved for affixing a label bearing the name of a correspondent, or the number of an order, or the title of a subject of some sort. The right side of the follow-up folder tab shows a series of numbers from 1-31 corresponding to days of a month over which a movable, colored signal can be placed to indicate a particular date. See Illustration 6-11 on page 82.

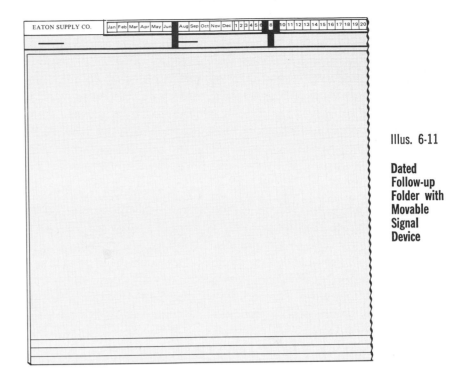

Illus. 6-11

**Dated
Follow-up
Folder with
Movable
Signal
Device**

When a follow-up filing system is composed of folders like the one shown in Illustration 6-11, each folder can be labeled with a typewritten gummed label on which appears a name or a number or a subject title depending upon the type of follow-up action being taken. For example, in a shipping-receiving department where a follow-up file is being used to trace deliveries, follow-up folders can be labeled to show shipping document numbers and expected delivery dates can be signalled on the top edge of follow-up folders. In other departments, such matters as dates for paying bills or for receiving payments of one sort or another can be marked for attention at future dates by using dated follow-up folders and labeling these with appropriate titles and marking dates by using signal devices as shown in Illustration 6-11.

When dated follow-up folders are used in the records department for handling future-order items, sheet requisition forms are used and one sheet is placed in each folder and request dates are marked by placing colored signals over numbers on folder tabs. Sometimes future-order items are handled by using photocopies or carbon copies of outgoing letters marked for future action. Such copies are placed in follow-up folders that have been signaled to note the requested delivery date for desired papers; when this time arrives, the photocopy or carbon copy is removed from the follow-up folder and sent, along with other papers as required, to the requester.

QUESTIONS FOR DISCUSSION

1. Why is the handling of requests for filed papers an important job in the records department?
2. There are six phases to a complete charge-out system. What are some of these phases of work?
3. What information is written on a completely filled-in requisition form?
4. When a request is made for only one piece of correspondence, would you use an out folder or an out card as a substitute for the borrowed paper in the files? Why?
5. What is one reason for using a follow-up system in the records department?
6. When a sheet requisition form is used, it is filed in the folder from which a paper has been taken. How are card out forms held in the files?
7. Why are out folders better to use than out guides when entire folders are borrowed from the files?
8. Both out cards and out folders have similar rulings and captions on them. Do both forms serve exactly the same purpose? Explain your answer.
9. In a system where out cards with printed fill-in sections are used, what is done to and with the card when a borrowed paper is returned?
10. In a system where out folders with pockets for holding requisition slips are used, what is done to and with the out folder and with the requisition slip when a borrowed file folder is returned?
11. Why is a follow-up filing system needed for records control?
12. When a follow-up file with requisition slips is being used, how is a requisition slip filed—
    a. by the date appearing on the borrowed paper?
    b. by the date on which the paper should be returned?
13. What procedure does a records control operator use when a request for the future delivery of a paper is received?
14. How are dated folders with movable signals used in a follow-up file?

FILING PROBLEM

Visit a local office and learn what methods are used for charge and follow-up controls. Write your report to be read, but be ready to make an oral report to the class if your teacher asks you to do so.

JOB 6 Requisition and Charge Procedures

At this time complete Job 6 in OFFICE FILING PROCEDURES, Fourth Edition. The instructions and supplies for this job are included in the practice set.

CHAPTER 7

TRANSFER AND STORAGE CONTROLS

If business organizations kept all the papers that they receive through the mail and all that they originate themselves, most organizations would be flooded out of operation in a relatively short time. It is not difficult to appreciate this condition because each of us as individuals has more or less the same problem as we attempt to control our personal records by eliminating some papers and keeping others.

In general, business organizations follow patterns of action somewhat like those used by individuals as they either retain or destroy papers and related materials. The procedures followed are these: (1) some papers are destroyed after a single reading; (2) papers relating to active and important matters are judged to have reference value and are kept "within reach" for a period of time; (3) some documents of legal or historic value are retained on an indefinite basis; (4) some papers, although not of current value, have future value and must be referred to occasionally beyond the period of their active use; these are, therefore, held for periods of time until their usefulness has ended.

In summary, business papers are held or disposed of under the following conditions: (1) Immediate disposal: When correspondence is received, the recipient or the secretary decides whether a paper has future reference value or not. If it has no further value, it is destroyed. (2) Active reference value: If it is decided that correspondence or other papers have future reference value, they are released for filing either in a departmental file or in a centralized filing department. (3) Permanent value: If material released for filing has legal value or historic value or will be used for extended reference purposes, it might be placed either in special sections in the active files or in a safe or vault type of file for an indefinite period of time. (4) Limited reference value or destruction: As the reference value of papers held in *active* files lessens over a period of time, some papers are removed from the active files and destroyed; others are transferred to *semiactive* files or are sent directly to an inactive *storage* file. (5) Final disposition: Papers held in semiactive files for a period of time are either destroyed or transferred to inactive storage files where they are held for a period of time and then destroyed according to a predetermined schedule.

Active files should contain only those records that are of immediate importance from a reference standpoint. Thus, as papers become older and less frequently referred to, and as new papers are being added to the active files, there comes a time when, to avoid overcrowding, the less useful papers must be separated and transferred to semiactive or storage files.

Bankers Box Co.

Illus. 7-1

Transfer Files for Semiactive Records in a General Storage Area

Transferring materials from the active files serves the following purposes: (1) It reduces the volume of papers in the active sections and makes for more efficient filing and finding of active materials. (2) Transfer makes additional space available in the active files. (3) Filing costs are reduced because transferred items may be stored in equipment less expensive than that used for active files. (4) Costs are further reduced because valuable floor space is not being used for semiactive or inactive records.

SECTION 1 EQUIPMENT AND SUPPLIES USED IN TRANSFER AND STORAGE

Active file materials must be kept in equipment that is easily operated and is located in readily accessible areas of an office. Semiactive or inactive materials must be held so as to be available when needed, but they need not be held in expensive cabinets fitted with easily accessible drawers or sections. Moreover, cabinets or drawer or shelf sections need not be located in areas of prime activity.

Sometimes, transfer materials that are frequently referred to are held in the same equipment as that used for active files; but, when this is done, the transfer file sections are located in the least available parts. For example, the top and the bottom drawers in cabinets could be used to hold transfer material, while the more accessible central drawers could hold active papers. Usually, however, transfer files are entirely

SAFCO Products Co.

Illus. 7-2

Transfer Boxes of the Type Used for Inactive Materials Taken from Vertical File Drawers (SAFCO's Saf-T-Lok Record Storage System)

Bankers Box Co.

Illus. 7-3

Transfer Boxes of the Type Used for Inactive Records Taken from Shelf Files and Certain Types of Lateral Files (Liberty Open-Shelf File Boxes)

separated from active files and are located in storage areas adjacent to them. When this is done, *transfer boxes* or cartons are used to hold inactive materials, while *transfer cases with sliding drawer sections* are used for semiactive materials stored in the same area in which the inactive materials are stored.

Transfer Boxes

When transferred records are kept apart from the active files, the type of equipment used for holding transferred materials depends upon how frequently these materials are used. If they are more or less inactive, that is, if there are relatively few requests for them, *transfer boxes* of the types shown in Illustrations 7-2 and 7-3 are frequently used.

Transfer boxes are relatively inexpensive and dust-free because they are constructed of heavy cardboard or fiberboard and are formed with lift-up tops that can be closed securely. However, transfer boxes have certain limitations, for they must be lifted completely out of their storage area (e.g., from a shelf); and the tops of the boxes must be opened before the records they hold are available for use. This factor of inaccessibility makes them most suited for holding only inactive records in a storage area.

Illus. 7-4

Transfer Cases for Semiactive Materials Which Were Transferred from Vertical File Drawers (StaxOnSteel Storage Units)

Transfer Cases

When active records are at first transferred to storage areas, these records frequently retain a degree of active reference value and are, therefore, usually kept in a *semi-active* state. This involves keeping records in accessible locations and holding them in types of equipment that are fairly easy to operate. Thus, if semiactive papers are not held in the same area and in the same cabinets as those used for active files, the semiactives are transferred to a storage area adjacent to the active area and placed in transfer cases. Transfer cases for material from vertical files are equipped with pull-out drawers like those shown in Illustration 7-4. When papers from shelf files are being held for semi-active reference, equipment similar to that shown in Illustration 7-3 is used.

Transfer cases are units made up of pull-out drawers held in shells or frames. Shells or frames are made of fiberboard that is bound with steel to form a framework which permits shells to be stacked to any desired height. Drawers can be moved in and out of shells with relative ease; thus, records held in transfer cases so equipped are much more accessible than are records held in transfer boxes with sealed tops. Transfer cases are therefore used for semiactive records, while inactive records are stored in transfer boxes.

Transfer Folders

Miscellaneous and individual folders are usually transferred from the active to the transfer files. However, specially made folders (with plastic tabs or other refinements) are too expensive to be transferred and, as a result of transferring, to be replaced in the active files. It is therefore more economical to prepare less expensive folders for transfer purposes. The active file guides are not usually taken with the folders when a transfer is made. Again, the guide sets are too expensive and, as a rule, more detailed than necessary for transfer needs. It is ordinarily advisable to have a single set of guides in transfer cases, although the notations on miscellaneous folders from the regular file may be sufficient for guiding purposes.

When the entire contents of folders are transferred (rather than individual documents), it is wise to examine the materials so that new active folders may be prepared for only those that were active during the preceding year or transfer period. This examination will prevent the files operator from preparing folders that are never used. It is also wise to examine carefully the miscellaneous folders being transferred to spot active correspondents for whom individual folders should be prepared. It is common practice to stamp each transferred folder with the words "Transfer File" or some similar notation to prevent transferred folders from being placed in the active file later in the event of removal from storage.

SECTION 2   TRANSFER METHODS

The two methods of transferring materials to inactive files are known as the *perpetual* and *periodic methods*. The choice of the specific method of transferring inactive records must be made by each firm in relation to its own needs and the nature of its business.

Perpetual Transfer

Some offices, such as those of lawyers, contractors, and architects, constantly transfer materials from active to inactive files because the work is completed in units; for example, in a lawyer's office when a case is closed or in an architect's office when a building has been finished. In such cases, there is no longer any immediate need to refer to these particular files, so the folders should be transferred. This method is known as the *perpetual transfer method*.

The perpetual transfer is not suited to usual business correspondence or documents since it involves the continual selection and marking of papers for transfer and creates additional work. To transfer records continuously in a normal office situation would be time consuming. Then, too, it is not always easy to decide when a single document is no longer needed for immediate reference and is ready for transfer. The perpetual transfer method is best used when work is handled or completed in easily defined units.

Periodic Transfer

Periodic transfer is the transfer of materials at stated intervals. In general, there are three plans of periodic transfer: (1) the one-period method, (2) the two-period or duplicate-equipment method, and (3) the maximum-minimum period method.

A-E ACTIVE	L-R ACTIVE
F-K ACTIVE	S-Z ACTIVE
A-E INACTIVE	L-R INACTIVE
F-K INACTIVE	S-Z INACTIVE

In 4-drawer files the upper two rows hold active papers, and the two drawers below, inactive records.

A-E INACTIVE	I-Q INACTIVE
A-B ACTIVE	M-N ACTIVE
C-F ACTIVE	O-S ACTIVE
G-L ACTIVE	T-Z ACTIVE
F-H INACTIVE	R-Z INACTIVE

In 5-drawer files, inactive files often may be contracted to fit less accessible space.

A-B INACTIVE	D-E INACTIVE	K-L INACTIVE	O-R INACTIVE
A-B ACTIVE	F-G ACTIVE	K-L ACTIVE	S ACTIVE
C ACTIVE	H-J ACTIVE	M-N ACTIVE	T-Z ACTIVE
D-E ACTIVE	F-G INACTIVE	O-R ACTIVE	S INACTIVE
C INACTIVE	H-J INACTIVE	M-N INACTIVE	T-Z INACTIVE

This arrangement of active and inactive papers in 5-drawer files allows current reference to drawers most easily reached, and easy reference to inactive papers located in equal, if less convenient space.

A-B ACTIVE	A-B INACTIVE	K-L ACTIVE	K-L INACTIVE
C ACTIVE	C ACTIVE	M-N ACTIVE	M-N INACTIVE
D-E ACTIVE	D-E INACTIVE	O-R ACTIVE	O-R INACTIVE
F-G ACTIVE	F-G INACTIVE	S ACTIVE	S INACTIVE
H-J ACTIVE	H-J INACTIVE	T-Z ACTIVE	T-Z INACTIVE

The "double-spread" plan for 5-drawer files need not involve drawer shifts at the time of transfer. The sketch illustrates a "side-by-side" treatment which saves end-of-year labor.

Sperry Remington, Office Systems and Machines, Sperry Rand Corporation

Illus. 7-5, **Periodic Transfer**

One-Period Method. When the one-period method is used, all materials are removed from the active files at a certain time (usually once or twice a year) and are placed in transfer cases. These cases are then sent to a records center. The older folders are usually placed in these cases. New folders are prepared and, for all practical purposes, a new active file is started. The chief objection to this method of transfer is that recent materials are suddenly placed in an inactive file and are not available for immediate reference. Frequent reference to the materials in the inactive files during the first few months following the transfer period is usually necessary.

Two-Period Method. Under the two-period method, duplicate files—one active and one semiactive—are maintained in the office. The semiactive files are usually maintained in the lower drawers of a filing cabinet or in adjacent filing cabinets. Let us assume that the file period is a year and that a new active file is started at the beginning of each calendar year. This means that in January of each year new folders are prepared, and a new active file is started for the new year. The materials for the preceding year remain where they are and the new file is placed in another cabinet, or the old materials are transferred to a nearby file drawer or to lower drawers in the same cabinet. In this way, a new file of materials for the current year is established, while the materials filed during the preceding year are readily accessible. At the end of the current year, the process starts again. A new file is set up for the new year, and the materials accumulated during the preceding year are left where they are or are transferred to another part of the filing cabinet. The materials for the previous year are now placed in transfer cases and are sent to the records center.

This system works very efficiently in smaller organizations where the amount of space occupied by the files is limited. In larger organizations where great numbers of records must be filed, it may be possible to use this method by reducing the length of the transfer period. Thus, new files might be prepared every six months rather than once a year. In turn, records would be transferred to the records center every six months instead of just once a year.

A high percentage of requests for filed materials is for records not more than six months old. A test of how well this statement applies to any given company may be made by saving the requisition forms used in the charge and follow-up system. A tabulation can be prepared to show the age of all papers requested from the files. The two-period plan using a year for each period will usually take care of practically all requests for filed materials. The two-period plan based on a six-month transfer period will take care of most file requests. There may be some disadvantage in maintaining a current file, a semiactive file, and a transfer file—all of which are the components of the system. However, the plan works very well in a large number of offices.

Maximum-Minimum Period Method. A transfer method that may eliminate the objectionable features of both the one-period transfer and the two-period transfer methods is known as the *maximum-minimum period method*. When this method is used, only the inactive material is transferred at regular intervals.

The following example illustrates how the plan works. In a particular office, the material is transferred once a year on June 30. All material dated during the current calendar year is left in the active files, while all material dated during the preceding year is transferred. This means that materials are kept in the active files at least six months (January 1 to June 30 of the current year, when the transfer is made) but not more than eighteen months (January 1 of the preceding year to June 30 of the transfer year). In other words, the material that is transferred is at least six months old, and it varies in age at the time of transfer from six to eighteen months. It is from these minimum and maximum periods of time that this method derives its name.

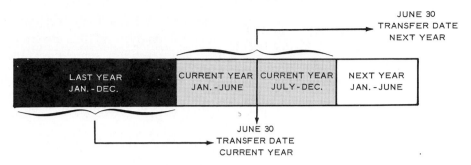

Illus. 7-6, **Maximum-Minimum Transfer Diagram**

**Transfer
Policies**

Regardless of the transfer method used, the following points should be kept in mind when transferring records:

1. Not every document is transferred. Many records are destroyed at the time of transfer because they are no longer of value. Others, because of their importance, are held in the active files for long periods of time.

2. The transferring of noncurrent records should take place during a slack period of the business year if at all possible. It is highly desirable to have as little interference as possible with the normal operation of the office.

3. An executive, before releasing a record for filing, may make a notation in one corner of the document to indicate the period of time the record should be held in the file. While this procedure will take more time when the document is released for filing, it will save considerable time when the transfer is made.

4. In transfer cases as well as in the regular files, those records to be retained for a longer period of time should be segregated from those of only temporary value. This procedure compensates greatly in saving storage space and transfer time.

**Records
Retention
Schedule**

There is no simple rule to follow in establishing a records-retention schedule. Every organization must study its own needs instead of adopting the retention schedule of another company. In a small office, this schedule might be developed by the owner of the company with the aid of the secretary and legal counsel. In a large organization confronted with a great volume of paperwork, a different approach is necessary. A records-retention program may be developed by a specially appointed committee composed of an officer of the company, the legal counsel, the files supervisor, and department heads. Many records authorities, however, believe the responsibility of developing an objective and realistic retention program should be delegated to only one person who is familiar with the entire operation of the organization.

An inventory of all records held by the organization, their volume and location, and a careful analysis of this inventory are usually the first steps in establishing a retention schedule. Once developed, the program will need the support of top management, and the schedule must be constantly reexamined and evaluated. Record requirements change, and the records retention schedule must be revised to meet the changing conditions.

It is assumed that records are retained because they serve some worthwhile purpose. Certain types of papers (some advertising materials, for example) should be destroyed immediately after they have been read; others could probably be destroyed after thirty days or so. Some offices have little use for many of their records after six months, but they must keep correspondence of a general nature for about two years. Certain documents, however, must be retained for long periods of time; some, even permanently.

SECTION 3   CONTROL PROCEDURES FOR TRANSFERRED RECORDS

There is little point in transferring papers to storage unless adequate controls are used for locating stored materials, for releasing them when requested, and for charging borrowers for materials removed from the transfer files. It is evident, therefore, that all the elements needed for records control in the active files are needed also to maintain order in the transfer or storage files. Such control requires that storage areas be identified, that boxes or drawers be labeled, and that central records of these matters be maintained.

Storage Areas and Boxes or Cases

The first step in controlling stored records is to know their exact location in the storage area so that they can be found easily. This can be a fairly simple process in a small storage area, but a more complex one as the space allotted for storage increases. In large storage areas, the aisles, shelf sections, and boxes or cases are all assigned numbers; and these numbers are written on the box labels as well as on storage record cards held at the control desk. Thus, the location of a particular box might be listed as: Aisle: 4 / Section: 12 / Box: 325.

In smaller storage areas, the boxes or cases are given consecutive numbers; and these numbers are written on labels affixed to the box fronts or on tags inserted into drawer fronts. Box or drawer labels show also the general contents of the boxes or drawers as well as the name of the department from which transfer materials were received. The

BOX NO.	CONTENTS	AREA NO.
629	*General Correspondence* *Sales Dept.* *19-- to 19--*	*5*
		AISLE
		A
DESTROY		ROW
		4
19--	From: *A* Thru: *Af*	TIER
		3

Illus. 7-7

Transfer Box Label

destruction date for materials held in the boxes or cases is usually written on the label or tag.

Storage Record Cards

These are sometimes known as "Catalog Cards," "Transfer Control Cards," or "Records Storage Index & Destruction Control Cards." However, whatever the name used, these cards are the most vital record kept by a control center (or desk) in a storage or transfer department. A storage record card shows when the records were received, by whom they were sent, the contents of the storage box, the location of the box, and the date set for the destruction of the contents of the box or case.

The storage record card in Illustration 7-8 is typical of the form used by many business organizations as well as by other types of organizations which maintain archives or records storage centers.

RECORD TITLE *General Correspondence*						RECEIVED FROM *Sales Department*					
DATE RECEIVED	FILE OR BOX NO.	CONTENTS ALPHABETIC NUMERIC FROM	TO	DATE FROM	TO	LOCATION BLDG. OR ROOM	AISLE	SECTION	DATE TO DESTROY	DATE DES-TROYED	CERTIFIED BY
5/10/74	*438*	*a*	*as*	*1/1/72*	*12/31/72*	*Base-ment*	*3*	*7*	*1977*		
5/10/74	*439*	*at*	*az*	*1/1/72*	*12/31/72*	*"*	*"*	*"*	*1977*		
5/10/74	*440*	*B*	*Ban*	*1/1/72*	*12/31/72*	*"*	*"*	*"*	*1977*		
5/10/74	*441*	*Bao*	*Bz*	*1/1/72*	*12/31/72*	*"*	*"*	*"*	*1977*		

FORM 1607

RECORDS STORAGE INDEX AND DESTRUCTION CONTROL CARD

BANKERS BOX ® record storage systems DIVISION OF TELLINGS MANUFACTURING COMPANY

Bankers Box Co.

Illus. 7-8, Storage Record Card

Depending upon the type of operations in a given organization, storage record cards are prepared by or completed by storage center personnel; and the cards usually are made in duplicate.

One storage record card is prepared for every transfer box or drawer in the storage system; or one line on a cumulative card like that shown in Illustration 7-8 is used for every box or drawer. When one box or drawer contains more than one type of material, a storage record card is prepared for each kind to be found in that box or drawer.

One of the primary advantages of using a storage record card system is that not all materials sent by one department need be placed in the same section of the storage area. This is possible because information posted on storage record control cards shows exact locations of carefully described materials—regardless of where they are located. This factor saves a great deal of time as papers are being stored, since all papers from one department are not necessarily sent at the same time and future volume cannot very well be anticipated by storage center personnel.

Filing Systems in Storage Center Operations

Four types of records are required for maintaining order and recording vital statistics in storage operations: (1) a master control file for locating and retrieving stored papers when they are requested for use by any department within an organization (such a filing system is known as a *retrieval control file*); (2) a charge-out system in connection with storage operations; (3) and (4) records that relate to the final disposition of stored records. These records and the types of filing systems needed in order to maintain them are described on pages 95 and 96.

It should be noted that when semiactive papers are kept in the same area as the active files (as is the case when the two-period method of transfer is used), there is no need for maintaining separate records or routines when transfer materials are being processed. Under such conditions, customary procedures in the filing department are sufficient for handling both active and semiactive file materials. However, when semiactive and inactive records are stored and processed independently, then all control procedures relating to transferred records become the responsibility of the storage center. In such cases, there must be procedures and records for controlling the storing, finding, lending, charging, and follow-up as well as the final disposal of stored records.

It is in such circumstances as these that the storage center must maintain the four types of records previously listed, and such records will now be considered in detail.

Retrieval Control File. This filing system is kept at the control desk in the storage center and is composed entirely of *storage record cards* of the type shown in Illustration 7-8. These cards are held in a system that is primarily alphabetic. Primary guides show names of departments from which file materials have been transferred. Secondary guides show names of types of records being held for particular departments, e.g., "CORRESPONDENCE," or "PURCHASE ORDERS," or "ACCOUNTS RECIEVABLE." Finally, series of guides for dates are used to show specific locations within a departmental group. For example, when a requisition is received from the Sales Department for correspondence material of a given date, the files operator scans the retrieval control file to locate a primary guide for "SALES"; then for a secondary guide for "CORRESPONDENCE"; and finally for a date guide corresponding to the date shown on the requisition form. Behind the date guide will be found the *storage record card* bearing the location information needed. Location data will be transcribed from the card to a routing slip, which will be taken to the storage section indicated. There, the storage box or case will be opened and the desired papers withdrawn and sent to the requester.

Charge-out and Follow-up File. The use of such a system in a storage center is exactly the same as that previously described for use in the filing department. A type of follow-up file similar to that shown in Illustration 6-10, page 78, is used for tracing as well as charging for borrowed materials that have been removed from the storage center.

Requisition cards or sheets are filed by the "date due" listed on them, and the follow-up file is checked daily in tracing due and overdue materials that should be returned to storage.

Tickler File for Destruction Dates. One of the most important services performed by the storage center as well as by the records department is that of finally disposing of all records held in storage.

Records are destroyed only after careful consideration has been given to the future usefulness of each type of record being sent for storage. Usually, destruction dates are determined after consultation by representatives from various departments has established guidelines to be followed and these have been approved by the executive and legal branches of an organization. The primary concern in a storage center or in a records department is that dates are established for the final disposal of various types of records and that destruction is carried out as scheduled.

In order to follow scheduled destruction periods, it is necessary for the responsible department, either records or storage, to keep a reminder or tickler file which is checked periodically to determine when destruction dates are scheduled. This filing system is called a *tickler file for destruction dates*; or it is called by some name that is similar to this (e.g., "destruction tickler" or "destruction follow-up"). The file holds only the carbon copies of *storage record cards* that are prepared in duplicate when transfer materials are received, and these cards are filed according to the "destruction date" given on them.

The tickler file for destruction dates is used in the same manner that any tickler or reminder type of filing system is used, and the follow-up file shown on page 78 is typical of the form in which such systems are usually found.

At the time indicated for destruction of a particular group of records, the department head whose papers are to be destroyed will be notified; and, unless complications arise, the records will be destroyed by shredding, burning, selling as scrap, or other approved means.

Destruction File. When materials are destroyed, there must be witnessed or certified proof of this action; and a record must be prepared and retained for an indefinite period of time. Destruction of records is a matter of vital importance and legally acceptable records must be kept by maintaining a *destruction file*.

The primary records held in a destruction file are completed copies of the *storage record cards* which were held in the tickler file for destruction dates. These cards are pulled from the tickler file when destruction dates are at hand; and when destruction and certification have been completed and recorded, these *storage record cards* are filed according to the name of the department and by the date of destruction.

Cycle of Records Control

A cycle of records control is completed with the destruction of records. This cycle includes all the procedures used in maintaining order during the useful life of those records. These procedures are as follows:

1. Control was started when papers released for filing were coded according to indexing rules and when necessary cross-referencing was completed.
2. Control was continued when papers were placed in a filing system according to predetermined coding.
3. Control was extended as papers were released from the files under a charge-out plan and returned under a follow-up system.

4. When papers were transferred from active files to semiactive files to inactive files, control was maintained by keeping records and following procedures designed to preserve order.
5. Control was continued as transferred materials were released, borrowers were charged, and return dates for released materials were checked by follow-up.
6. Finally, stored papers were destroyed according to a predetermined time schedule, and records of this action were made. This step represented the concluding phase of records control.

QUESTIONS FOR DISCUSSION

1. Are all papers received by an organization kept in the filing system?
2. Who decides whether or not to keep a paper for filing purposes?
3. Name at least three reasons for transferring materials from an active file to a less active one.
4. Why are semiactive transfer materials usually held in transfer cases rather than in transfer boxes?
5. What is the one-period method of transfer?
6. What is the two-period method of transfer? For a small office, what is the advantage in using a two-period instead of a one-period plan at transfer time?
7. What advantage has the maximum-minimum transfer plan over the one-period and the two-period plans?
8. What purpose is served by labels on drawers and on boxes in the transfer files?
9. What is a storage record card, and what information is kept on this type of record card?
10. What type of record is kept in a retrieval control file, and how is such a file used?
11. What is a destruction file, and why is it maintained?

CHAPTER 8

TYPES OF ALPHABETIC FILING SYSTEMS

Filing Systems in General

If, on your first job, you are asked to use one of the many types of filing systems in operation in modern offices, it will be greatly to your advantage to know something about the system—how it is planned; why it is assembled as it is; how to get the greatest benefit from its special features. Thus, a careful study of the representative systems described and illustrated in this chapter will "pay off" for you in your first job. Your knowledge of these systems will be advantageous later when you are asked to improve an old system or to install a new one.

Either of two approaches to installing an alphabetic system for correspondence filing may be taken: A complete system can be purchased from a manufacturer's representative, or an individualized system can be planned and assembled by qualified personnel in the filing department. In either approach, those responsible for selecting or for planning and assembling a system must have a lot of information.

1. They must know the requirements that will be made of the records storage and control system adopted by their company.
2. They must be thoroughly familiar with the kinds of filing systems and equipment that are available and must have determined which of these will most nearly meet the needs of the office or company in which the system is being installed.
3. They must know all the elements that are essential for an adequate system of storage and control and how these can be varied and used to best advantage in solving particular filing problems.

Guides and folders, for example, may be positioned in a variety of arrangements in file drawers. The system planner, therefore, must be able to answer the question: Which way would be best for *this* office? There are also various ways of using alphabetic notations, colors, and numbers to identify parts of a system. All these elements are basic to the efficient functioning and usefulness of a filing system, and the reasons behind their use should be known to those who use the system or who plan to improve it.

A

RECORDING X-Ray Company

RAPAPORT Van Marvin

RAMSEY Underwriters

RADIO Wado

REED Thomas

RAPPAPORT Toy Bazaar

RADIO Steel Company

RABHOR Sportswear Inc

RECORD Press

RAW Rubber Engraving Co

RALEIGH Paper Company

RADIANT Quilting Company

RESEARCH Programs

ROVER National Motor Inn

RENDEZVOUS National Originals

RACEWAY National

RAYBURN Mfg Co

RAYBURN Mfg Co Jan.-June

RICH Marvin

RAWLINGS Martin

REYNOLDS Manual

RAYBURN Nancy

REDDY Kilowatt Inc

RAINBOW Knitting Mills

RABIN John

RADIO Land

RATHSKELLER German American

RAPAPORT Isadore

RADIO Hawaii Inc

RABB George

RAT Fink Room

RAMSET Fastening System

RAHR Export Clinic

RADIANT Dress Company

REED Cuff (&) Associates

RAYTHEON Company

RAHR Clor Clinic

RADIO City

RAWLINGS Albert

RIDDLE Albert

RATHMAN Albert

RADIO Amusement Corp

RABBITT Byron

RABBINECAL Assembly

RAB Alice

REYNOLDS Aluminum Co

RAAB

RAC

RAB

REL

Tabs (left): U to Z · R S & · P Q R · National · Rayburn Mfg. Co. · M-N-O · G-H-I · D-E-F · C · Albert · A-B · R

Tabs (right): U to Z · ST · PQR · M-N-O · OUT J-K-L · G-H-I · D-E-F · C · A-B · SINGLE NAME

R

Remington Rand's COLORSCAN SYSTEM

B

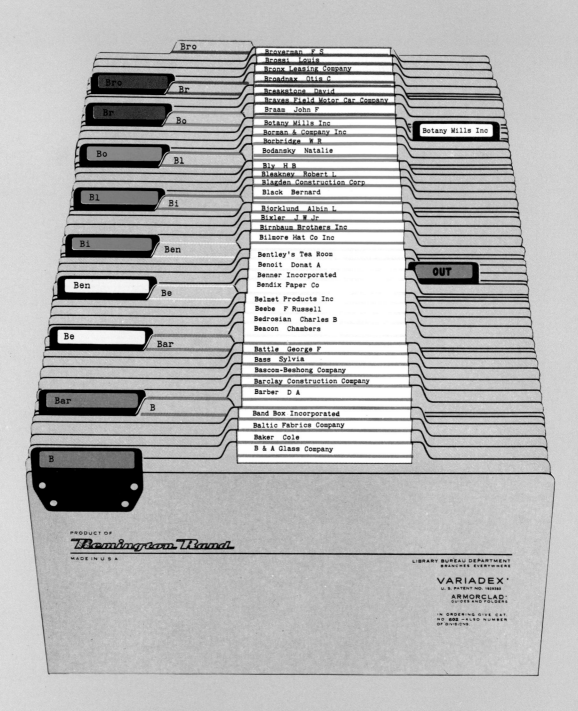

Remington Rand's VARIADEX SYSTEM

Shaw-Walker's SUPER-IDEAL SYSTEM

D

TAB Products' ALPHA CODE SYSTEM

Commercial Systems

Four commercial systems have been selected for illustration, analysis, and comparison in this chapter. They were chosen because they are widely used and because each is representative of a different plan or approach to the problem of handling correspondence in an alphabetic system. Planned and developed by experts in systems engineering, each of these systems includes elements that perform definite functions. The four systems (illustrated in color preceding this page) are:

A. *Colorscan System,* by Remington Rand, Office Systems and Machines, Sperry Rand Corporation, Marietta, Ohio.
B. *Variadex System,* by Remington Rand, Office Systems and Machines, Sperry Rand Corporation, Marietta, Ohio.
C. *Super-Ideal System,* by Shaw-Walker, Muskegon, Michigan.
D. *Alpha Code System,* by TAB Products Company, Palo Alto, California.

An analysis of the four systems will be made from three standpoints: (1) the positioning of guides and folders, (2) the use of notations, and (3) the uses made of color.

Guide and Folder Positions

Colorscan System. The Colorscan System, shown on illustrative page A, is a color-control system with guides and folders arranged to make maximum use of the color features of the system.

1. Primary alphabetic guides occupy first position, which is used also for special name guides (e.g., Rayburn Mfg. Co.).
2. Secondary alphabetic guides are placed in second position; these are used to index *second* units in names. Second position is used also to show special section titles (e.g., National).
3. Individual folders with double-width tabs occupy the third-fourth position and are placed "in-line."
4. Miscellaneous folders are placed in line in fifth position. OUT guides also are placed in fifth position.

This system has been planned so that each major section is placed in-line; that is, each has a location straight back through the file drawer. This positioning makes each section stand out clearly from all others; and since blocks of color are important features in the Colorscan System, the in-line placement makes for the greatest possible visibility throughout the system.

Variadex System. The Variadex System, shown on illustrative page B, is a Remington Rand color-control plan for filing in vertical or open lateral types of equipment and is made also for shelf-filing purposes.

The vertical filing system shown on illustrative page B, being definitely keyed to a color coding plan, uses the various positions in the file drawer to advantage for locating color blocks as well as alphabetic subdivisions. In order to do this, guides and folders are located in "in-line" arrangements, just as they are in the Colorscan System. However, positions used for Variadex guides and folders follow a pattern different from that found in Colorscan because of fundamental differences between the two systems. In Variadex, guides and folders are set as follows:

1. All primary guides are in first position, first position being considered by the system designers as the most likely position from which to move across the drawer to other sections in searching for a needed miscellaneous or individual folder.
2. All miscellaneous folders are placed in line in second position. Here they are close to primary guides but are not confused with them because they are in a different position.
3. Individual folders in central position have tabs cut two positions wide.
4. Special guides and OUT guides are placed in fifth position. Here they are readily visible and accessible.

Super-Ideal System. The Shaw-Walker Super-Ideal System, shown on illustrative page C, is designed to be used for vertical systems ranging from one drawer to four drawers in size. The Super-Ideal System is also available for vertical systems up to 1,000 drawers in size.

In contrast to the Colorscan System, the use of color in the Super-Ideal is of a supplementary nature; that is, color is used to assist in the finding of particular sections within the system. The positioning of guides and folders is very important to the efficiency of the Super-Ideal. Thus, most major sections are placed in staggered positions in order to gain maximum visibility for the items in each section of the system.

In the Super-Ideal System, the items are arranged in positions across the file drawer as follows:

1. Primary guides are alternated in a slightly overlapped arrangement in first and second positions so that the greatest degree of visibility will be made available to files operators.
2. All miscellaneous folders (blue) are placed in an in-line arrangement in first position so that reference to them can be made quickly by looking down only one position in the file drawer.
3. Individual folders with tabs cut double width are placed in alternating arrangement in slightly overlapped positions 3 and 4 and positions 5 and 6. This provision for large numbers of individual folders is in the interest of keeping the use of miscellaneous folders to a minimum and holding the bulk of material either in individual folders or in special section folders. (Note the red strip labels.)

4. Special guides with tabs somewhat more than double width are placed at the right of the drawer.

Out guides (not illustrated) are placed in the center of positions 3 and 4 occupied by individual folders.

Alpha Code System. TAB's Alpha Code System, shown on illustrative page D, is made up entirely of guides and individual folders for use in either shelf or open lateral types of equipment. Because of this use, guides and folders are tabbed and labeled in a vertical style. In such an arrangement, first position can be considered as being at the top section of the exposed edge of a guide or folder; second position is the next lower cut; third position and others are in successively lower positions.

Alpha Code, being a system in which various blocks of color are used as the primary means of locating folders, does not depend upon positioned folders or specially cut folder tabs to provide visibility across the file sections. Thus, only straight-cut tabs and a basic positioning of folder tabs are used as follows:

1. First position (the top position) is reserved for primary guides.
2. Second position is used for individual folder titles (in white).

Out guides are placed in the center of second position; their tabs, projecting beyond those of individual folders, can easily be seen.
3. Third position is used to identify the *first* letter in the key unit of a name.
4. Fourth position is used to identify the *second* letter in the key unit of a name.
5. In fifth position, the lowest section of out guides can be seen because individual folders are cut back in fifth position.

Comparison of Notation Styles

Each of the four systems being considered uses either an entirely different style of notation from that used by the others or a variation of a common style.

As notations in the systems are analyzed, reference will be made to terms that are used to define the standard forms of notations: single-letter, single-unit, double-closed, and multiple-closed.

Single-Letter Notations. Single-letter notations consist of single letters of the alphabet. They are easily read and sometimes are used to form combinations, such as G-H or XYZ, for use in very small filing systems of one- or two-drawer size. The Colorscan System (shown on illustrative page A) and the Alpha Code System (shown on illustrative page D) use single-letter notations on guides.

Single-Unit Notations. Single-unit notations are formed when two or more single letters of the alphabet are shown as a single unit on guide and folder tabs. The Variadex System (shown on illustrative page B) uses this style of notation, e.g., Bar, Be, Ben.

Double-Closed Notations. These notations show the beginning and the closing letters in each alphabetic section of the file. An example of a double-closed notation is *Aa-Al 1*. This is desirable because complete boundaries for each segment of the system are given. The Super-Ideal System (shown on illustrative page C) uses a form of double-closed notations. For example, the notation on the second primary guide is read as "Ba-Bl."

Multiple-Closed Notations. Multiple-closed notations are commonly used in several forms. One of these forms shows multiple-closed notations in this manner:

$$Aa - Ac - Ag$$

This notation indicates that this particular alphabetic section starts with "Aa" and progresses through "Ag." Included in this alphabetic section is the important subsection "Ac" which, when shown in this manner on a guide, is made easier to locate in the file drawer.

Another form of multiple-closed notation is illustrated in the Super-Ideal System shown on illustrative page C. This illustration shows a 25-division (25-guide) unit in which three types of notation forms are used on guides and miscellaneous folders. For example, the first primary guide and the first miscellaneous folder show a single-letter notation; the second and the fourth show double-closed notations; the third and the fifth show multiple-closed notations. This combination of forms is used because the system illustrated is a small one, designed for a single file drawer containing 25 guides. Thus, several guides show only single letters, and only the most active letters ("B," for example) have more than one guide in an alphabetic division. Super-Ideal systems for larger files (75-division units, for example) have more of the multiple-closed notations and fewer (or none) of the single-letter notations.

The first guide used in each of the most active divisions carries a double-closed type of notation; for example, guide 2 shows "B" followed by "A" on the upper left side of the tab label, and "L" on the lower left side. These notations show that this section starts with names beginning with "Ba" and includes the important alphabetic subsection "Bl." This guide also shows notations on the right side of the center (dividing) line which include the word "Also" followed by such notations as "B &" and "B -." These indicate that single-letter names such as "B & W Supply Co." and "B - G Stores" are to be filed behind this guide.

Guide 3 marks a subdivision of the primary "B" section. This guide and all similar guides show a form of multiple-closed notations which indicate the beginning letters of a subsection, e.g., "Bo," and also show the most important alphabetic sections included in it, e.g., "Br," "Bu," and "By."

Use of Color in Alphabetic Systems

Color is used in two different ways by the designers of alphabetic systems, and the *systems* included as illustrations in this chapter reflect this condition. In these systems, the two uses of color are: (1) as an accenting device in order more clearly to define the separate parts of a system and (2) as an integral part of the coding phase of a system. "Color-accent" and "color-code" are the terms frequently used to designate the two phases of color usage.

A color-accented filing system is planned so that the use of a particular color for a particular section or segment in the system will give an additional identity to it and thus make it easier to locate that section or segment.

In a color-coded system, each of a series of colors is identified with a particular alphabetic section in the system, thus giving it a positive color code by which identification of a given alphabetic section can be made more easily than otherwise would be possible.

Thus, a color-accented system assists filing and finding by such means as showing contrasting colors on *various types of folder and guide tabs*; while a color-code plan uses colors on guides and folders according to a scheme in which a color is always associated with the *same alphabetic designation* in a system. Thus this use of color becomes a code, because a code is a systematized pattern of identification.

The TAB Products Company Alpha Code System and the Remington Rand Colorscan and Variadex systems are all color-code filing plans, while the Shaw-Walker Super-Ideal is a color-accented system.

Colorscan System. The Colorscan System is a color-code system for shelf filing and for vertical and open lateral types of filing. The system uses first-position primary guides to show major alphabetic sections and secondary guides to signal both alphabetic and color blocks within a major alphabetic section. By the use of a color code, folders can be located with greater ease and can be filed at random within a given color block.

Color coding in the Colorscan System requires the following procedure and equipment:

1. Primary guides in first position have white labels and signal the main alphabetic sections throughout the system. For example, in the illustration, the first guide shows the start of the "R" primary section in this filing system. First position also holds primary guides which are used to mark special sections of the system. The guide for Rayburn Mfg. Co. illustrates this use of a primary guide.
2. Secondary guides in second position perform three functions:
    a. They divide primary sections into smaller alphabetic sections.
    b. They show a particular color which is the color-code for that particular section of the system.
    c. They include special name guides which show the location of special name sections in which the *second* unit in a name is used and is listed on the guide tab. The guides marked "Albert" and "National" are examples of this use of secondary guides.

This combined alphabetic (a) and color (b) plan for the secondary guides is for the first letter in the *second* unit in a name. For example, in the name "Reynolds Aluminum Co.," the "A" in the second unit "Aluminum" determines which of the secondary guides to use in filing this name.

In any major alphabetic section, 9 secondary guides are used; and each is given a color which differs from that assigned to any other guide. The 9 colors used are: for A - B, red; for C, yellow; for D - E - F, pink; for G - H - I, green; for J - K - L, brown; for M - N - O, blue; for P - Q - R, orange; for S - T, purple; for U - Z, tan. Thus, the color block in which the name "Reynolds *A*luminum Company" will be found is *red*.

Other examples of names color-coded for the Colorscan System are:

2 *Raleigh P*aper Co.	(filed in the orange block)
2 Thomas *Reed*	(filed in the purple block)
2 *Ratheon C*ompany	(filed in the yellow block)
2 *A*lice *Rab*	(filed in the red block)

Single-unit names are filed in white labeled folders directly behind the primary guide for a particular section. In the "R" section, the name

"RACO" would be filed in its own folder directly behind the "R" guide. This would also be true for names such as "Royalcrest," "REDline," and all other single-unit names coming within the "R" section of the Colorscan System.

Remington Rand suggests that when Colorscan is used, folders can be filed at random within color blocks. When this is done, the more active folders tend to be located near the front part of a color section and thus are more readily found than they would be if filed strictly in alphabetic order within color sections. Having blocks of color in a system is a deterent to misfiling since a color out of place is easily seen and thus a folder out of place is easily corrected.

Variadex System. Variadex is a Remington Rand color-code system for use in vertical, open lateral, and shelf types of equipment.

This system is based upon, or keyed to, a definite color plan that is related not only to the identification of sections and items in the system but also to the guiding plan of the system and to names that are being processed for filing.

The color plan for Variadex has been devised in the following manner: Five different colors are used for marking five different alphabetic subdivisions between any two primary letters in the alphabet. The letter that is used to determine the color is the *second* letter appearing in a name or in a notation. For example, in a name beginning with the letters "Be," the "e" would determine the color used; or, in the name "Bowman," the "o" would determine the color used. The five secondary letters that are used as subdivision breaks are: a, e, i, o, and r. To understand how this plan is used, consult the illustrative page B as you read the following description.

> The initial letter "B" when followed by "a," "b," "c," or "d" is indicated by a tab with the color *orange.*
> The initial letter "B" when followed by "e," "f," "g," or "h" is indicated by a tab with the color *yellow.*
> The initial letter "B" when followed by "i," "j," "k," "l," "m," or "n" is indicated by a tab with the color *green.*
> The initial letter "B" when followed by "o," "p," or "q" is indicated by a tab with the color *blue.*
> The initial letter "B" when followed by "r," "s," "t," "u," "v," "w," "x," "y," or "z" is indicated by a tab with the color *violet.*

In the illustration, which shows the "B" to "Bro" portion of the 125-division file, all items in each section are marked with the same color, either by a solidly colored tab or by a colored bar across a tab.

With this color scheme used in processing names for filing, the colors would be as follows for names on materials going into the system illustrated:

James A. B*a*rton	would be filed in the orange section (Bar section)
Willis B*e*nson	would be filed in the yellow section (Ben section)
J. R. B*i*llings	would be filed in the green section (Bi section)
A. S. B*o*wman	would be filed in the blue section (Bo section)
Charles B*ro*wn	would be filed in the violet section (Bro section)

Single-letter names (B-O-A Corp.) are filed in the orange section.

Super-Ideal System. The Shaw-Walker Super-Ideal System has a color-accent plan in which colors are used on guides and folders in order to make each type of item in the system stand out from all others and thus be more readily located.

Primary guides, which are staggered in first and second positions, show primary section notations in red letters. All other notations are given with black letters on a white background.

Miscellaneous folders in first position have blue tabs and thus stand out from other items in the file drawer because of a contrast between colors used on these folders and on guides and other folders. Miscellaneous folders for primary alphabetic sections have red notations which correspond to those on the guides for those sections.

Secondary guides staggered in 1st and 2nd positions show black notations on white backgrounds in contrast to primary guides with red on white.

Special section guides are placed in overlapping fifth-sixth position, which lends distinction to these items as does the use of heavy black tabs and black-on-white notations.

Individual folders have color strips across the top of tabs and these, in addition to the offset arrangement of these folders, provide contrast and excellent visibility for individual folder tabs.

Alpha Code System. This TAB Products Company filing system combines alphabetic symbols with color patterns to form a code for each folder in the system. (1) Each letter in the alphabet has its own color pattern; for example, an *A* is always printed in *red* on a label showing a *solid red* patch of color; a *B* is always *yellow* on a label with a *solid yellow* patch.

There are *two* alphabetic-color labels on each folder. The *upper* of the two is used for the *first* letter in a name. The lower label is for the *second* letter in a name. Thus, the name "Abbott" would have a *red upper* label, and a *yellow lower* label. All names with the first two letters "Ab" would have upper red and lower yellow labels; thus a red-yellow block of color would be formed in the system.

In such a system as the Alpha Code, when folders are accurately filed, all identically coded folders will appear in the same section and any misplaced folder will be out of its color block and will be easily seen as a misfile.

Refer to the illustration of the Alpha Code System and follow these examples of coded names:

1. In the primary H section, in the center part of the lower shelf, notice that *all* folders behind the H guide have upper tabs colored in solid violet. Violet is the color for the letter H, and the pattern used is a solid patch of the color violet. Then notice that the lower tabs of folders in the violet H section show several patterns and colors. These are used to show color blocks for the various second letters in names; for example, the first five folders in the section show solid red lower tabs—the pattern and color for the letter "a." Thus, such names as *Ha*ll and *Ha*rrison are found in this violet-red (solid) section.

2. In the B primary section, notice that:
   a. All upper tabs are solid yellow—the color and pattern for the letter B.
   b. The first five folders in the B section have solid red lower labels for "a." Such names as *Ba*iley, *Ba*nks, and *Ba*tes would be found in this color block.
   c. The second block of folders have two-part blue labels in lower position because two-part blue is the pattern and color for the letter "o." Such names as *Bo*oks, Incorporated, and *Bo*rden, L. R., would be found in this color block.
   d. The next 14 folders have two-part brown labels in lower position because this is the pattern and color for the letter "r." Such names as *Br*idges, *Br*een, and *Br*ennan are found in this color block.

There are no miscellaneous folders in the Alpha Code System; each folder is for an individual correspondent and is labeled with the name of that person or company.

Three different patterns and ten colors are used in covering the alphabet from A to Z. The patterns are: (1) solid-color labels for letters A to H; (2) two-part colored labels for letters I to R; (3) three-part colored labels for letters S to Z. The colors used are those shown at the top of page 108.

Letter	Color	Letter	Color
A	Solid red	N	Two-part dark green
B	Solid yellow	O	Two-part blue
C	Solid orange	P	Two-part purple
D	Solid light green	Q	Two-part violet
E	Solid dark green	R	Two-part brown
F	Solid blue	S	Three-part pink
G	Solid purple	T	Three-part red
H	Solid violet	U	Three-part yellow
I	Two-part pink	V	Three-part orange
J	Two-part red	W	Three-part dark green
K	Two-part yellow	X	Three-part blue
L	Two-part orange	Y	Three-part purple
M	Two-part light green	Z	Three-part violet

QUESTIONS FOR DISCUSSION

1. When a filing system is to be installed or improved, why is it necessary to know what types of systems and equipment are available?

2. Why is an in-line positioning of guides and folders especially effective for a color-control system like Colorscan?

3. Why are guides and folders placed in staggered positions in the Super-Ideal System?

4. How do single-unit notations differ from single-letter notations?

5. What are double-closed notations?

6. What advantage might there be in using multiple-closed notations?

7. What are the two ways of using color in alphabetic systems?

8. What is the principal difference between the two ways of using color in alphabetic systems?

9. In the Colorscan System, how are first-position guides used?

10. How are secondary guides used in Colorscan?

11. There are two alphabetic-color labels on Alpha Code folders. For what purpose is the upper of the two labels used?

12. In the Alpha Code system, how are second letters in key units of names used?

13. In the Variadex system, why in your opinion are changes in colors based upon the second letters in names rather than on first letters?

FILING PROBLEMS

1. Assume that letters from the correspondents in the following list are to be filed according to the Variadex System.

   A. Write each name in correct indexing order.
   B. List the names in correct filing order.

C. Indicate after each name the color used on the guide behind which the correspondence would be filed and on the folder in which the correspondence would be filed.

1. N. T. Boswell & Sons
2. Bi-Monthly Journal
3. The Black & Dekker Co.
4. B & E Railroad
5. Benson & Hedges Company
6. Brother Bear Motel
7. Bhankohleing Canning Co.
8. Bavarian Lines, Inc.
9. J. F. Banning-Brown
10. Brite Enamel Company

2. If you were making a random refile of folders in a Colorscan filing system, under which color and alphabetic sections would folders be replaced if each was labeled with one of the names in the list below? (See first name on list for example.)

Names	Primary Alphabetic Section	Secondary Alpha-Color Section
(Example) 2 Paul M. Roth	R	P = orange
1. Alex M. Roth		
2. Rothman & Clark		
3. Rudell Tool Company		
4. Quality Discount Stores		
5. Rath's		
6. Radio City		
7. Radio Station WTRA		
8. Spring Lake Lodge		
9. Roth-Inland Corp.		
10. Raymond, Harris & Co.		

3. Assume that papers sent to and received from persons and firms whose names are given below are to be filed in an Alpha Code System. Proceed as follows:

   1. Prepare a form like that shown below as an example.
   2. Write each name in indexed form and list it in alphabetic order on the form you have prepared. Include in your list the number assigned to each name.
   3. Indicate in the "Upper Label" column the letter and color pattern which would be used on the upper label for each of the names on the list.
   4. Indicate in the "Lower Label" column the letter and color pattern which would be used on the lower label for each of the names on the list.

   List of names:
   1. Healy-Hayes Insurance Company
   2. Olive Halls
   3. HALL's
   4. Hallmark House, Inc.
   5. Hip-O-Potamus Creations, Inc.
   6. Dennis Hirsh
   7. Hitachi American Ltd.
   8. Hideo Hayachi
   9. Iaconis & Angelo
   10. Niki Iacona

No.	Names	Upper Label Color-Code	Lower Label Color-Code
3	HALL's	H = solid violet	A = solid red

CHAPTER 9

GEOGRAPHIC SYSTEMS AND PROCEDURES

The secret to an effective filing system is to be able to locate materials immediately whenever they are requested by authorizd personnel. The manner in which records are requested and how they are normally used should determine the type of filing system. If records concerning correspondents of a company are generally requested by the names of the correspondents, the records should be filed according to those names. On the other hand, if the locations of the correspondents are of greater importance than the names of the correspondents, it is better to file such records geographically, that is, by locations. In the former case, for example, the records of the Dr. Alexander Pet Foods Co., of Tucson, Arizona, would be filed under the company name. In the latter case, however, the records of this company would be filed first under the key unit "Arizona," then by the city name "Tucson," and finally according to the name of the company.

Nature and Uses of Geographic Filing

Geographic filing is an alphabetic method based principally upon the geographic locations of correspondents. The exact organization that is used in a geographic system depends upon the type of business in which the filing is done, the geographical districts in which correspondents are located, and the use that is to be made of the filed material. For example, correspondence that is international in scope can be held in a system that is based *primarily* upon an alphabetic arrangement of names of countries. For a country-wide system, names of states or provinces that are arranged in alphabetic order can serve as primary titles in the system. For regional or local geographic systems, names of cities and/or streets can be used as primary titles throughout the system.

In all such types of systems, names of correspondents are used as captions on individual folders. Miscellaneous folders bearing location names are used to close sections within geographic systems.

The geographic method has distinct advantages for those businesses that classify their records by geographic districts rather than by individual names. Since the work in sales departments is frequently organized by geographic areas, correspondence files organized on the same basis make it possible to check, control, analyze, and summarize the activities of the departments most efficiently. For example, emphasis on the sections of the country or state that produce the most business may be of greater significance than are the names of the customers, for with the former information advertising campaigns or sales structures can be adjusted to appeal to those areas most in need of additional effort.

Another example of a situation in which geographic filing is advantageous involves companies that mail large quantities of materials at second-class postal rates. The United States Postal Service Corporation requests that all second-class mail be separated by state, town, and ZIP Code before delivery to the post office. Many such companies file their address plates or stencils geographically. Thus, as the mail is addressed, the items are automatically arranged in proper mailing order.

Public utility companies servicing large areas frequently arrange their files geographically to speed up their reference work. Mail-order houses, publishing companies, steamship lines, and large wholesale houses, among others, find geographic filing advantageous.

Arrangements of Geographic Files

In general, there are two basic arrangements of geographic files, each with several possible variations: (1) the lettered guide plan and (2) the location name guide plan.

Lettered Guide Plan. The lettered guide plan (Illustration 9-1, page 113) is very similar to an alphabetic filing system in that free use is made of alphabetic guides. The system is designed as follows:

1. The key title, a state name in this instance (Texas), is indicated by a state name guide with a double-width tab in central position.
2. The primary guides are alphabetic guides staggered in first, second, and third positions. Each primary guide indicates the alphabetic range of the city names that are filed behind it. The primary guides are numbered consecutively to aid the files operator in keeping them in proper order.
3. A miscellaneous alphabetic folder is provided for each primary guide. It bears the same caption and appears in the same position as the guide it follows. This positioning of the folders assures that no miscellaneous folder will obstruct the view of the guide behind it. Notice in the illustration that both guide *A 1* and miscellaneous folder *A 1* are in first position, while both guide *B 2* and miscellaneous folder *B 2* are in second position.
4. The fourth position is reserved for (1) special guides that identify the cities for which there is considerable material; (2) special letter guides, which follow the special city guides and provide an alphabetic

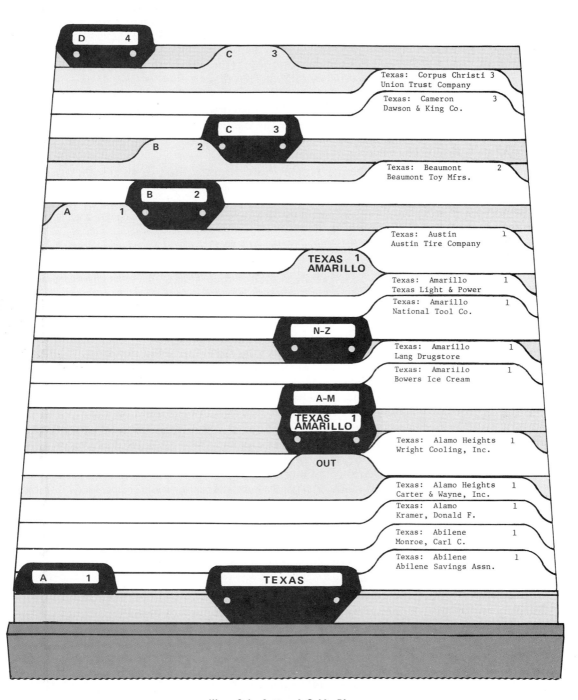

Illus. 9-1, **Lettered Guide Plan**

breakdown of the names of correspondents within the cities (notice the special city guide captioned *Amarillo* and the two special letter guides *A-M* and *N-Z* in the illustration); (3) miscellaneous city folders corresponding to the special city guides (see the folder for *Texas: Amarillo*); and (4) Out guides to indicate materials that have been borrowed from the files.

5. Fifth and sixth positions are reserved for individual folders with double-width tabs. Note that the tab for an individual folder has a two-line caption with the names of the state and city on the first line and the name of the correspondent on the second line.

Location Name Guide Plan. Illustration 9-2 shows the same file as that in the lettered guide plan just described but arranged according to the location name guide plan, that is, according to the names of the various cities in Texas. The system is designed as follows:

1. The key title (Texas) is indicated by a state name guide with a double-width tab in second and third positions.
2. The primary guides are city name guides placed in first position— *Abilene, Alamo, Alamo Heights, Amarillo, Austin, Beaumont, Cameron, Corpus Christi,* and *Dallas.* These guides indicate cities in which are located correspondents with sufficient correspondence so that frequent reference is made to them.
3. Letter guides are placed in second position to denote alphabetic breakdowns of correspondents' names filed behind city name guides. (See guides *A-M* and *N-Z* behind the Amarillo guide.)
4. Miscellaneous folders are placed in third position. The miscellaneous folders in Illustration 9-2 are of three types:
   A. A city miscellaneous folder is provided for each city guide and is placed immediately behind the last individual folder in the section. *Abilene* and *Alamo* are examples.
   B. When a city name guide is followed by letter guides (second position), a separate miscellaneous folder is provided for each section indicated by the letter guides. (See *Amarillo* sections.)
   C. A state miscellaneous folder is provided for each major alphabetic division. In the portion of the file drawer pictured in Illustration 9-2, a state miscellaneous folder is provided at the end of each of the *A, B,* and *C* sections; they are labeled *Texas A-Az, Texas B-Bz,* and *Texas C-Cz.*
5. Individual folders with double-width tabs are in fourth and fifth positions. These folders are opened for correspondents whose correspondence is active enough to warrant individual folders. The tabs for these folders show on the first line the names of the state and the city and on the second line the names of the correspondents.
6. Out guides with single-width tabs are placed so that the word "OUT" is in the center of the two positions occupied by tabs of individual folders.

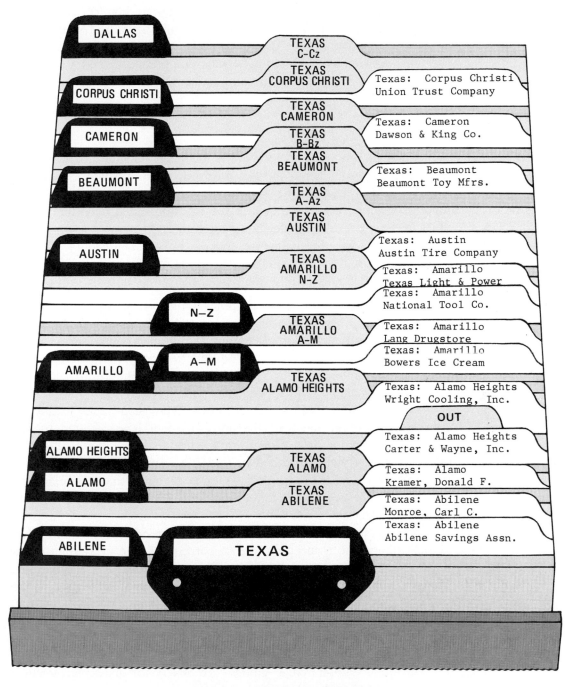

Illus. 9-2, **Location Name Guide Plan**

Some alphabetic systems include numbers on the tabs of guides and folders in addition to the alphabetic designations, names, or location notations. Such numbers are used to help avoid misfiling folders. Other systems omit the numbers because numbers take additional space on the tabs, consume time when new tabs are prepared, and/or become complicated in a rapidly expanding system.

Geographic Filing Procedure

Inspection. Each incoming letter should be checked to see that it has been released for filing.

Coding. Inasmuch as geographic locations constitute the first titles for filing correspondence by this method, such locations should be clearly marked. (See Illustration 9-3.) An effective coding procedure for a geographic name is to circle the location name and number the units in the name to indicate their index order.

After the location name is coded, the correspondent's name is coded in the usual manner, that is, by separating the units by diagonals, underlining the first unit, and numbering the others in their index order.

Cross-References. In geographic filing, as in alphabetic filing, there are times when cross-references must be prepared. For example, if a letter gives information pertaining to another company or to one of the branches of a company, and that information is of such importance that reference may be made to it in the future, a cross-reference is prepared. In a geographic filing system, a cross-reference is filed in the same manner as a letter: The geographic location is considered first; the name of the correspondent is considered second.

Cross-references in a geographic file are of three types: (1) cross-reference sheets that are placed in folders to refer to specific pieces of correspondence, (2) visible cross-reference guides that are placed in the file drawers as permanent references, and (3) cross-reference notations on folder tabs.

Some offices prefer not to use a cross-reference sheet in one folder to call attention to a specific piece of correspondence in another folder because they want the information in each folder to be complete. Therefore, instead of cross-referencing correspondence, they make facsimile copies of incoming letters and extra carbon copies of outgoing letters, the copies being filed in the appropriate folders. This practice eliminates the necessity of referring from one folder to another because each folder contains all pertinent information.

Visible cross-reference guides are used, for example, when a correspondent has branches in several cities and, as a result, the

Texas/Light (and) Power

7391 SOUTH EIGHTH STREET AMARILLO, TEXAS 79103
806-861-4548

MAY 7 19-- P.M.

May 6, 19--

Mr. Santos Ibera
Security Engineering Co.
4285 East Potter Street
Amarillo, TX 79105

Dear Mr. Ibera

One of our customers, Mr. Sam Appleman, of Bushland, Texas, has a problem we believe you can help solve.

Mr. Appleman is erecting a new plant and would like to install a new electronic warning device to give an advance signal should one of the plant boilers become overheated. He wishes to have this device sealed into the building when it is being erected, but he requires that it have a sufficient number of inspection outlets so repairs can be made easily. Furthermore, because of the nature of his business, there must be no danger of the electricity igniting the highly combustible gas used in the manufacturing process.

Will you please have one of your engineers arrange an appointment with Mr. Appleman and me to discuss this problem. We should meet within the next week or ten days so that construction can proceed soon thereafter.

Sincerely yours

Carl C. Dawes
Carl C. Dawes
Customer Service

dk

Illus. 9-3

Letter Coded for Placement in a Geographic File

CROSS-REFERENCE SHEET

Name or Subject ___Texas, Bushland___
___Sam Appleman___

Date of Item ___May 6, 19--___

Regarding ___Electronic warning device___
___for overheated plant boilers___

SEE

Name or Subject ___Texas, Amarillo___
___Texas Light and Power___

Authorized by ___Joan Conrad___   Date ___5/9/--___

Illus. 9-4

Accompanying Cross-Reference Sheet

correspondence in one folder frequently pertains to problems and conditions in other branches.

This filing problem may be handled also by the use of a permanent cross-reference notation on the tab of each folder that contains correspondence pertaining to materials in other folders. Assume, for example, that the correspondent Jones Equipment Co. has its main office in Detroit, Michigan, and branch offices in Spokane, Washington; Denver, Colorado; Tampa, Florida; and St. Louis, Missouri. The tab of each folder would show a reference to the other offices. The tab of the Detroit folder would show the following:

```
Michigan:  Detroit
Jones Equipment Co.
SEE:  Wash.:  Spokane;  Colo.:  Denver;
      Fla.:  Tampa;  Mo.:  St. Louis
```

The tabs of the folders filed under Spokane, Washington; Denver, Colorado; Tampa, Florida; and St. Louis, Missouri, would be labeled in a similar manner.

Sorting. Letters are sorted by geographic units, starting with the key unit for the first sorting and continuing until all the units involved in the filing system have been used. For example, the first sorting might be on the basis of states, the second sorting on the basis of cities or towns, and the final sorting on the basis of names of correspondents.

Placing Material in Folders. The first step in placement of material in folders is the location of the proper folder for each item. The files operator locates (for example) the state drawer by reading the drawer labels; he or she finds in that drawer the guide that indicates the proper section in the state. This guide usually lists an alphabetic range in which the city name would fall (Illustration 9-1) or an actual city name (Illustration 9-2). Ordinarily this is as far as the guides can be used in locating folders, although there may be a further breakdown. (See the *Amarillo* and *A-M* guides behind the *A-1* guide in Illustration 9-1 and the *A-M* guide behind the *Amarillo* guide, Illustration 9-2.)

Lettered Guide Plan. Next the files operator examines the alphabetic section in which the city name falls to see whether there is an individual folder for the correspondent. If there is such a folder, he places the communication in it by date, the most recent date in front in the same manner in which a communication is filed in an individual folder in an alphabetic file.

If there is no individual folder, the files operator places the communication in a miscellaneous folder. If there is a miscellaneous folder labeled with the name of the city in which the correspondent is located, the material is placed in that folder. If there is no such folder, the material is placed in the miscellaneous folder with the alphabetic caption indicating the alphabetic section in which the city name falls. At this point the rules for alphabetic correspondence filing must be followed. The letters in a miscellaneous folder are grouped alphabetically first by the city names, then by the names of the correspondents, and last in each group by date with the latest date in front. If there are several correspondents with the same name in the same city, the identical names rules are followed (Rules 6 and 20).

Location Name Plan. After locating the city section in which the correspondence should be filed, the files operator looks for an individual folder for the correspondent. If there is such a folder, the communication is filed in it.

If there is no individual folder, the files operator places the material in a miscellaneous city folder if there is one. In this folder the letters are grouped first in alphabetic order by correspondents' names and then in each group by date. If several correspondents in the same city have the same name, the rules for identical names are followed (Rules 6 and 20).

If there is no miscellaneous city folder, the communication is placed in the miscellaneous state alphabetic folder (such as *Texas A-Az*), in which the correspondence is grouped first by city or town; next, in each city group by names of correspondents; then, by address, if necessary; and, finally, in each correspondent's group by date with the latest date forward.

Supplementary Card Index

In a geographic filing system, problems sometimes arise because correspondence is not filed primarily according to the names of correspondents. For example, a person who requests material from the files may have forgotten the address of the correspondent, or a correspondent may write from a location other than his business address. To handle situations such as these, a supplementary card index is maintained. This index is needed, not in filing materials, but in finding them when the address is unknown or is in doubt.

If, when filing material, the files operator finds no previous correspondence for that correspondent, he prepares an index card showing the name and address of the correspondent. Since the material will be filed in a miscellaneous folder, the files operator types the letter "M" in the upper right corner of the index card to indicate the type of folder in which the material is to be filed. The card is then placed in the supplementary card index.

When the volume of correspondence with a correspondent accumulates to the number of pieces that require the opening of an individual folder, the files operator removes the correspondence from the miscellaneous folder, opens an individual folder and transfers the correspondence to it, and changes the "M" in the corner of the index card in the supplementary card index to "I" to indicate that the correspondence is now filed in an individual folder.

Expansion in a Geographic System

In the lettered guide plan, when the number of correspondents in one city has increased sufficiently to justify the opening of a miscellaneous city folder, a guide bearing the name of the city is placed in fourth position; the correspondence pertaining to that city is removed from the miscellaneous alphabetic folder; a miscellaneous folder bearing the name of the city is opened and placed in fourth position behind the city guide; and the correspondence is transferred to it. When the pieces of correspondence with one correspondent increase to the number justifying an individual folder, the correspondence is taken from the miscellaneous alphabetic folder or the miscellaneous city folder, as the case may be; an individual folder is opened; and the correspondence is transferred to it.

In the location name guide plan, when the number of correspondents in one city has increased sufficiently to justify the opening of a miscellaneous city folder, a city guide is added to the file, the correspondence pertaining to that city is removed from the miscellaneous state folder; a new folder with a caption indicating the name of the city is opened; and the correspondence is transferred to it. When the number of pieces of correspondence with one correspondent increases to the number justifying an individual folder, the correspondence is taken from the miscellaneous city folder or the miscellaneous state folder, as the case may be; an individual folder is opened; and the correspondence is transferred to it.

Geographic Filing in an Alphabetic System

It is sometimes practical to add special geographic sections to an alphabetic file. This is accomplished, for example, in the portion of an alphabetic file shown in Illustration 9-5. The guiding system is alphabetic, with primary guides in first position. Miscellaneous folders in second position are provided at the end of each alphabetic section just as they are in any regular alphabetic system. Special guides in third position identify special sections by name (for example, Kolfax) and by

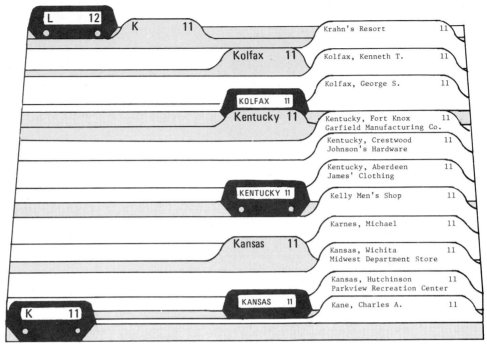

Illus. 9-5

Geographic Filing in an Alphabetic System

geographic locations (Kansas and Kentucky). Miscellaneous folders are provided at the end of each special section with tabs in third position. Individual folders are in line in fourth and fifth positions and use double-width tabs.

For incidental (special) geographic filing in an alphabetic system to be useful, one or more of the following conditions are generally present: (1) business correspondence and related papers are concerned with sales in given geographic areas; (2) services are performed in relation to geographic areas; (3) organizations are formed and operated in relation to geographic regions or districts; (4) political or social agencies and activities are related to geographic boundaries.

In Illustration 9-5, correspondence with customers only in Kansas and Kentucky are grouped together because these two states are serviced by regional representatives; all other customers are serviced by the home office, and a special geographic section is not necessary.

Papers are coded for filing in special geographic sections of an alphabetic system in the same manner as they would be coded for a complete geographic file. (See Illustration 9-3.)

If material to be filed geographically in an alphabetic file is not recognized by code clerks and properly marked for geographic filing, the value of the geographic section is lost as are the papers which will have been filed alphabetically rather than by geographic location.

Subject Filing in a Geographic System

As in alphabetic correspondence filing, there is occasionally an advantage in a geographic system in having a special subject folder for certain correspondence more likely to be called for by subject than by geographic location or by individual name. Examples would include correspondence concerning advertising, job applications, tax returns, and financial reports.

In a geographic system the difficulty encountered is that of giving a geographic location to correspondence that is related because of its subject matter but that involves a number of different locations. The best solution for this problem seems to be that of grouping all special subject folders in one part of the files separate from ordinary correspondence. If it is considered desirable to maintain the geographic arrangement for all materials, regardless of type, the special subject folders can be arbitrarily assigned the geographic location of the business that maintains the filing system.

QUESTIONS FOR DISCUSSION

1. What is geographic filing? Under what conditions might a company prefer to use it?

2. Name a few of the types of businesses that find distinct advantages in filing by a geographic method.

3. Describe (a) the lettered guide plan and (b) the location name guide plan (illustrated on pages 113 and 115).

4. Explain the coding procedure in a geographic file.

5. What three types of cross-references may be used in a geographic file?

6. Why are facsimile copies or extra carbon copies sometimes used instead of cross-reference sheets in folders?

7. On what basis are letters sorted after they have been coded geographically?

8. When filing coded materials, how does the files operator locate the proper folder for each item in a lettered guide plan?

9. How does the files operator locate the proper folder when the location name plan is used instead of the lettered guide plan?

10. In what order are letters filed in (a) a miscellaneous city folder? (b) a miscellaneous state folder?

11. For what purpose is a card index file used in a geographic filing system?

12. When would it be practical to use special geographic sections in an alphabetic file?

13. How is correspondence pertaining to a special subject handled in a geographic file?

FILING PROBLEMS

1. A. Type or write each of the following names and addresses on a 5″ by 3″ index card or on a slip of paper cut to that size. Place in the upper right corner of the card the number that identifies the name. Type each name in proper indexing order for a geographic filing system by writing the state and then the city on the first line, and the correspondent's name in indexing order on the second line.

B. After you have typed all the cards, arrange them alphabetically, first according to states, then according to cities, and finally according to correspondents' names.

C. Prepare an answer sheet similar to the one illustrated on page 19. Type or write the numbers 1 to 15 in one column and the numbers 16 to 30 in a second column. After the numbers on the answer sheet, list the numbers representing the names in the order in which you have them arranged.

1. The Von Wald Company
   Camden, AR 71701

2. Byers' Barber Shop
   St. Petersburg, FL 33738

3. Nelson Clothing Company
   Gainesville, GA 30501

4. Blue Star Drum Corps
   Coral Gables, FL 33134

5. Penline Graphics, Inc.
   Jacksonville, AR 72076

6. Cass Apartments
   Little Rock, AR 72203

7. Hosch Marine Sales
   Decatur, GA 30031

8. Family Veterinary Clinic
   Bradenton, FL 33505

9. Swartz Cabinet Shop
   Savannah, GA 31402

10. A-1 Office Equipment Co.
    Fort Smith, AR 72901

11. Fran's Bake Shop
    Jacksonville, FL 32201

12. Redi-Products Company
    El Dorado, AR 71730

13. Climatrol Air Conditioning
    Jonesboro, AR 72401

14. Blue Moon Supper Club
    Athens, GA 30601

15. Best Building Supply
    Jonesboro, GA 30236

16. Hope Accoustical Tile Co.
    Hope, AR 71801

17. Max's Auto Wrecking Company
    Orlando, FL 32802

18. Gordie's Men's Hair Styling
    Atlanta, GA 30304

19. C & G Claim Service
    Jacksonville, AR 72076

20. American Roofing Company
    Jacksonville, FL 32206

21. ADT Protection Service
    Macon, GA 31201

22. Renners Flower Shoppe
    Clearwater, FL 33515

23. Drapps Container Company
    Jacksonville, GA 31544

24. Arkansas Air Lines
    Little Rock, AR 72201

25. A to Z Beverage Depot
    Gainesville, GA 30504

26. Tampa State Bank
    St. Petersburg, FL 33731

27. Assured Abstract and
       Title Co.
    Fort Smith, AR 72901

28. Badger Bearing Company
    Atlanta, GA 30306

29. Genuine Auto Parts
    Gainesville, FL 32601

30. Brite-Way Signs Co.
    Hot Springs, AR 71901

2. A. Type or write each of the following names and addresses on a 5″ by 3″ index card or on a slip of paper cut to that size. Place in the upper right corner of the card the number that identifies the name. Type the names and addresses in proper indexing order for a geographic filing system.

B. After you have typed all the cards, arrange them alphabetically, first according to states, then according to cities, and finally according to correspondents' names and addresses.

C. Prepare an answer sheet similar to the one illustrated on page 19. Write the numbers 1 to 25 in one column and the numbers 26 to 50 in a second column. After the numbers, list the numbers representing the names in the order in which you have them arranged.

1. Freedom Baptist Church
   99 Church Street
   Altoona, PA 16601

2. Nu-Way Dry Cleaners
   3718 Silver Lane
   Lancaster, NY 14086

3. Tom Cat Hamburgers
   401 Maple Street
   Greenville, SC 29609

4. Charles S. Chambers
   132 College Street
   Oswego, NY 13126

5. North Side Jewelers
   918 Ace Avenue
   Bethlehem, PA 18017

6. Coulee Tool & Die
   1232 Clinton Street
   Syracuse, NY 13204

7. Oliver A. Stoffer
      Electronics
   230 Lark Lane
   Norristown, PA 19401

8. Royal Engraving Co.
   214 Copeland Avenue
   Spartanburg, SC 29301

9. Long Beach Communications,
      Inc.
   312 State Street
   Albany, NY 12210

10. Tom's Speedometer Shop
    27 Elm Drive
    Greenville, PA 16125

11. Northeast Furniture Sales
    278 Washington Street
    Jamestown, NY 14701

12. Bruce Termite Protection
    417 Exchange Bldg
    Charleston, SC 29401

13. Sheppard's Coffee House
    7311 Center Drive
    Rochester, NY 14609

14. Dun's Eatery
    23 Main Street
    Johnstown, PA 15901

15. Rev. T. P. Bruce
    527 Cass Building
    Charleston, SC 29401

16. Free Way Department Store
    415 Brown Street
    Altoona, PA 16601

17. Wil-Kil Pest Control Co.
    3602 Washington Avenue
    Newberry, SC 29108

18. Top's Apple Orchard
    Farm Lane
    Middletown, NY 10940

19. Boyds Sporting Goods
    7231 West Salem Road
    Williamsport, PA 17701

20. Nu-Way Dry Cleaners
    9310 Silver Lane
    Lancaster, NY 14086

21. Northside Department Store
    739 North Street
    Bethlehem, PA 18018

22. Speed-O-Meter Race Track
    Highway 18
    Greenville, SC 29602

23. Charles-The-Barber
    279 Prince Street
    Oswego, NY 13126

24. Nut-All Peanut Shoppe
    2716 Washington Avenue
    Lancaster, PA 17602

25. Wehrs Electric
    1102 Charles Street
    Reading, PA 19606

26. Albrecht's Duraclean
       Services
    1973 A Street
    Buffalo, NY 14211

27. New Style Clothing Company
    27 Crocket Lane
    Lancaster, SC 29720

28. Tony's Barber Shop
    28 Main Street
    Middletown, PA 17057

29. C. H. Sheppard Manufacturing
    Co.
    89 Newton Square
    Rochester, NY 14618

30. Wilki Leather Shop
    94 Race Street
    Newberry, SC 29108

31. North Star Car Wash
    97 Copeland Avenue
    Altona, NY 12910

32. Northey's Diaper Service
    416 Mountain Road
    Bethlehem, PA 18016

33. B & B Root Beer
    18376 Highway 12
    Newburgh, NY 12550

34. Bond-Well Dry Walls
    415 Nelson Place
    New Castle, PA 16101

35. Lancaster News
    62 Circle Drive
    Lancaster, SC 29720

36. Sheppard's Coffee House
    73 Quarry Lane
    Rochester, NY 14603

37. Pennsylvania State
       Employment Service
    39 Main Street
    Scranton, PA 18505

38. John A. Dundee
    2613 Hawthorne Street
    Johnstown, NY 12095

39. New Style Clothing Company
    5672 Custer Blvd.
    Lancaster, NY 14086

40. Larry S. Nutall
    1819 Madison Street
    Lancaster, PA 17602

41. Tom Speed
    4819 Jefferson Street
    Greenville, SC 29602

42. Welton Bond
    415 Nelson Place
    New Castle, PA 16101

43. North East Travel Bureau
    63 Spruce Street
    Jamestown, NY 14701

44. Earl A. Dunn, M.D.
    76 Easton Road
    Johnstown, PA 15901

45. Rev. Cal H. Sheppard
    308 Losey Boulevard
    Rochester, NY 14603

46. Terrance Bruce
    813 Easy Street
    Charleston, SC 29405

47. Top Hat Ceramics
    163 South Leonard Street
    Middletown, NY 10940

48. Marie Women's Wear
    176 Market Street
    Schenectady, NY 12302

49. Dun-Rite Garage Doors
    501 Gillette Street
    Johnstown, PA 15901

50. Oswego Chamber of Commerce
    712 Main Street
    Oswego, NY 13126

JOB 7 Geographic Correspondence Filing

At this time complete Job 7 in OFFICE FILING PROCEDURES, Fourth Edition. The instructions and supplies for this job are included in the practice set.

CHAPTER 10

NUMERIC SYSTEMS AND PROCEDURES

Nature and Uses of a Numeric File

As stated earlier, records should be stored in such a manner that they can be located easily and quickly when they are needed. When the number of files is large and when names of some correspondents are similar, as they are often likely to be in a large filing department, locating specific folders and pieces of correspondence may become a slow, inefficient process. To overcome such inefficiency, the *numeric filing method* was devised. This method of filing is easy to identify because it is a system in which numbers rather than letters or names are used for guide and folder captions.

Numeric filing is found in a great number of everyday experiences. For example, banks now identify the checking accounts of their depositors by numbers. An individual account number is assigned to each depositor, and this number is printed with a special ink on a set of blank checks before the checks are given to the depositor. After a check has been drawn, cashed, and returned to the bank, a machine automatically "reads" the number and locates the account of the depositor. Social security numbers are used for an increasing number of purposes, including federal income tax returns. Other examples of situations in which numeric filing is used to advantage are:

1. Charge accounts for gasoline purchases and for department store buying, credit cards, and many other types of transactions involving credit, all of which are identified by number.
2. Orders for merchandise from a mail-order house, which places its items by number on the stockroom shelves and lists its items by number in its catalog.
3. Orders for automobile replacement parts to be sent by manufacturers.
4. Premiums on life insurance policies that are filed by policy numbers.
5. Factory jobs that are identified by numbers.
6. Installment loans and mortgages.
7. Legal cases, which are assigned consecutive numbers in the order in which they are initiated; legal clients, who are assigned numbers by the attorneys handling their cases.
8. Jobs undertaken by building contractors.
9. Districts or territories, such as sales districts or distribution areas.

**Organization
of a
Numeric
File**

A numeric correspondence file usually consists of four parts:

1. A main correspondence file in which guides and folders bear numeric captions.
2. A supplementary index card control file in which correspondents' names or subject titles are arranged alphabetically.
3. A miscellaneous alphabetic file in which are housed (1) materials pertaining to new correspondents for whom the volume of future materials is not known or not anticipated to be extensive enough to warrant the assignment of a number immediately or (2) materials from past correspondents whose correspondence has not yet reached the frequency requiring a separate folder and an assigned number.
4. An accession book, a consecutive record of assigned numbers.

In the main numeric file each important correspondent is given an individual folder that has a numbered caption. The folders are numbered in sequence, beginning with a predetermined number such as 100 or 1000, with little or no regard for the alphabetic order of names.

If the volume of correspondence with a certain person or company is small, infrequent, or inactive, the correspondence is housed in a separate miscellaneous alphabetic file. But when the volume of correspondence with that person or company increases sufficiently to warrant the opening of an individual folder, that folder is given the next unassigned number. All materials to, from, or about this correspondent are always placed in this folder, with the most recent material in front.

A number may be assigned also to a subject or a group classification such as "Applications." In such a case all materials relating to this subject are filed in folders bearing this subject title. Within such folders the correspondence is filed in alphabetic order according to the names of the applicants, and all letters pertaining to each application are arranged by date.

**Advantages of
Numeric
Filing**

There are many advantages to a numeric filing system. Among them are the following:

1. All papers pertaining to a certain job or to related activities are brought together.
2. A certain degree of privacy is possible because only numbers are visible to someone looking at the files. Ordinarily neither names nor titles are written on the guide or folder tabs.
3. Numbered folders or cards that are out of place can be located more rapidly than is possible in most alphabetic systems.
4. Almost unlimited expansion is possible in a numeric filing system.
5. Cross-references are not needed in the numeric section of the files because they are conveniently located in the alphabetic card index.

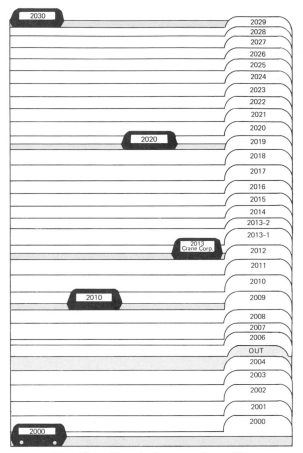

Illus. 10-1, **Numeric Correspondence File**

Disadvantages of Numeric Filing

In spite of the advantages of numeric filing, there are disadvantages to consider, the most important of which are listed below.

1. Numeric filing systems are indirect systems in that the files operator, before filing or seeking correspondence, must first consult an alphabetic index card control file to determine the proper code number for each correspondent. This is in contrast to direct alphabetic systems in which the files operator can go directly to the file drawer and file or find the record.

2. Numeric files provide only for active correspondents. Alphabetic files are still necessary for miscellaneous folders to accommodate materials received in such limited quantity that individual folders are not necessary. When the volume of these materials from any one source increases, the method of coding of the correspondence must be changed and numbers assigned.

Arrangement of a Numeric File

The guides in a numeric file may appear in any of the available positions. One arrangement of guides and folders in a numeric correspondence file is shown in Illustration 10-1. The primary guides are staggered in first, second, and third positions; special guides for very active correspondents are placed in fourth position; individual folders and out guides are placed in fifth position. The special guides in fourth position call immediate attention to folder numbers for which correspondence is so frequent that more than one folder bearing the same basic number is needed to house the correspondence.

The guides are numbered by 10's. Consequently, unless correspondence with a single firm is so active as to require more than one folder bearing the same basic number, there would never be more than ten folders between two numbered guides. The folders are placed in the drawer in strict numeric order. The tabs of the folders bear only the numbers assigned to the various correspondents so that no correspondents' names are visible except on special guides.

Index Card Control File

Since guide and folder tab notations show only numbers, an alphabetic file card control is essential to the operation of a numeric file. The card control consists of an alphabetic arrangement of the names of the correspondents and of subjects. The names are typed on cards, which are filed behind alphabetic guides in a special card drawer or in a file box. Each card gives the name of a correspondent or a subject title and shows the number of the folder that has been assigned to the name or subject; for example, Astrolite of New York—folder No. 100. Thus, if the number of the folder given to that company has been forgotten, the files operator can consult the card index control file to get the number of the folder.

The cards in the index card control file are usually prepared in the form of the one in Illustration 10-2.

```
┌─────────────────────────────────────────┐
│ Astrolite (of) New York           100    │
│                                          │
│ Astrolite of New York                    │
│ 150 Lafayette Street                     │
│ Utica, NY  13516                         │
│                                          │
│                                          │
│                                          │
└─────────────────────────────────────────┘
```

Illus. 10-2

Index Card in Card Control File

Miscellaneous Alphabetic File

Numeric folders are not usually prepared for correspondence that is inactive or infrequent. Such papers are held in a miscellaneous alphabetic file until they accumulate to a point where it is practical to prepare individual folders for them in the numeric file.

The miscellaneous alphabetic file is often placed in the front part of the first file drawer of the regular numeric file. It may, however, be kept in a separate filing cabinet or drawer. The miscellaneous alphabetic file usually consists of guides and miscellaneous folders with alphabetic captions only.

Materials that are filed in the miscellaneous alphabetic file may or may not be listed in the index card control file. If these materials are listed in the index card control file, each card that serves as an index for this type of material is marked with the letter "M," instead of a number, in the upper right-hand corner to indicate that the correspondence is in the miscellaneous alphabetic file.

Accession Book or Register

Many users of a numeric system keep an *accession book* or *register,* a consecutive record of numbers assigned to folders, similar to the one illustrated below.

NUMBER	NAME	DATE
1209	Corwin + Adams Co.	Feb. 3, 19--
1210	Abbott, Richard K.	Feb. 3, 19--
1211	Kline Television Service	Feb. 4, 19--
1212	Durban-Smith Variety Store	Feb. 5, 19--
1213		

Illus. 10-3, **Accession Book**

Numeric Filing Procedure

Inspection. Each incoming letter should be checked to see that it has been released for filing.

Preliminary Name Coding. Each letter must be read carefully by the files operator to determine which name is to be used as a basis for numeric coding. The files operator must then code the name in the usual manner by (1) marking off the units in the name with diagonals, (2) underlining the key unit, and (3) writing above the remaining units the numbers that indicate their position or rank in the index order of the name. Such detailed coding is not necessary for assigning the folder number. It is essential, however, in preparing the index card control cards to assure their correct place in the card control file and to assure correct placement of correspondence in miscellaneous folders. Other names that will be used for cross-reference purposes should be marked also in the usual manner.

Alphabetic Sorting. After all names to be considered in filing the correspondence have been coded, the files operator sorts the pieces of correspondence alphabetically in preparation for the numeric coding process. This step need not be done if the volume of correspondence is small.

Numeric Coding. The first step in the numeric coding process includes checking the index card control file for every name to be coded. If the name appearing on a piece of correspondence is listed in the card index file, the files operator notes the number already assigned to that name and uses it to code the letter. In the upper right corner of the letter, the number that has been assigned to that particular correspondent is written. The files operator should be absolutely certain to write the correct number in clear, easily read style. Failure to do so may result in misfiling the correspondence. A careless operator will sometimes write a digit inaccurately, occasionally drop a digit (record 2586 as 258, for example), and all too often transpose figures (record 392 as 329). Such errors make the filing system ineffective.

If no number has been assigned to the correspondent because his correspondence is inactive or new, the letter is coded by writing the letter "M" in the upper right-hand corner of the letter to indicate that it is to be filed in the miscellaneous alphabetic file. Every piece of correspondence, whether it is an incoming letter or the carbon copy of an outgoing communication, must be coded. If a record of miscellaneous correspondence is kept in the index card control file, a card should be prepared for the correspondent and the letter "M" should be assigned as the code.

Cross-References. Cross-references are usually made in the index card control file. They are used when a firm is known by two different names or has changed its name, or when individuals connected with the firm are likely to be thought of in connection with the correspondence.

If, in January, 1974, the Bowman Hardware Co. (Folder 251) changes its name to the Fairmount Hardware Co., a new card showing the new name but the same number should be prepared, as shown below. (A new card is prepared so that the new name of the company will

Illus. 10-4, **Original Card**   Illus. 10-5, **Cross-Reference Card with Notation**

appear on the original card in the control file.) The old card for the Bowman Hardware Co., showing the number 251, should be changed into a cross-reference card by adding an "X" to the number. The notation "Fairmount Hardware Co., Successors" and the date of the name change should be typed on the card to complete the information.

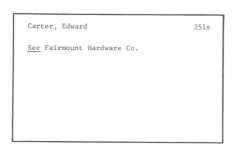

```
Carter, Edward                        251x

See Fairmount Hardware Co.
```

Illus. 10-6, **Cross-Reference Card under the Name of an Individual**

If correspondence with the Fairmount Hardware Co. is likely to be called for under the name of Edward Carter, the president of the company, a second cross-reference card should be prepared as shown in Illustration 10-6.

Sorting for Numeric Filing. After all the communications have been coded, the files operator sorts them: first by hundreds, then by tens, and finally by units. All pieces coded "M" are placed in one pile to be filed at one time in the miscellaneous alphabetic file.

Placing Material in Folders. All materials bearing code numbers are placed in folders bearing those same numbers. If two or more pieces of correspondence have the same code number, they are placed in the folder according to date, with the latest date in front. All materials coded "M" are filed alphabetically in the miscellaneous alphabetic section of the file.

Adding Individual Folders

Individual folders are assigned only to correspondents whose correspondence is frequent and active. The reason for this restriction is that unnecessary time would be spent in filing and finding materials if every new piece had to be filed in a separate folder. Furthermore, it would be too expensive to buy enough folders so that one could be assigned to every correspondent. The matter of determining which correspondents and which groups of materials are important enough to warrant the opening of individual folders must be decided in each office.

If a new correspondent is believed to be important, or if the communications with a correspondent have accumulated in the miscellaneous alphabetic file to the minimum number of pieces established by the business for the opening of an individual folder, the files operator assigns to the correspondent the first unassigned number. The communications are then coded with the newly assigned number in the upper right corner of each piece. If there is no card in the supplementary card index file for the correspondent, the files operator prepares a file card and puts it in correct alphabetic sequence in the index card control file. If there already is a card in the control file, the files operator merely erases the "M" and writes the new folder number in its place.

For example, if the correspondence of Larry Bryan Associates, which is housed in the miscellaneous alphabetic file, becomes active enough to warrant the opening of an individual folder, and if the last number assigned is 519, the files operator (1) removes the correspondence with this firm from the folder in the miscellaneous alphabetic file, (2) assigns number 520 to this correspondent, (3) makes up a file card for it if there is no such card in the control file (if there already is a card in the control file, the files operator changes the "M" code to "520"), (4) erases the "M" code on each piece of correspondence and substitutes the numeric code 520 in the upper right-hand corner, (5) files the card alphabetically in the control file, and (6) files the correspondence in the numeric correspondence file by opening a new folder bearing the caption 520.

Terminal Digit Filing

Terminal digit filing is a method of numeric filing designed to reduce the possibility of misfiling because of the difficulty encountered in reading and remembering large numbers. In terminal digit filing, the numbers are assigned in the same manner as described for consecutive digit filing, but the numbers are read from right to left in small groups beginning with the terminal group, hence the name *terminal* digit filing.

Terminal digit filing is used when numbers contain five or more digits. In the number 742618, for example, the digits could be separated into two groups of three digits or three groups of two digits each. The two-digit groups would be filed in this manner:

3	2	1
Final	*Secondary*	*Primary*
74	26	18

The files operator would first locate the drawer containing those materials or records whose numbers end with 18. A search would then be made down the guides in that drawer for guide No. 26. Lastly, the material would be filed in numerical order in back of the number 73. Numbers of less than six digits are brought up to that figure by adding zeros to the *left* of the number. For example, the number 28753 would be written 028753.

Terminal digit filing is used in filing such items as checks, mortgages, letters of credit, insurance policies, hospital case records, purchase orders, and various government documents.

Terminal digit filing has several advantages over consecutive digit filing. These are listed below.

1. Filing errors are more easily avoided because only the primary digits need be considered in locating the drawer; and only the secondary digits need be considered in locating the guide.
2. Records are more easily obtained because the most current materials are more evenly distributed throughout the file. If several files operators are working at the same time, they are less likely to need the same file drawer at the same time.
3. Sorting and handling of records is more efficient. Time savings of 25 to 50 percent have been realized by some companies.

Middle Digit Filing

One modification of terminal digit filing is middle digit filing. In this system, the middle series of digits is considered first, then the series at the left, and lastly (if necessary) the final series (the series at the right). The primary guides are prepared for the middle series of digits.

In using the middle digit system, the number 742618 would be filed in this order:

2	1	3
Secondary	*Primary*	*Final*
74	26	18

The files operator would first locate the drawer or primary guide for those materials or records whose primary digits are 26 and search down the guides for guide No. 74. The materials would then be filed in the proper order according to the number 18.

Middle digit filing has the same advantages and uses as terminal digit filing. In addition, the following advantages are claimed for it.

1. If the filing system is being changed over from a consecutive digit system, it is easier to change to middle digit filing than to terminal digit filing because entire blocks of 100 numbers are moved as a single group. For example, all records numbered 74 26 00 through 74 26 99 remain in the same sequence after the move and can therefore be moved at one time.
2. In terminal digit filing it is necessary to consider 10 different places to find 10 documents in consecutive order; in middle digit filing, only

1 place would be necessary, each place representing 100 consecutive numbers, as the folders are already arranged in consecutive order.

3. If the company prefers to assign the numbers in blocks rather than singly, it is possible in middle digit filing to have the entire block filed in one place. For example, a sales organization may wish to assign all records with the middle digits of 50 to the main branch, all records with the middle digits of 51 to Massachusetts, and so on. In middle digit filing 100 different folders could have the middle digit of 50, and all would be located in the same section of the files.

Comparison of Consecutive, Terminal Digit, and Middle Digit Sequences

The following table compares the sequence of seven numbers filed in consecutive, terminal digit, and middle digit files. The same numbers are used in the three columns.

Back	Consecutive Number Filing	Terminal Digit Filing	Middle Digit Filing	Back
↑	74 27 18	12 34 56	53 96 24	↑
	53 96 24	34 37 49	53 95 27	
	53 95 27	34 34 49	34 37 49	
	46 29 18	53 95 27	34 34 49	
	34 37 49	53 96 24	12 34 56	
	34 34 49	46 29 18	46 29 18	
Front	12 34 56	74 27 18	74 27 18	Front

Folder or Card Guide Drawer   Guide Drawer Folder or Card

Use of Color in Numeric Filing

Color coding is frequently used in numeric filing systems as an aid in quick identification of groups of numbers and in identification of misfiled folders. There are many color systems in use for numeric filing systems. One system uses a different, clearly identifiable color on the tab of each folder. The color used is determined by the *next to last* digit. In this system, each group of ten folders is one color with a second contrasting color for the next ten folders. If ten colors are used, the color group will repeat itself in only one group out of each ten groups of ten folders.

Just where the color is applied to the tab depends upon the design of the filing system. In some systems, the entire tab is colored; in others, a thin strip of color covers the top of the tab. A third method uses a colored plastic clip over a particular number on the tab or a particular number is printed in the appropriate color. In each case, the files operator must know and understand the exact color coding being used. It is reported that the use of color could reduce misfiling by up to 80 percent.

Shaw-Walker

Illus. 10-7, **Numeric-Name System**

Numeric-Name System

In this system, made by the Shaw-Walker Company, numbers are printed on the folder tabs, which are wide enough to accommodate gummed labels indicating the name or subject of the folder. By showing both a number and a name, additional identity is given to each folder and makes filing and finding faster and surer. Another feature of this system is that even numbers are given to folders with tabs on the left side and odd numbers are given to folders with tabs on the right.

In Illustration 10-7, notice that the arrangement is determined by the numeric sequence, not by the alphabetic sequence of names. Thus, the system is primarily numeric and indirect, requiring a supplementary alphabetic card file for identification purposes.

Soundex and Triple Check Automatic Systems

There are many possible variations of alpha-numeric filing systems. Two such variations are the Soundex system and the Triple Check Automatic system, both of which are manufactured by the Remington Rand Division of Sperry Rand Corporation.

The Soundex system is designed to bring all names that sound the same but are spelled differently (such as Patin, Paton, Patten, and

Patton) into one section of a file by assigning alpha-numeric codes to the names on the basis of pronunciation rather than spelling.

The Triple Check Automatic system is based upon a system of alpha-numeric codes assigned to correspondence according to a chart for coding primary indexing units and a chart for coding secondary indexing units. Filing of papers is done on the basis of the codes assigned rather than on the basis of the alphabetic units themselves. Color is also used to aid in the filing and finding of folders.

Both Soundex and Triple Check Automatic are highly specialized systems and are typically used in large filing departments with special problems that these systems are designed to solve. Before a files operator is assigned to the operation of such a system, he or she is given careful in-service training. For that reason these systems are not covered in detail in this book.

QUESTIONS FOR DISCUSSION

1. What is a numeric file?
2. Of what four parts does a numeric correspondence file usually consist?
3. In a numeric file, what bearing has the alphabetic order of names on the assigning of numbers to new correspondents?
4. In what order are letters filed in a numbered subject folder?
5. What are the advantages and disadvantages of a numeric file?
6. Describe the arrangement of the numeric file illustrated on page 128.
7. Explain the use of the supplementary card index file.
8. Why is a miscellaneous alphabetic file used in a numeric filing system?
9. What is the purpose of an accession book or register?
10. What three steps are followed in preliminary name coding?
11. Why are the pieces of correspondence sorted alphabetically before they are coded numerically?
12. Describe the entire numeric coding process.
13. How is a cross-reference handled when a firm is known by two different names?
14. Where and how are materials coded "M" filed?
15. To what type of correspondents are individual folders assigned?
16. Describe the process of opening an individual folder.
17. How is a number read for filing in terminal digit filing?
18. What are the adavntages of terminal digit filing over consecutive digit filing?
19. In what way does middle digit filing differ from terminal digit filing in the reading of numbers?
20. What is the advantage of using color coding in numeric filing systems?

FILING PROBLEMS

1. A. Assume that individual folders are to be opened in a numeric file for the names in the following list in the order in which the names are listed. Type or write each name on a separate 5″ by 3″ index card or on a slip of paper cut to that size. Keep the names in the order listed. Assume that the accession book indicates that the next number to use is 728. Assign a number to each name and write that number in the upper right-hand corner of the card.

   B. After you have typed the 40 cards and assigned the numbers, arrange the cards in alphabetic order in preparation for filing in the supplementary index card control file.

   C. Prepare an answer sheet similar to the one illustrated on page 19. List the folder numbers assigned to the names in the order in which you have arranged the names.

Couturiers Shoppe
Charles Ullmann Associates
    Clothing Displays
Young Men's Sport Coats
Bill & Paul's Sporthaus
New Rochelle Debutante Shop
Midway Bootery
FLA Winter Wear
Zugelter Apparel
Mountain View Swim Suits
Toggery, Inc.
Charles L. Sprayer Dress
    Clothes
LeBaron Gentlemen's Coats
Tall Girls' Shop, Newark,
    New Jersey
The Modern Woman's Shop
Stanford Sport Center
6th Avenue Tie Shop
Midwest Shoe Shop
Dorothy Ullmann Bridal Shop
Tall Girls' Shop, New York,
    New York
The Moderne Shop
The Pre-Teen Shop

Alcorn-Waite Corp.
VanHattem Hosiery
Mid-Atlantic Swim Suits
Jerry Madison and Sons,
    Boys' Wear
A-One Bargain Center
Kay-Lynne Formal and Bridal
    Home
Rite-Fit Women's Wear
Cardinal Tie and Shirt Shop,
    Inc., Mobile, Alabama
Lloyd's Men's Shop
Bunny Cleaners and Tuxedo
    Shop
Elizabeth Sterling Apparel
The Nu-Look Bootery
Tall Girls' Shop, Newark,
    Delaware
MacKay & Floyd Co.
John's Men's Suits
Wepman's Men's Wear, Inc.
Ann's Used Clothing
Johns Cut-Rate Clothing
D. R. Norris and Bros.

2. A. Assume that each of the following 50 numbers is the numeric code for a piece of correspondence that has been removed from the files. The files are arranged according to a consecutive digit system. Type or write each number on a separate 5″ by 3″ index card or on a slip of paper cut to that size. Type the digits in each number in pairs by skipping a space after the second and fourth digits.

   B. After you have typed all the cards, arrange them in the proper order for consecutive digit filing. Your first number will be 13 25 26, the lowest number; it will appear after No. 1 on the answer sheet.

   C. Prepare an answer sheet similar to the one illustrated on page 19. After the 50 numbers on the answer sheet, list the numbers on the cards in the order in which you have them arranged.

```
71 48 26    26 48 02    26 18 02    32 18 44    26 53 76
49 25 16    13 53 56    49 25 39    13 25 76    49 07 16
82 37 78    49 07 56    32 37 46    67 82 04    13 25 48
49 07 78    67 25 16    82 07 21    13 25 26    13 53 73
71 37 26    55 18 32    55 82 39    55 18 44    67 64 44

32 48 59    55 64 60    55 48 02    71 37 44    71 37 76
82 37 56    13 37 16    67 82 21    82 07 44    49 25 78
82 07 78    13 37 02    82 07 56    32 37 21    13 25 65
49 25 73    67 82 16    82 37 44    13 37 39    82 07 16
26 18 59    32 53 39    55 64 39    67 64 76    26 48 44
```

3. A. Using the same index cards that you prepared for Problem 2, rearrange the numbers for a middle digit file. Your first number will be 49 07 16; it will appear after No. 1 on the answer sheet.

   B. Prepare an answer sheet.

4. A. Using the same index cards that you prepared for Problem 2, rearrange the numbers for a terminal digit file. Your first number will be 26 18 02; it will appear after No. 1 on the answer sheet.

   B. Prepare an answer sheet.

JOB 8   Numeric Correspondence Filing

At this time complete Job 8 in OFFICE FILING PROCEDURES, Fourth Edition. The instructions and supplies for this job are included in the practice set.

CHAPTER 11

SUBJECT SYSTEMS AND PROCEDURES

The topic to which particular correspondence refers is frequently more likely to be remembered when the correspondence is requested than is the name of the writer of the material. In such cases, it may be better to file the correspondence by its subject title. A subject filing system is one in which the captions on the guides and folders are based on subject titles rather than upon correspondents' names. In many subject files, a strictly alphabetic method of coding is used. This system is known as *direct subject filing*. In other files, both letters and numbers are used in the guide and folder captions. This system is known as *alpha-numeric subject filing*.

SECTION 1 DIRECT SUBJECT FILING

Nature of Subject Filing

When most of the correspondence in a file is likely to be requested by the titles of the subject matter of the correspondence rather than by the names of the correspondents, it is generally better to file the correspondence under the subject titles in a subject file. The subject titles may correspond to those that make up an alphabetic arrangement of the activities, the departments, or the problems of a business or an office. Frequently this arrangement resembles an outline of the activities of the business. For example, a subject filing system might be based upon the following alphabetic list of activities or departments in a particular company:

Accounting	Personnel
Administration	Production
Credit	Purchasing
Filing	Sales
Orders	Shipping

Each one of the main subject headings listed above would probably be separated into subdivisions; and these subdivisions, in turn, might have to be broken down further into smaller subject areas. For example, a more complete subject breakdown of Sales might be developed, such as the one shown on page 141.

```
S A L E S                        Conferences
        Advertising                  Managers
            Direct-mail              Office Supervisors
            Magazines                Salesmen
                National         Customers
                Trade                Inquiries
            Newspapers               Special Orders
                Daily            Exhibits
                Sunday               Conventions
                Weekly               Sales Offices

        Branch Offices           Salesmen
            Inspections              Full-time
            Managers' Reports        Part-time
                                     Trainees
```

Uses of Subject Filing

Subject filing can be used to advantage whenever it is desirable to have all correspondence pertaining to one subject grouped in one place in the files rather than separated under many different names. This is especially important when all the records pertaining to one product or one activity are needed at the same time. This situation is generally more typical of single departments in a business than it is for a centralized file of an entire business. The correspondence of one department is usually concerned with a relatively small number of subjects with few divisions and subdivisions. These fit into a simple classification that everyone in the department who has occasion to use the file understands thoroughly.

Subject files are frequently found in: (1) research departments where materials are filed under particular studies being undertaken—a research director for new products development, for example, may file research reports first by product name and second by the specific report name; (2) executive offices where the interest is not so much in a particular correspondent as in the overall picture—a purchasing agent for office equipment, for example, may be more concerned with the types of office equipment available than with the names of the manufacturers of such equipment; (3) offices that keep instructional data—teacher files, for example, in which data relating to various subjects are held under topical headings; and (4) institutions and companies where work requires that the items which are handled be identified by name or by group titles—art galleries, museums, libraries, and many commercial supply houses, for example.

Subject Filing in a Centralized File

When subject filing is used in a central filing department, all customer material is filed according to the names of the customers; but all matters dealing with the operation of the business are filed by subject according to a classification that has been designed to meet the needs of the business. The subject file brings together all material in such areas as advertising, sales, personnel, taxes, insurance, and office procedures. This material is often kept longer than customer material, and segregating it into a subject file gives it the protection it warrants.

Arrangement of a Subject File

The guides in a subject file may appear in one, two, or three positions, depending upon the number of headings, subdivisions, and smaller subject areas in the outline of subjects pertaining to the activities or departments of the business. For example, primary guides might be used in first position to indicate the subjects representing the main headings of the outline; auxiliary guides might appear in second position to represent the subdivisions of each main heading in the outline. If the subdivision headings in the outline are in turn subdivided, guides in third position could carry suitable captions.

All folders in a file may be of one type with captions consisting of subject headings only; or folders of a second type may be included for names of individuals and businesses. In a subject file there is generally no miscellaneous folder similar to that in an alphabetic file. Each letter is coded according to its content.

There are two types of alphabetic subject files: (1) The *direct alphabetic* or *dictionary method* has all major subjects arranged in alphabetic order. In this system minor subjects are filed behind the proper major subject guide, but they also are arranged in an alphabetic order. (2) The *encyclopedic method* has usually only a few major subjects but many subdivisions. The major subjects and minor subjects may follow an alphabetic order, or they may follow an order indicating the relative importance of the major subjects.

Direct Alphabetic Method

One type of direct alphabetic subject file is shown in Illustration 11-1, page 143. In this file the primary guides in first position are alphabetic guides. After the first guide *A 1* and in second position is the first main subject guide, *Auditing.* The individual folders following the guides are in the last two positions. An individual folder has a double-width tab with a caption that consists of (1) the main subject heading given on the guide preceding the folder and (2) the secondary subject title of the materials filed in the folder. The first such folder is captioned *Auditing-Cash Receipts.*

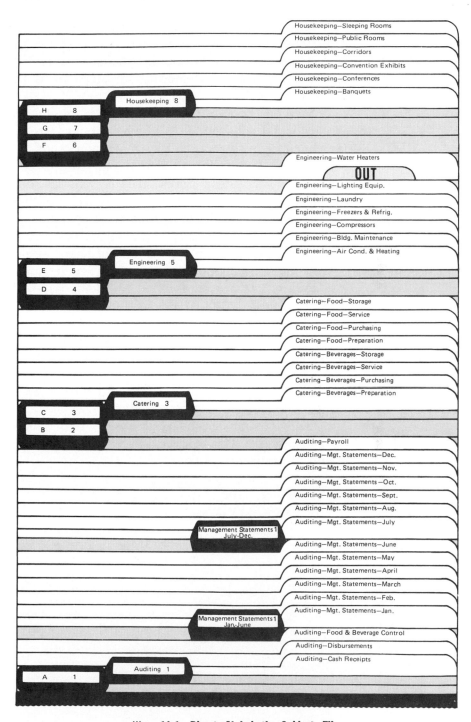

Illus. 11-1, **Direct Alphabetic Subject File**

The first auxiliary guide, *Management Statements—January-June,* is in third position. It indicates the months of the year covered by the individual folders filed behind it. Auxiliary guides (monthly, quarterly, alphabetic, or other breakdown) are prepared as necessary to set off the required individual folders.

Note that none of the guides requires an alphabetic breakdown in this particular company at this time. Should there be at a later date a large number of folders behind a main subject guide, alphabetic guides could easily be added in third position. No miscellaneous folders are provided in the system. Should they be required, one would be placed immediately after the last individual folder in each section and would be labeled with the appropriate main subject guide or with the primary alphabetic guide, whichever better serves the purpose. The miscellaneous folders would be placed so that their tabs would show in the same position as the individual folders. OUT guides are also placed in the last position to mark the location of folders removed from the file for temporary use.

Encyclopedic Method

The encyclopedic method of alphabetic subject filing is shown in Illustration 11-2, page 145. This is known also as the *closed method* or *group method*. When the file in the illustration was established, the materials were first sorted according to the major headings of the subject outline. These four headings were then arranged in alphabetic order and subdivided into secondary groups. A third subdivision could be set up if necessary. The headings in the portion of the drawer illustrated would be outlined as follows:

I. Auditing
   A. Cash Receipts
   B. Disbursements
   C. Food and Beverage Control
   D. Management Statements
      1. January-March
      2. April-June
      3. July-September
      4. October-December
   E. Payroll

II. Catering
   A. Beverages
      1. Preparation
      2. Purchasing
      3. Service
      4. Storage

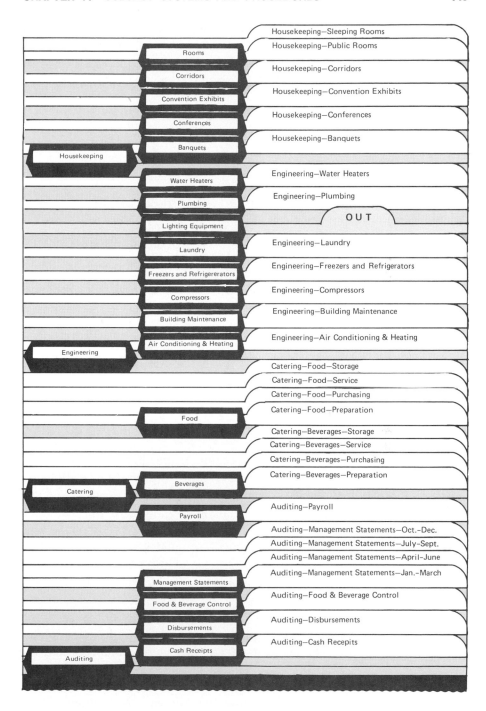

Illus. 11-2, **Encyclopedic Alphabetic Subject File**

B. Food
    1. Preparation
    2. Purchasing
    3. Service
    4. Storage

III. Engineering

A. Air Conditioning and Heating

B. Building Maintenance

C. Compressors

D. Freezers and Refrigerators

E. Laundry

F. Lighting Equipment

G. Plumbing

H. Water Heaters

IV. Housekeeping

A. Banquets

B. Conferences

C. Convention Exhibits

D. Corridors

E. Rooms
    1. Public Rooms
    2. Sleeping Rooms

The primary guides in the illustration, *Auditing, Catering, Engineering,* and *Housekeeping,* are placed in first position. After the first primary guide, *Auditing,* and placed in second position, are the captions of the five auxiliary guides for this section of the file.

The tabs of the individual folders appear in the last position after the corresponding auxiliary guides. The individual folders are prepared with half-cut tabs because of the long captions frequently required for an encyclopedic alphabetic subject file. The captions for the individual folders are complete so as to indicate their exact location. When a folder is removed from the file, an out card is substituted with the caption in the same position as the individual folders.

The months of the year can be incorporated into an encyclopedic alphabetic file. The section *Auditing—Management Statements* has a different folder for each quarter of the year, and the captions on the folders indicate this breakdown. An alphabetic breakdown can be identified in the same manner. If additional folders with the same subject headings are required in other sections, a second folder could be labeled with a number *2;* a third folder with *3;* and so on. If miscellaneous folders are desired, they can be added immediately after the last folder in the appropriate sections and labeled with the captions identifying the sections.

The encyclopedic alphabetic subject file in Illustration 11-2 utilizes the same subject classifications used in the Direct Alphabetic Subject File. It may be noted that both systems do not always work equally well with the same type of filing situation because an arrangement that fits well with the direct alphabetic subject file may produce a disproportionate number of guides with the encyclopedic system. The system to be used should be selected with the individual filing requirements clearly in mind.

Subject Filing Procedure

Inspection. Each incoming letter should be checked to see that it has been released for filing.

Coding. In many cases the correspondence is coded by an executive or a secretary before it is sent to the filing department. If a letter has not been coded in this manner, the files operator must read it carefully to determine the subject classification to be used as a basis for coding. If the subject appears in the letter in a form identical with that on the caption of the folder in which the letter should be filed, the coding may be done by underlining the subject wherever it appears in the letter (Illustration 11-3). In most cases, however, it is necessary to code the letter by writing the subject classification at the top of the letter or in the upper right corner. The units in the subject title are coded by numbering them to indicate their position or rank in the index order.

To prevent errors in coding, a master record of the subject captions and the kinds of correspondence filed in each of the folders bearing these captions should be available at all times in the filing department. This master record may be in the form of a typewritten outline with explanatory comments, in the form of a card index file with all subject captions arranged alphabetically, or in both forms. Unless some type of supplementary record is kept, two files operators may use two different subjects for coding letters of the same type. More differences of opinion arise regarding the coding of letters for a subject file than for any other type of file. Thus, in addition to using a master record, it is advisable to have one person take responsibility for making final decisions on subject coding problems.

Cross-References. A cross-reference should be prepared if more than one subject is involved in the same piece of correspondence. In Illustration 11-3, the information on the cross-reference sheet indicates (1) that a letter from Hotel Suppliers, Inc., discussed two things—information concerning building maintenance and information concerning lighting; (2) that the letter was filed in a folder bearing the caption *Engineering—Lighting;* and (3) that the cross-reference should be filed in the folder headed *Engineering—Building Maintenance* so that anyone who looks in that folder for the correspondence with Hotel Suppliers, Inc., will know that he should look also in the other folder.

In some businesses a photocopy is made of the original letter, and the copy is filed in the cross-reference location. When this is done, a cross-reference sheet is not prepared. The coding of the letter remains the same so that it is evident where the copies are filed.

Sorting. After all material has been coded, it should be sorted first according to the main subjects of the file and second by the first subdivisions. This means that if the file is based upon an outline consisting of five main headings, the first sorting would be on the basis of such headings. For each of these sorted groups, the second sorting would be based upon the subdivisions of the main heading in the outline.

Placing Material in Folders. Material in a subject folder should be arranged first by the alphabetic order of subjects if more than one subject is involved. The first basis for arrangement of materials in a single subject folder, however, is the alphabetic order of the names of the correspondents so that all correspondence with one person or company is grouped together in the folder. Different pieces of correspondence for the same correspondent are arranged within that group by date, with the latest date in front. Material that is placed in an individual folder is arranged in the same manner as that in an individual folder for an alphabetic name file, that is, the latest date in front.

Index to Subject File

A subject system is difficult to hold under control; but such a system can hold papers and records efficiently. One way to gain control over a subject file is to prepare an index card control file and use it in conjunction with the subject system. This procedure requires preparing cards which show descriptions of each major subject in the system and which list the subtopics under each subject. It is useful to prepare a control card for each correspondent on which are shown his name and the subject name under which his papers are filed.

hotel suppliers, inc.

3351 Commonwealth Avenue
Philadelphia, PA 19133
(215) 857-3446

APR 26 19-- A.M.

April 25, 19--

Mr. Donald C. Worth, Manager
The Worth-Bryan Hotel
1012 Euclid Avenue
Cleveland, OH 44102

Dear Mr. Worth

Would you like to reduce your lighting expense by 15 percent without a comparable increase in other costs? Our engineers have been working on such a project for more than ten years, and they have finally announced the results of their study.

It is a known fact that the engineering of proper lighting involves not only the fixtures but also the color of the surrounding areas and the presence of natural daylight. The automatic control of these three factors had not been known prior to the completion of this study.

When poor lighting is evident, electric power costs rise. In addition, the color of the surrounding areas fades and looks dull, drab, and worn, especially when conventional paints are used.

Our engineers have combined the type of illuminating equipment needed with a new formula of long-wearing paint. The results are astonishing.

Mr. James K. Ferguson, one of the engineers on this project, will be in Cleveland next week. He would like to discuss these findings with you and your staff. He is a specialist in the painting problems as well as the lighting problems of your section of the country. He will telephone you as soon as he arrives to arrange an appointment at your convenience. Naturally, there is no obligation on your part.

We do hope you will find time in your busy schedule to visit with Mr. Ferguson.

Sincerely yours

Anthony C. Brake
Anthony C. Brake
Sales Manager

rde

Engineering/ Lighting 1
Building Maintenance 3

Illus. 11-3, Incoming Letter with Subject and Cross-Reference Coding

---

CROSS-REFERENCE SHEET

Name or Subject *Engineering-Building Maintenance*
Hotel Suppliers, Inc.
Philadelphia, Pennsylvania

Date of Item *April 25, 19--*

Regarding _____

_____

_____

SEE

Name or Subject *Engineering-Lighting*
Hotel Suppliers, Inc.
Philadelphia, Pennsylvania

Authorized by *Alice Evans* Date *4/29/--*

Illus. 11-4, Subject Cross-Reference Sheet

Subject Sections in Alphabetic Filing Systems

Subject sections can be added to alphabetic filing systems whenever and wherever they are needed without disrupting the efficiency of the alphabetic system. However, this is true only when correspondence that is to be filed by subject title is properly coded before being filed. Material to be filed by subject must be recognized by code clerks, and the subject title must be underlined if it appears in the paper, or written and underlined on the upper right-hand side of the paper if it does not appear in the paper. If some papers which should be a part of a subject section are by mistake filed by company names, then the value of the subject section is lost and so are the papers which have been filed by company names rather than by subject.

SECTION 2　ALPHA-NUMERIC SUBJECT FILING

Subject Numeric File

The use of numbered notations on guide and folder tabs has increased during the past several years. This increase has undoubtedly been caused in part by the rapid adoption of the use of mechanized office data processing. Punched cards are more easily processed by number; electronic computers operate through numbers; and the reference to information is increasingly being done through the use of various numbering systems. Even when there is a clearly labeled alphabetic name on a card or a record, the number of that card or record must also be known.

In many situations the files are organized primarily by subject, but numbered notations on guide and folder tabs are used just as they sometimes are used in alphabetic name files. The simplest type of numbering is that used in the example at the top of page 151 in which the subject titles are the same as those used on pages 140 and 141. The numbered notations may be used as follows:

1. As a part of the subject captions to facilitate filing. Subject titles are frequently quite long and seldom appear in their exact form in correspondence. Considerable time can be saved, therefore, if numbers instead of words are used in coding and in locating folders in the files.
2. As a substitute for subject captions. When only numbers are used for captions, then subject headings, divisions, or subdivisions that are closely related can be grouped together in the files even though the subject titles do not fall in the same alphabetic section. When this plan is followed, a supplementary card index file, arranged alphabetically by subjects, is necessary and is used in a manner similar to that for numeric correspondence files. This is an indirect method of filing, however, and is not commonly used.

No.	Heading	No.	Division	No.	Subdivision
100	Accounting				
200	Administration				
300	Credit				
400	Filing				
500	Orders				
600	Personnel				
700	Production				
800	Purchasing				
900	Sales				
		910	Advertising		
				911	Direct-mail
				912	Magazines
				912	National
				912	Trade
				913	Newspapers
				913	Daily
				913	Sunday
				913	Weekly
		920	Branch Offices		
				921	Inspections
				922	Managers' Reports
		930	Conferences		
				931	Managers
				932	Office Supervisors
				933	Salesmen
		940	Customers		
				941	Inquiries
				942	Special Orders
		950	Exhibits		
				951	Conventions
				952	Sales Offices
		960	Salesmen		
				961	Full-time
				962	Part-time
				963	Trainees
1000	Shipping				

One example of using only numbers for captions is called *Co-ordinate Indexing* and was designed by the Office of Aerospace Research, United States Air Force. It is recommended only for a large subject file containing many items each covering several subjects rather than just one subject per item and which would require extensive cross-referencing. A card file can be constructed to contain cross-references to several subjects. This avoids the need for cross-reference sheets or photocopies which, when used, add considerably to the volume of the main file.

Three things are necessary for a coordinate indexing subject file: (1) a simple numeric coding according to the subject, (2) a word list containing the filing words (subject titles) and alternate words to enable the files operator to locate the key title under which the subject is coded, (3) a word card file, which contains one card for each key title and the indexing numbers of all filed items containing information covered by this title. This serves as the cross-reference notation necessary to locate one or more items pertaining to a particular subject.

Subject Decimal Filing

A simple numbering system is adequate for most subject files. When the outline upon which a subject filing system is based is more complicated or detailed, however, a decimal system is advantageous.

Perhaps the most widely known and used decimal system is that devised by Melvil Dewey. It is used by libraries to classify books, catalogs, pamphlets, and all related materials. Dewey's system divides all human knowledge into nine main groups and one general group. The arrangement of numbers and subjects is as follows:

000	General Works	500	Natural Science
100	Philosophy	600	Useful Arts
200	Religion	700	Fine Arts
300	Sociology	800	Literature
400	Philology	900	History

These major groups, in turn, are divided into nine subdivisions and one general division. For example, the "Useful Arts (600)" section has these subdivisions:

600	General	650	Commerce
610	Medicine	660	Chemical Technology
620	Engineering	670	Manufactures
630	Agriculture	680	Mechanical Trades
640	Domestic Economy	690	Building Trades

These sections are further subdivided into groups of ten. Then, by the use of decimals, the subdivisions can be continued indefinitely.

The Dewey Decimal System, or some adaptation of this system, can be employed to advantage in business filing when provision for expansion in the files must be made and when detailed subdivisions in a filing system are needed. To be efficient, such filing systems must be carefully organized and the files operators must be thoroughly familiar with the subject outline upon which the system is based.

Direct Decimal-Subject Filing

The principal advantages of the direct decimal-subject system over the alphabetic system for certain kinds of materials are illustrated by the Yawman and Erbe direct subject filing system shown in Illustration 11-5. It is possible to group related materials in this file, as shown by the series of folders in Section 705. These folders, in a straight alphabetic system, would be spread from the "A" to the "G" sections of the system. Also, the coding of papers for the decimal-subject system is easier and faster than coding in an alphabetic system because only the code numbers need to be written on file materials. It is advantageous to have decimals showing on guide and folder tabs so that numbers and titles can be identified as a unit.

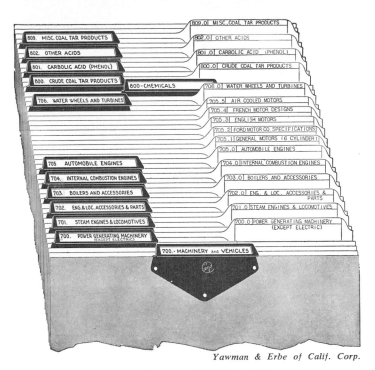

Illus. 11-5, **Direct Decimal-Subject Filing**

Yawman & Erbe of Calif. Corp.

Armed Forces Decimal Filing

The basic filing system of the Armed Forces, as described in *War Department Decimal File System* and *Navy Filing Manual*, is adapted from the Dewey Decimal System. The classification of the topics in the correspondence records and reports of the Armed Forces is based upon the main groups listed below.

000	General	500	Transportation
100	Finance and Accounting	600	Buildings and Grounds
200	Personnel	700	Medicine, Hygiene,
300	Administration		and Sanitation
400	Supplies, Equipment,	800	Rivers, Harbors, and
	and Services		Waterways

Other Captions for Subject Files

Several other systems for subject caption notations are becoming more commonly used. The first of these is known as Duplex-Numeric. The following example indicates the nature and use of the system.

Subject Outline	Primary Guide Notations	Secondary Guide Notations	Folder Notations
Employee Training	50		
Types of Training		50-1	
On-the-Job			50-1-1
Company Courses			50-1-2
School-College Courses			50-1-3
Union Coordination		50-2	
Planning			50-2-1
Administration			50-2-2

SUBJECTS AND SUBDIVISIONS	SIMPLE NUMERIC	DECIMAL	DUPLEX-NUMERIC	DUPLEX-ALPHABETIC	ALPHA-NUMERIC
ADVERTISING	100	100.	10	A	A
Rates	110	110.	10-1	A-a	A-1
Magazine	111	111.	10-1-1	A-a-a	A-1-a
Newspaper	112	112.	10-1-2	A-a-b	A-1-b
Outdoor	113	113.	10-1-3	A-a-c	A-1-c
Copy	120	120.	10-2	A-b	A-2
Magazine	121	121.	10-2-1	A-b-a	A-2-a
American	*No numbers are available for these items*	121.1	10-2-1-1	A-b-a-a	A-2-a-1
January		121.11	10-2-1-1-1	A-b-a-a-a	A-2-a-1-a
February		121.12	10-2-1-1-2	A-b-a-a-b	A-2-a-1-b
Time		121.2	10-2-1-2	A-b-a-b	A-2-a-2
January		121.21	10-2-1-2-1	A-b-a-b-a	A-2-a-2-a
February		121.22	10-2-1-2-2	A-b-a-b-b	A-2-a-2-b
OFFICE MAINTENANCE	200	200.	20	B	B
Typewriters	210	210.	20-1	B-a	B-1

Illus. 11-6, **Comparison of the Various Notations Used in Subject Filing**

This system is capable of indefinite expansion and can be used to advantage when subject classifications are numerous and detailed or when an alphabetic arrangement would be impractical, as in an architect's office, where a file would logically follow the sequence of the erection of a building. The system is extensively used in law offices, where the client is assigned a number, and every case handled for the client is assigned an auxiliary number based on the client's number.

If letters are substituted for numbers in the Duplex-Numeric system, the method is known as Duplex-Alphabetic. In the example used for the Duplex-Numeric system, the Duplex-Alphabetic caption for Employee Training would be "E"; for Types of Training, "E-a"; for On-the-Job, "E-a-a."

Another system, the Alpha-Numeric, is a combination of the two preceding systems in that capital letters are used for the main headings of the outline; numbers are used for the first divisions of the main headings; and small letters are used for the subject subdivisions. In other words, letters and numbers are used alternately to determine the captions.

Illustration 11-6, page 154, indicates the application of five different systems of coding the same items in a subject outline. Notice that some of the coding systems are not adapted to the subject outline given in the first column. The simple numeric outline is not adequate, and some of the duplex outlines appear unwieldy. However, these systems are very useful in certain situations.

QUESTIONS FOR DISCUSSION

1. What is a subject filing system?
2. When is it advantageous to use a subject filing system?
3. Where might we frequently find a subject file in use?
4. What are the two types of alphabetic subject files?
5. Describe the direct alphabetic method of subject filing illustrated in this chapter.
6. Describe the encyclopedic method of alphabetic subject filing illustrated in this chapter.
7. Why do the encyclopedic filing system and the direct alphabetic filing system not always work equally well?
8. What is the purpose of the master record of the subject captions and the kinds of correspondence filed in each of the folders bearing these captions?
9. When should a cross-reference be prepared in subject filing?
10. What three items of information are available from a cross-reference sheet?

11. If a photocopy is made of an original letter, is a cross-reference sheet necessary? Where is the photocopy filed?
12. After materials have been coded, how should they be sorted?
13. How are materials placed in folders?
14. What is the purpose of maintaining an index to a subject file?
15. What is a subject numeric file?
16. How are numbers used in a subject file?
17. What is a subject decimal file?
18. When would the Dewey Decimal System be used in business filing?
19. Describe the general nature of the Duplex-Numeric System.
20. In what way is the Duplex-Alphabetic System similar to the Duplex-Numeric System?
21. What is the Alpha-Numeric System?

FILING PROBLEMS

1. An executive file in the personnel office of a certain company contains information grouped under the following general subject captions:

Employee Testing   Job Evaluation
Sources of Potential Employees   Employee Training
Employee Selection Devices

The following subdivisions are used sufficiently to require separate folders in the file:

Application Blanks   Company Courses
Combination Tests   Personal Investigations
Visual Aids   Selection of Evaluators
Labor Unions   Present Employee Recommendations
Factor Comparison Evaluation   Job Grading Evaluation
Planning for Training   School-College Courses
Employment Agencies--Private   Intelligence Tests
Point System Evaluation   High Schools
Former Employees   Instructional Materials
Follow-up on Training   Job Ranking Evaluation
Achievement Tests   Physical Examinations
References Submitted by   Aptitude Tests
   Applicants   Selection of Trainees
Labor Scouts   Walk-in Applicants
On-the-Job Training   Supervisory Training
Employment Interviews   Employment Agencies--Government
Wage Evaluation   Social Interest Tests
Administration of Training   Teacher Education
Colleges   Advertisements
Trade Journals

Prepare, on an 8½" by 11" sheet of paper, a master record of the subject captions and the subdivisions that logically fall under these captions. Arrange both the subject captions and the subdivisions in correct alphabetic order.

2. The files in the office of the purchasing agent of a manufacturing concern need to be rearranged. The purchasing agent wants to use the encyclopedic method of subject filing and then to add a duplex-numeric system to the captions.

Prepare a master record of the primary guides, secondary guides, and folders in alphabetic order on 8½″ by 11″ sheets of paper. Use duplex-numeric notations on the outline.

The primary guides have the following captions:

```
10  Office Equipment
20  Office Furniture
30  Office Supplies
```

The secondary guides show the following subtopics:

Dictating Machines	Binders	Bookcases
Blotters	Adding Machines	Ink
Chairs	Desks	Addressing Machines
Ribbons	Pens	Paper
Typewriters	Bookkeeping Machines	Calendars--Calendar Pads
Bookends	Carbon Paper	Duplicators
Copying Machines	Calculators	Miscellaneous Supplies (Place this guide at the end of the Office Supplies section.)

The folder tabs have the following captions:

Offset Duplicators	Wood Bookends
Accounting Desks	Tissue Paper
Battery-Operated Dictating Machines	Rotary Calculators
Check Binders	Photocopy Carbon Paper
Full-Bank Adding Machines	Fountain Pens
Metal Bookends	Xerography Copying Machines
Perpetual Calendars	Addressing Machine Ink
Conference Desks	Typewriter Ribbons
Nylon Post Binders	Typewriting Desks
Thermographic Copying Machines	Accounting Books
Desk Pad Blotters	Telephone Book Binders
One-Time Carbon Paper	Dye-Transfer Copying Machines
Duplicator Paper	Executive Chairs
Metal Plate Addressing Machines	Catalog Binders
Fountain Pen Ink	Diaries
Secretarial Desks	Leather-Covered Bookends
Bond Paper	Memo Calendar Pads
Folding Chairs	Pencil Carbon Paper
General Use Carbon Paper	Billing Machine Desks
Ledger Binders	Photocopy Paper
Tape Dictating Machines	Ten-Key Adding Machines
	Indelible Ink

Interoffice Paper
Executive Desks
Storage Binders
Magnetic Ink
Typewriter Paper
Plastic Belt Dictating Machines
Ball Pens
Diazo Process Copying Machines
Address Labels
Spirit Carbon Paper
Transcribing Desks
Cement and Glue
Stencil Duplicators
Airmail Paper
Clerical Desks
Staplers
Plastic Bookends
Offset Pens
Metal Post Binders
10-Key Calculators
Second Sheet Paper
Drawing Ink
Rocker Blotters
Electric Typewriters
Desk Calendar Pads
Spirit Addressing Machines
Newspaper Binders
Marking Ink

Letterhead Paper
Disc Dictating Machines
Paper Clips
Clip and Spring Binders
Book Blotters
Carbon Paper Packs
Photocopy Machines
Ceramic Bookends
Fluid Duplicators
Receptionist Desks
Adding Machine Paper
Secretarial Chairs
Carbon Paper Ribbons
Stamp Pad Ink
Calculator Desks
Cartridges, Ball Point
Key-Driven Calculators
Wrapping Paper
Prong Binders
Manual Typewriters
Wall Calendars
Facsimile Copying Machines
Duplicator Ink
Nonrefillable Ball Pens
Wire Dictating Machines
Ring Binders
Adding Machine Ribbons
Appointment Calendars

JOB 9   Subject Correspondence Filing

At this time complete Job 9 in FILING OFFICE PROCEDURES, Fourth Edition. The instructions and supplies for this job are included in the practice set.

CHAPTER 12

CARD RECORDS AND SYSTEMS

Importance of Card Records and Systems

Card record systems of one type or another are used in almost every business office as well as in professional offices and in service and governmental organizations. Vital records in many forms are kept on cards. So diverse are these records that they vary from the recording of such simple data as the names and addresses of persons to the posting of such complex data as production costs. Among the offices, organizations, and professional people that rely on card records to a considerable degree are libraries, schools, research groups, dentists, doctors, hospitals, and all kinds of business, industrial, and public utility organizations.

Since card record systems are vital to operations in so many organizations, it is essential to efficiency that office personnel understand the principles of card filing as well as the types of systems used and the equipment available.

Supreme Equipment & Systems Corporation

Illus. 12-1, **Card Files**

In this card file section of a metropolitan bank, more than 600,000 signature cards are held for frequent reference. This system was installed by the Supreme Equipment & Systems Corporation.

Nature of Card Record Systems

Some of the many commonly used systems of card filing have already been described and illustrated in previous chapters of this text. In Chapter 1, an alphabetic card file for names and addresses is described and illustrated; in the chapters on numeric, geographic, and subject correspondence filing, other card indexes are described as auxiliary parts of the systems. But these represent only a few of the total uses of card systems. There are hundreds of methods of using cards to show a great variety of reference information or to carry statistics that are vital to business operations. Some of the more common types of card records are: stock records; payroll records; personnel records; repair and maintenance records; inventory and purchasing records; shipping and receiving records; bookkeeping and accounting records; hospital, dental, and medical records; and records pertaining to scientific and industrial research operations.

Equipment for Card Record Systems

Usually, the kind of equipment that holds a card file is directly related to the manner in which the system is used. For example, cards used for such data as names and addresses are primarily for reference purposes, and only three or four lines of data are given. Thus, such a system can be based on 5″ x 3″ cards, which can be held in shallow trays or in specially designed visible equipment. Cards carrying records to which continuous posting is made must be held in convenient positions and frequently must be accessible to several persons working in a centralized area. Sometimes, systems of the latter type use large open tubs that hold a number of overlapping cards in vertical position; other such systems utilize large rotating units that house series of card trays. Posting and reference systems may use rotating units that hold a series of bound books containing many sections of visible cards. Thus, because there are many types of card records, the equipment to house the cards varies to a considerable degree; and there is much specialized equipment available to those who plan and assemble card record systems. In general, however, equipment can be considered as being in one or the other of two classes: equipment designed to hold cards in a vertical position or to hold them in a horizontal position.

In the vertical method, cards are placed on edge; and vertical guides are used to mark sections in the file drawer in a manner similar to that used in all types of correspondence files.

In the horizontal method, cards are placed flat, in overlapping position; and they are usually held in long, shallow trays that can be stored in cabinets. The overlapping of the cards makes the lower edge of each card visible when the tray in which the cards are held is pulled out from the cabinet. (See Illustration 12-7, page 169.) For this reason, horizontal card files are called *visible card files* or *visible files*.

Because the equipment and the guiding systems for vertical and visible files are so dissimilar, separate consideration is given to each type in this chapter.

SECTION 1   VERTICAL CARD FILES

In general, the plan used for a system of guides in a vertical file may be as standard as that used for correspondence files. On the other hand, it may be as diverse as need be to guide with efficiency any of the many types of card systems described previously. Thus, a guiding plan can be a standard alphabetic, numeric, geographic, or subject plan; or it can provide combinations of any of the standard plans, including such auxiliary code systems as alpha-numeric or decimal codes.

The vertical card file shown in Illustration 12-2 is an example of an alphabetic system of guiding as applied to records relating to names of firms or of individuals.

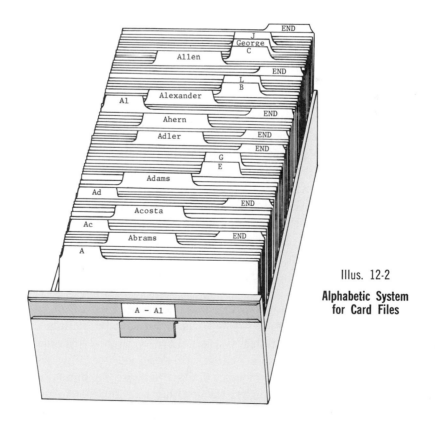

Illus. 12-2

Alphabetic System for Card Files

In Illustration 12-2, notice that the system includes the following sections:

1. Primary alphabetic section guides are located in first position and show single-unit notations from "A" to "A1."
2. Special guides for commonly found names are given prominence by having tabs of two-position width covering positions 2 and 3 in the file drawer.
3. Common name sections are further subdivided by guides in fourth position for commonly found second units in names.
4. "END" guides are shown in fifth position. These are used to mark the close of particular name groups within a given alphabetic section. END guides eliminate the need to search through a number of cards in order to locate the close of a special section and the resumption of the major alphabetic sequence. For example, the last index card bearing the name "Abrams" would be filed before the "END" guide; and the card following this "END" guide would show a name such as Abramson, T. L.

Alphabetic systems for card files are used extensively to hold records relating to names of customers, or of personnel, or of suppliers of goods and services. Alphabetic systems are also used in conjunction with files that are primarily concerned with subject titles or with geographic locations or with numeric correspondence files. Indexes for automatic or electrically processed data are frequently held under alphabetic systems.

The section of a card filing system that is shown in Illustration 12-3 is typical of many that are based upon the encyclopedic subject method. In this, primary guides are used to designate such major divisions within the system as those in Illustration 12-3 which appear in the central position and are labeled "Filing Supplies" and "Filing Systems." The first subdivisions of these two major divisions are signaled by three guides in first position labeled "Folders," "Guides," and "Alphabetic."

The second and third subdivisions in the system are marked by series of guides located in second and third positions. These guides provide an outline sufficiently detailed to permit the easy retrieval of any particular card in the system.

Subject Systems for Card Records

The subject system shown in Illustration 12-3 is used to hold stock record cards for items held for sale by a filing equipment and suppliers dealer. In this system, there is a card for each type of stock that is carried. These cards are designed to show such information as how many units of a particular item are on hand; how many units to order; when to reorder; from whom to reorder.

```
┌──────────────────────────────── Letter Size
├────────────────────────────── Legal Size
│              20-Division
  Alphabetic   ┌─────────────────
             FILING SYSTEMS
                              Letter Size
                              Legal Size
              Vertical File
              Shelf File
                                 Vertical
                                 Shelf
                                 Lateral
                 OUT Guides
                              Letter Size
                              Legal Size
     Guides    Lateral File
                              Letter Size
                              Legal Size
              Vertical File
              Shelf File
                                 Vertical
                                 Shelf
                 OUT Folders     Lateral
                              Letter Size
                              Legal Size
              Lateral File
     Folders  FILING SUPPLIES

     Correspondence Filing Supplies & Systems
```

Illus. 12-3

Subject Guiding Plan in a Vertical Card Filing System

A person seeking a particular card in such a subject system would (1) locate the desired drawer in the system by scanning the drawer labels; (2) within the drawer, scan the primary guides and locate the desired major division; (3) scanning from left to right across the drawer, find the location of a block of cards which would include the one desired. Search for the particular card within the block of cards would involve riffling through the cards and locating the one bearing the desired title— all cards being arranged in alphabetic order according to names of items held in stock.

In a large stock record system, numeric notations in the form of stock record numbers usually are included as titles on cards and the final arrangement of cards is one of numerical order.

Subject systems which have been organized in much the same manner as the one shown in Illustration 12-3 are commonly used to control many types of business, industrial, and scientific records. Subject systems may be used for storage record cards, for purchasing and

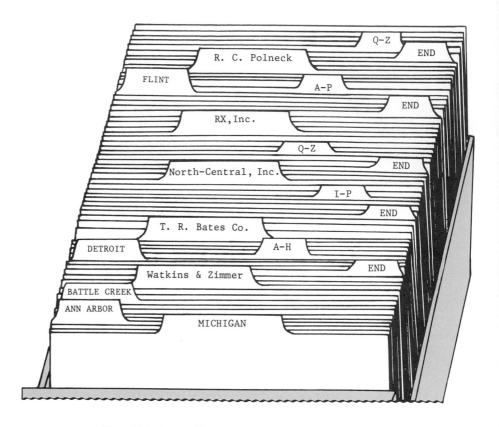

Illus. 12-4, **Geographic System for Controlling Card Records**

stock records, for inspection and maintenance records, for quality control data, and for material control systems. Also, master indexes for many types of records are kept in card form under the control of a subject system.

Geographic Systems for Card Records

Geographic guiding systems are frequently used to control card records because the nature of many business operations is such that locations of customers or suppliers or of operations are of primary importance. Thus, names of districts within a city or in a region sometimes are used as notations for the guiding plan in a card filing system. In other cases, names of cities and states or provinces serve as guiding notations. In this respect, geographic card systems and geographic systems for correspondence have much in common, including the fact that the primary guiding plan can be either the lettered guide plan or the location name plan (see pages 113 and 115).

Illustration 12-4 shows a section of a geographic system for cards in which the location name plan is used. A centrally located primary guide denotes the primary title, "Michigan." A series of secondary guides in first position show various city names: Ann Arbor, Battle Creek, Detroit, and Flint. Special name guides cut to two positions in width are shown in second and third positions combined. These guides are labeled to show names of important individuals and companies—those to which frequent reference is made.

Fourth and fifth positions are reserved for special alphabetic sections, which are marked by guides bearing such double-closed notations as A-H, I-P, and Q-Z. These subsections are used to divide what otherwise would be overcrowded sections of cards.

End guides are used in last position to mark the close of special sections and to mark the resumption of alphabetically filed cards.

By using such special sections as those just outlined, card filing systems can be made more useful because filing and retrieving processes are made easier. However, it must be recognized that a limit must be placed on the use of special sections and special guides. Otherwise more guides might be added to a system than would be justified, and filing and finding would be made more difficult and costly. Usually, special name guides, like those shown in combined second and third positions, are not added until about 20 cards have accumulated for a particular name. Also, such alphabetic subdivision guides as those shown in Illustration 12-4, positions four and five, are not added until about 50 cards have gathered behind a city guide. Notice that the Detroit section in Illustration 12-4 is of sufficient size to require the use of both alphabetic and special name subdivision guides.

Signals for Vertical Card Files

Card filing systems can be made more efficient through the use of equipment and methods for signalling the more important data that are held in the system. By means of signalling devices, different types of information or data can be more clearly marked and thus be more readily located and summarized when needed. A few examples of the many types of signalling devices available for office use are:

1. When guides having hollow tabs are used, variously colored insert strips or slips can be used to mark major sections of the system as well as special sections within it. Insert slips can be purchased in printed form from dealers, or they can be typed so that desired notations will appear. Slips are inserted into the hollow tabs of guides in order to form desired parts of the system.
2. Cards of different colors can be used. For example, in a personnel file, cards of one color can be used for men and those of another color for women. Also, a manufacturing business that sells to both wholesalers and retailers might use cards of one color for wholesalers and cards of a second color for retailers.

3. Some cards have special code symbols printed across the top edge. The file clerk selects the proper code for the information on the card and cuts from the top edge of the card all of the other codes, so that the one selected is left as a signal tab.

4. Small, colored movable signals may be attached to the tops of the file cards so that the position as well as the color classifies the information on the card. In a credit file, for example, a red signal could be attached in a particular position on a card to indicate that an account was one month overdue. A black signal could be attached in another position to indicate that an account was two months overdue. In this manner a credit manager could tell at a glance the number of delinquent accounts and the age of each account. Furthermore, credit references could be made much more easily than would be possible if each card had to be pulled from the file and read in detail to secure the desired information.

Equipment for Vertical Card Files

Vertical card systems are held in two types of equipment: (1) stationary cabinets or shelves and (2) power-driven movable shelves.

Stationary Cabinets or Shelves. For many years, stationary cabinets with pull-out drawers have been used for housing both large and small filing systems. Stationary cabinets with drawers are still being used to hold such card records as those alphabetic, subject, and geographic systems shown in the first part of this chapter. In addition to these types of card records, punched cards, microfiche, and index control systems are frequently housed in cabinets with drawers. A small index control system in a cabinet is shown in the lower right side of Illustration 13-19, page 191.

In recent years, equipment for holding card systems on stationary shelves has been developed and is widely used. In this method, shallow trays holding cards are placed in rows on stationary shelves. The trays hold cards which are controlled by guides bearing such captions as those you have seen in Illustrations 12-2, 12-3, and 12-4. A large system of this type is shown in Illustration 12-1, page 159, in which depositors' record cards are held in trays on stationary shelves.

Power-Driven Movable Shelf Equipment. When this type of equipment is used, cards are held in shallow trays which are placed on movable shelves. The shelves are mounted on a framework held inside a cabinet shell, and the framework is geared to revolve in a manner similar to the motion of a ferris wheel. Any particular shelf can be brought into and held at a working position by pressing one of a series of push buttons mounted on a panel in front of the machine operator. Illustration 12-5 shows a room full of power-driven movable shelf units.

Wheeldex, Inc.

Illus. 12-5, **Power-Driven Card File Units**

In Illustration 12-5, notice that each shelf holds twelve card trays in a side-by-side arrangement. Each tray holds a set of guides in addition to holding the required cards. These trays can be removed from shelves, but usually the operator can refer to or otherwise process the cards without taking a tray out of the shelf area. The push-button control panel for a power-driven unit is shown in Illustration 12-6.

Illustration 12-6 shows details of a push-button control panel and of a shelf holding a series of trays for a numeric card system. The panel

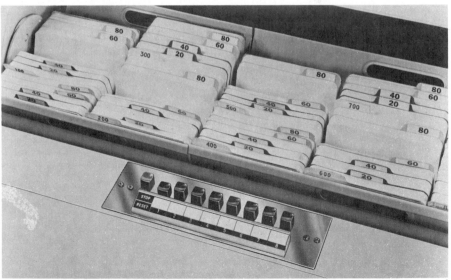

Diebold Inc.

Illus. 12-6, **Push-Button Control Panel for a Power-Driven Card File Unit** indicates that there are eight shelves in this particular unit and that button #1 has been pressed and shelf #1 is now in position for reference by the operator. Notice that this numeric system uses primary guides in first position (100 to 700 show in this picture); secondary guides, which are blocked by twos in second and third positions, divide each primary section into four subsections. Thus, cards are more-or-less evenly divided and controlled within a given section in this system.

Advantages of Power-Driven Equipment

The relative advantage of power-driven equipment over manually operated equipment varies according to certain conditions existing in various types of business operations. For example, in some companies reference to card records is infrequent, while in others card records are vital to operations and are referred to continually. Also, in some organizations relatively few card records are needed, while in others card systems are complex and voluminous. Thus, as business conditions vary, the relative value of power-driven equipment for card systems varies; and when records are required in volume and/or are very active, power-driven equipment has these advantages:

1. A volume of cards is held in compact, easily accessible form.
2. Working time is saved by having cards brought to the operator's station rather than having the operator move from his work station into the filing area.
3. Use of floor space is improved by the use of power equipment because records can be held in tiers rising to heights which would not be possible to use if manual operations were relied upon.
4. Because fast retrieval of cards is made possible by power equipment, desired information can be transmitted rapidly; therefore, service to customers or to company personnel is made more efficient.

SECTION 2   VISIBLE CARD FILES

Types of Visible Systems and Equipment

There are three major types of visible record systems, and each is distinguishable because of certain features which are to be found only in that particular type of system. The systems are: (1) visible card files, (2) loose-leaf visible books, and (3) vertical-visible files.

Brief descriptions of each type of system include the following salient features: (1) Visible card files are formed by a series of cards being held in a flat position in shallow trays, with each card being positioned so that one or more edges are always visible. (2) Loose-leaf visible books are formed by cards or sheets of paper held flat and set in a staggered position, allowing an edge of each card or sheet always to be visible. (3) Vertical-visible files are formed of cards especially cut to permit an upper, angle-cut corner to be seen at all times when cards are held in vertical rows across the width of a wide drawer or tub-like container. The margin of each card on the right side is also visible because of the offset positioning of cards in the rows.

Systems for Visible Card Files

In visible card files the primary guiding notations appear on labels which are inserted into holders on the outside of the drawers or trays in a cabinet. Captions on these labels show the range of the group of cards held in each tray.

Inside the tray the visible edge of each card shows an identifying mark which assists in finding cards and keeping them in an orderly arrangement. The mark of identification will correspond to the major system used in a particular file, whether it is alphabetic, numeric, geographic, subject, or a combination of these.

Illustration 12-7 shows the structure of a typical visible card filing system. In the illustration, notice that one of the shallow trays held in

Victor Systems & Equipment
Sperry Remington

Illus. 12-7, **Visible Card Cabinet**

the cabinet has been pulled out in a position for reference or for posting purposes. Also observe that the cards in this tray have been opened so that a particular section is exposed, the section being composed of a face of one card (in vertical position) and a face of another (in horizontal position). The two faces of these cards are used to hold a single record in common.

Cards held below the open section are in an overlapping position which allows the lowest line on each card to be seen thus providing the visible element in this type of card system. The overlapping factor is portrayed most precisely in Illustrations 12-8 and 12-9.

Visible card files can be controlled by any of the systems known and used in filing. Any of the following types of titles can be used as captions: personal names, names of stock items, dates, decimal or serial numbers, geographic names, and subjects. Two such systems are indicated in Illustrations 12-8 and 12-9.

The segment of a system given in Illustration 12-8 indicates that a numeric system is being used. This is evident because the visible edge of each card shows a number in the left corner and these numbers are arranged in sequence (385, 386, 387). Had this been an alphabetic system, the descriptive titles which follow the numeric ones would have been listed in alphabetic order and the numbers would have been out of sequential order. The system indicated in 12-9 shows that this file is governed by an alphabetic arrangement in which descriptive titles are arranged in alphabetic order.

Signal Systems for Visible Records

One of the most useful and distinctive features of visible records is that they can be signaled (marked) to show a great variety of summary information. When visible cards are so signaled, many vital facts can be determined without recourse to a detailed examination of the data on a whole card or a series of cards. Signal marks can be made on the cards by hand, or signal devices can be selected from a variety of types manufactured of metal or plastic materials.

Signals can be used to show such information as the amount of stock on hand at any given time (stock record cards), the volume of sales or the percentage of quota on sales (sales record cards), the number of overdue accounts and the length of time each is overdue (credit and collection cards), and the date for follow-up on any matter concerning accounts, contacts, and so forth.

Illustration 12-8 shows the lower visible edges of three cards and the types of signalling devices used to flash notice of vital information to persons who scan these cards. Two types of signals are shown. Those

TAG NO.	DESCRIPTION			MONTHLY INSPECTION CONTROL
385	Bench Grinder			JAN FEB MAR APR MAY JUN JUL AUG SEP OCT NOV DEC
386	Rivetting Machine			JAN FEB MAR APR MAY JUN JUL AUG SEP OCT NOV DEC
387	Knob Machine			JAN FEB MAR APR MAY JUN JUL AUG SEP OCT NOV DEC

Acme Visible Records, Inc.

Illus. 12-8, **Lock-In Chain and Progressive Signals for Visible Card Records**

(4 in number) closest to the description titles (e.g., Bench Grinder) are called "Lock-In Chain" by their producer, Acme Visible Records, Inc. These are colored, movable plastic strips which are fixed in slots at the lower edge of the card and can be moved up-and-down to signal vital information of one kind or another as desired. The signals to the right of the Lock-In Chain ones are known as Progressive signals by the manufacturer (Acme) because they can be moved by a sliding motion progressively from one notation to another, e.g., from one month to the next, or from one number to the next, etc. These signal marks are used to show a variety of spot information of vital importance to those who refer to the cards. For example, the cards shown in Illustration 12-8 are concerned with an inspection schedule in a preventive maintenance system. In this, the Lock-In Chain signals are used to signal the week during which an inspection will be made of Bench Grinders. Progressive signals are used to show the month during which the inspection must be made. Thus, it is signaled that Bench Grinders will be inspected during the first week of February. When this inspection has been completed and data have been posted to the cards, a new signal will be set for the week and month for the next inspection.

Illustration 12-9 shows a typical signalling device used in many visible record systems. The signals consist of strips of plastic material

ITEM	PART NO.	WEEKS SUPPLY ON HAND											
Cam Shaft Gear	398	1	2	3	4	5	6	⑦	8	9	10	11	12
Crank Shaft Gear	225	1	2	3	4	5	⑥	7	8	9	10	11	12
Driving Shaft	187	1	②	3	4	5	6	7	8	9	10	11	12
Feeder Arm Right	339	1	2	3	4	5	6	⑦	8	9	10	11	12
Feeder Cam	358	1	2	③	4	5	6	7	8	9	10	11	12
Feeder Pump Cover	186	1	2	③	4	5	6	7	8	9	10	11	12
Impression Cylinder	116	①	2	3	4	5	6	7	8	9	10	11	12

Acme Visible Records, Inc.

Illus. 12-9, **Transparent Signals for Visible Card Records** which might either be clear or opaque, colored or plain, depending upon the particular use to be made of them in the signal system. These plastic strips are fitted into the lower edge of the card and under the flap of the pocket in which the card is held. Strips can then be moved along a horizontal path to desired locations on the face of the card. In the cards illustrated, signals are used to show the weekly supply on hand of each item of stock; and as the supply is lowered, the signal is moved to a lower number to flash this fact to those who refer to this card to determine when to reorder a particular item. Many variations of this type of stock control record are widely used not only in business but also industrial organizations.

Power-Driven Visible Card Unit

A recent event in the area of visible card equipment has been the introduction by Sperry Remington of an automated system for visible card retrieval. The unit which performs this action is known as the VIS-U-TRIEVER.

The VIS-U-TRIEVER is composed of a closed section and a work station or console, somewhat like that in the illustration of the power-driven unit for handling trays of cards (page 167). The action of the VIS-U-TRIEVER is somewhat like that of the power-driven unit except that panels of visible cards are brought to the work station area and returned to storage after work on a particular card has been completed.

Such a system is especially useful for holding very active records because the efficiency of a visible card system is heightened by the immediate delivery of records. In order to get this service, the operator stationed at the console has at her disposal a 10-key unit on which she can press out signals for the retrieval from the storage area of a given panel of visible record cards. Then, upon the completion of posting or reference work with cards on a particular panel, it can be returned to storage by pressing out another signal on the 10-key control unit.

Visible Panels for Reference Records

Many types of business records are used as sources for quick reference purposes that require only names and addresses, or index numbers, or some similar brief notation. For such reference purposes, the use of an entire card form would be unnecessary and costly. There has, therefore, been developed a visible system for the necessary one-or-two-line reference which does not justify the use of a whole card. The system uses visible panels into which are inserted single-line strips of card material on which have been typed the "flash" data required.

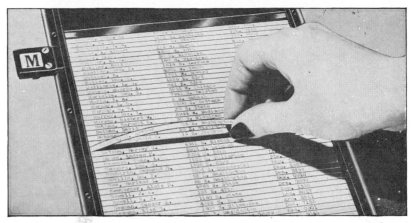

Illus. 12-10, **FLEXOline: Visible Panel for Reference Records**

Panels of the type shown in Illustration 12-10 are usually mounted in vertical position upon a center post around which the panels can be moved in a manner similar to that of turning pages in a book.

In addition to being easy to operate and to view, visible panels can be changed readily by inserting or removing listing strips as desired. Listing strips or slips are made in sheet form which can be fed into a typewriter and labeled with one line or more of information for a visible quick reference system.

Loose-Leaf Visible Systems

Loose-leaf cards or sheets that are held in prong binders or ring binders are widely used where voluminous data must be kept in a relatively small space. An advantage of this system is that the binders are portable.

Loose-leaf visible cards are available in several forms. Some binders hold cards so that bottom edges are visible. Others hold them so that top edges show, while still others are arranged so that the side edges are visible.

The types of records kept in loose-leaf form are as varied as those kept in visible card files. They include cards for records of stock, data on purchasing, accounting or record-keeping data, and many other types of records.

Vertical-Visible Files

Essentially, this type of visible equipment represents a combining of the vertical and the visible systems of filing cards by holding especially cut cards in vertical position across the width of tub-like containers. In this arrangement, one visible edge of a card is formed by a diagonal cut having been made across the upper corner of the card. A second

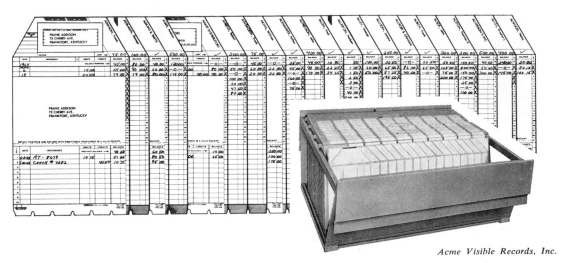

Acme Visible Records, Inc.

Illus. 12-11, **Vertical-Visible Card File**

visible edge results from each card being placed in an overlapping position in relation to other cards held in the same row. An unusually wide cabinet called a "tub" is the receptacle used to hold rows of vertical-visible record cards.

Types of Signals for Vertical-Visible Files

Like all other visible record systems, vertical-visible ones can be signaled to show and to feature key data of one kind or another; and the kinds of data that can be held on cards can take any of a number of forms so that signal devices are found in great variety. For example, cards can be used in conjunction with integrated data processing systems by having edge-punched common language strips form a part of the card. These can show on a visible part of the card, or the card can be marked to show that a common language tape is included with it. Colored signals can be clipped to any visible surface to indicate such data as a summary total, a due date, a reorder date, etc. Also, cards of different colors can be used to indicate types of major items being handled by records in the system.

Wheel Equipment and Systems for Card Records

In addition to the type of equipment that holds cards in trays which can be set into mechanically powered units, cards are also affixed directly to wheel-like frames which are manually operated. These are known as *wheel files* and are made in a variety of forms. They have the advantage of being relatively simple to operate and yet capable of showing all faces of cards for posting or for reference purposes.

Wheel files are generally of two types: (1) The open wheel type (without cabinet enclosure) has cards attached in vertical position. The whole file is rotated into a desired position by hand action. (2) The enclosed wheel file is held in a cabinet equipped with a work-station shelf area. Cards are brought into alignment with the shelf area by manually turning the wheel upon which cards are affixed.

The open wheel system shown in Illustration 12-12 is a portable unit which holds 2,000 cards (6″ x 3″) and an A-Z index of 60 divisions. Both larger and smaller units are available in this type of equipment for cards of varying sizes and in quantities varying from 1,000 to 7,000.

The cards and guides that are used in all types of wheel files are cut and perforated so that they can be fitted around the twin rails that are formed around the core of the revolving central section of the wheel.

When the wheel is turned to a desired position, cards are spread into a wide "V" section. This permits either direct reference to a given card or reference and posting without having to remove the card from the wheel. Posting is possible because the revolving central core is not free-wheeling; it is held under limited pressure by a ratchet-like arrangement within the central section of the unit. Illustration 12-12 shows the posting or reference position of a wheel file.

Illus. 12-13

Random Filing System for Card Records

Many kinds of "quick reference" data are kept in open wheel systems. Among these are name and address lists, inventory records, wage rates, price lists, and item location lists of various kinds.

Some of the larger enclosed wheel files operate in the same manner as that described for the portable open wheel type. Enclosed units usually hold more cards of larger sizes than those held in portable open wheel types. Enclosed wheel equipment usually is of "desk height" and includes either a shelf-like work station, or can be operated from a desk station.

Random Filing of Card Records

By using a specialized type of equipment, the ELECTROFILE by Acme Visible Records, Inc., it is possible to file cards in a random fashion and retrieve them by mechanical means. (See Illustration 12-13.)

The principle of this system is that each card has attached to it at the bottom edge a strip of 30 metal teeth resembling those in a comb.

These teeth can be cut to any desired coding pattern for any given card so that each has a unique code retrieval mark. The coded cards rest upon rods which, when activated by depressing keys on the control panel keyboard, will push upward any desired card from the stack of cards held in the unit or section of the file. Or blocks of cards can be pushed into an upward, retrievable position. This operation is performed regardless of the location of a card or a block of cards in the filing system; thus, no pattern need be followed in replacing (or in placing) cards within an ELECTROFILE unit.

QUESTIONS FOR DISCUSSION

1. What are some of the kinds of card records kept by many business organizations?
2. Why might it be more efficient to keep stock records on cards rather than on sheets in bound-book form?
3. What two general types of equipment are used to hold card records?
4. How many kinds of guiding plans can be used for vertical card systems?
5. Why are END guides used in card files and not in correspondence files?
6. Why is the subject system shown in Illustration 12-3 said to be based on the encyclopedic subject method?
7. Mention several types of records for which subject guide plans for card files might be used.
8. In a geographic card system, when and how do subdivisions of special sections make filing and finding easier?
9. How can colored, movable signals be used to advantage on cards?
10. What are some advantages in using power-driven equipment for files?
11. What are the three major types of visible equipment?
12. What distinguishes each of the three major types of visible equipment from the others?
13. Why are visible systems more efficient for certain types of records than index card systems would be?
14. Why are signals an important feature of visible card systems?
15. What are some of the reasons for using loose-leaf visible systems?
16. Why are insert strips in visible panels better than index cards for quick-reference records?
17. What particular advantages do vertical-visible systems have over other types of visible systems?
18. What are two common uses for wheel files?
19. What are some of the advantages of being able to file cards at random?

CHAPTER 13

EQUIPMENT AND SYSTEMS IN RECORDS CONTROL

Place of Equipment and Systems in Records Control

The need for systematic procedures and for systems in records control has been emphasized throughout all sections of this textbook, and a variety of plans and techniques have been presented for controlling records. Now, another area will be presented for study; it involves the relationship between systems development and the use of equipment.

Before the specifics of equipment and systems are described, brief consideration should be given to the importance of these factors. In this regard, both equipment and systems are critical factors in controlling records; they require that attention be given to the varying problems or situations of each individual company. Each company, or each office, usually has records control problems of its own that cannot be entirely solved by applying only those general principles which govern records control practices common to many types of businesses and offices. As an example of this, you will find that, when field trips are made, no two offices have exactly the same types of records; nor is it likely that their records will be held in exactly the same types of equipment or processed by using exactly the same procedures.

Thus, it becomes evident that you must know the general principles and procedures in records control, and you must also recognize that these must be adapted, in varying degrees, to meet the particular needs of a given company or office. Those who are prepared to make such adjustments will have control of their records; those who are not so prepared will have, at best, only a partially effective records control program.

These statements concerning the need for both general as well as specific knowledge about records control apply directly to the matter of knowing the "how and why" of equipment usage and the selection of equipment and supplies which will be best suited to the needs of a particular office or organization.

In the field of equipment, manufacturers provide a wide range of quality materials for use; and the more typical of these will be illustrated and described in the sections of this chapter. However, it is necessary first to present a few specific points to be considered before equipment and supplies can be selected for any given office.

Planning for Records Control

What do you need to know about a particular situation before an efficient records control plan can be developed? In general, you must know: (1) What kinds of records are to be filed and controlled. (2) How frequently each kind of record will be handled—constantly during the day or only intermittently. (3) How many people will be working at the files. (4) What volume of material will be handled in a given period of time—every six months or every year. (5) Which method of filing will be best suited to the material that will be filed—straight alphabetic, geographic, subject, numeric, or some combination of these systems. (6) What type of charge-out and follow-up will be most satisfactory. (7) What transfer plan (described in Chapter 7) will be used. (8) If records control will be centralized, or departmentalized, or handled through a combination of these plans. Not all these matters will have to be considered in every situation, but in general all of them must be considered at one time or another before a system can be properly planned and controlled.

Specific problems must be solved before suitable equipment and supplies are ordered. For example: (1) When various types of filing cabinets are considered for installation, it might be determined that some three-drawer cabinets should be purchased so that they could be used as counters. Other two-drawer cabinets might be selected for use as desk-side units. (2) Open-shelf units might be selected in preference to vertical cabinets because the records to be handled are of the semi-active variety. (3) Guides with hollow tabs might be purchased if a system is to be constructed for a particular office. (4) For a relatively small but very active file for an executive, a subject guiding system might be found most suitable; and hanging folders might be used because of the increased accessibility that this type of equipment can give.

Equipment for Correspondence and Document Filing

Many types of equipment are available for document and correspondence filing purposes, and each type has certain advantages as well as disadvantages over others in comparable types. It is well, therefore, to be generally informed about the relative merits of particular types of equipment because the efficiency and cost factors of a filing system depend, in large part, upon the relationship between the kinds of records kept and the types of equipment used.

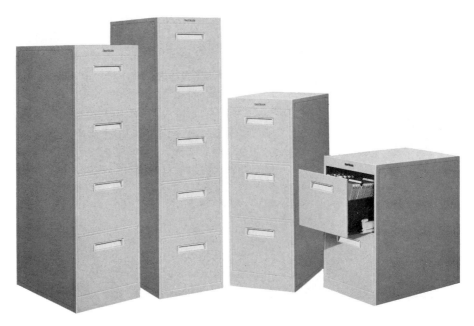

Shaw-Walker

Illus. 13-1, **Two-, Three-, Four-, and Five-Drawer Vertical File Cabinets**

The general types of equipment available for housing correspondence and documents are (1) vertical cabinets, (2) shelves, (3) lateral cabinets, (4) hanging-folder equipment, (5) rotary equipment, and (6) mechanized equipment. Of the hardware used in filing, these six types of equipment are not always entirely separate or equally divided, as following parts of this chapter will explain.

Vertical Cabinets

Vertical cabinets are composed of rectangular shells in which are held a series of large, bin-like drawers that are constructed so that papers can be filed in a vertical position with writing facing forward toward the files operator.

Vertical cabinets have the advantages of providing closed, convenient, and relatively compact storage space in drawers that can be organized under any of a variety of systems for guiding purposes. Vertical cabinets are most useful when individual papers are being handled rather than when entire folders are to be taken from the files.

The principal disadvantage of vertical cabinets is their bulk. They occupy a great deal of floor space; and, when very active files are in operation, they require wide aisles to allow the pulling out of the file drawers. As a result, much floor space is lost.

Because cabinets are available in various sizes, they can be adapted for use in a number of ways: (1) One- and two-drawer units may be used near desks to augment paper storage and to make for easy reference to very active papers. (2) Three-drawer cabinets are frequently used as work counters and as dividers between sections in an office. (3) Four- and five-drawer cabinets may be used as blocking partitions in an office area. Frequently, units of these sizes are selected because active and semiactive materials can be handled in the same cabinets. (This procedure is described in Chapter 7.) (4) Cabinets designed primarily to hold correspondence are flexible in the sense that they can be changed to house a variety of other types of materials. This adaptation is accomplished by using substitute drawers of various sizes in the place of the correspondence-size drawers. In this way, two check-holding drawers or two card file drawers can be inserted into the space occupied by one correspondence drawer.

Some cabinets are made of very heavy metal, and the cabinet shells are insulated to provide some degree of fire protection for valuable papers and documents. Heavy cabinets are also made with combination locks and with the reinforcement necessary to permit their use as safes for the storage of vital and valuable documents and papers.

Shelf-Filing Equipment

In an effort to minimize some of the disadvantages of filing certain types of records in vertical cabinets, various forms of shelf-filing equipment have been developed and are widely used.

The equipment and supplies used with shelf filing differ from those used with vertical filing cabinets because folders are placed on open shelves with the visible portion of each folder along the side edge rather than across the top. Thus, tabs on both guides and folders must be cut so that their notations show vertically (down the side) rather than horizontally (across the top).

On the upper shelf in Illustration 13-2, tabs on guides and folders are shown in two positions. Side-tabbed guides are in first position

Illus. 13-2, **Shelf File with Removable Sections**

TAB Products Co.

(the upper position), and side-tabbed folders are in second position (the lower position). Captions on both guides and folders are written in a vertical style.

Folder-supporting devices of one kind or another are usually included as part of an open-shelf filing system. The supporting device pictured on the third shelf from the top of Illustration 13-2 is a small bin-like section that can be removed by the operator. Such sections are used to hold guides and folders in an upright position as well as to serve as dividers and carriers of file materials.

Uses for Shelf Files. Very active papers are not usually held in shelf files mainly because entire folders must be pulled out of the shelf area before papers can be filed or found. Furthermore, guide and folder notations are not as readable as are those on top-tabbed guides and folders in vertical cabinet filing systems. Therefore, semiactive materials are more apt to be held in shelf files, which are more economical in cost of equipment and in the use of valuable floor space. Some types of insurance papers, case histories in hospitals, legal papers, and contract job records can be most profitably held in shelf files.

Advantages of Shelf Files. In general, the advantages of shelf filing over cabinet filing are: (1) Floor space is saved because room for the pulling out of drawers is not needed; therefore, aisles between shelves can be narrower than aisles between vertical cabinets. (2) Direct access to folders is easier because these are held on open shelves and are always visible. (3) Costs for shelf filing equipment are much less than those for vertical cabinet filing since the shelf equipment is relatively simple in construction.

Disadvantages of Shelf Files. The disadvantages of shelf filing over cabinet filing are: (1) An entire folder must be withdrawn from a shelf before any action can be taken to find or file papers. (2) Open shelves do not provide adequate protection from dust. (3) Notations on folders and guides are not as readable as those on the top edges of guides and folders in vertical cabinets. (4) Open shelves are not always neat in appearance.

Lateral Filing Equipment

A lateral file is one in which folders and guides are held in pull-out drawers constructed to hold papers in a lateral direction. Lateral cabinets are constructed in either of two styles: (1) with drawer fronts that can be opened to expose the contents of the drawer, as in a shelf file, or (2) with drawer fronts that are fixed parts of file drawers and thus

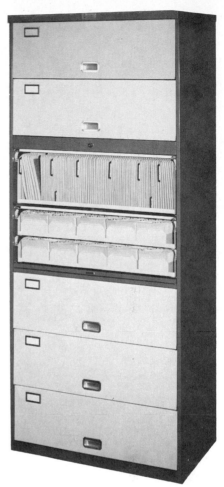

Oxford Pendaflex Corporation

Illus. 13-3, **Five-Drawer Lateral Cabinet with Solid Drawers**

Supreme Equipment & Systems Corporation

Illus. 13-4, **Lateral Filing Cabinet with Sliding Front Panels**

move as the drawers are being pulled out of the cabinet area, as in a vertical file cabinet. This factor is important because the system of guides and folders varies with the type of drawer being used in a lateral cabinet. A lateral file with solid drawers can use only top-tabbed guides and folders (see Illustration 13-3), while a lateral file drawer with a sliding front panel can be equipped with both top-tabbed and side-tabbed guides and folders (see Illustration 13-4). The contents of the drawer with top- and side-tabbed guides and folders can be arranged so that the tabs can be read either from right to left or from left to right. This factor can be used to advantage to gain maximum working space when several lateral units are being placed in a filing area.

The lateral cabinet shown in Illustration 13-4 shows two open drawers and five closed drawers. In the top part of the upper open drawer, six primary side-tabbed guides are visible. Between these primary guides are sets of top-tabbed folders. The two tabs in the lower part of the drawer are tabs of out guides. The drawer has not been pulled forward out of the cabinet shell, but this is the action which is taken in order to get access to the folders in this file. The closed drawers are opened by pulling the front panel up and sliding it back into the body of the cabinet shell. The two card file sections shown below the open correspondence drawer are auxiliary parts that can be ordered and fitted into the space that usually would be occupied by a single correspondence drawer. Cabinets with exchangeable sections are advantageous when there is a need for combination files in an office.

A comparison of lateral cabinets with vertical cabinets and shelf units shows that the laterals require less floor space than do the verticals because less aisle space is needed to accommodate the opening and closing of drawers. Since shelf units do not require any aisle or floor space for drawer action, these are the most economical in terms of floor area required. Top-tabbed guides and folders used in solid drawer laterals are similar to those used for vertical files but are usually considered better than the side tabs needed for shelf files. Guides and folders in lateral cabinets equipped with sliding front panels can be tabbed on the side edge or across the top or in both positions. For very active files, this is an advantage to be gained from the greater visibility of all guides and folders held in open-front, pull-out drawers.

Evaluating Equipment for Correspondence Filing

The use of any particular type of equipment depends primarily upon the kind of records being held and the frequency of reference to them. For example, very active records are not usually held in shelf files because entire folders must be pulled before search can be made for a specific paper. Conversely, it is costly to file semiactive or inactive records in vertical cabinets when floor space is at a premium. Thus, it is evident that decisions regarding types of equipment to be used should relate directly to the kind of filing to be done as well as to the relative value of each type of equipment in terms of costs and efficiency.

Hanging Folder Systems and Equipment

The hanging folder (or suspended folder) method of holding papers represents a very adaptable and widely used form of records control. There are two types of hanging folder equipment. One type has folders constructed with metal or plastic strips across the top edge of the front

Supreme Equipment & Systems Corporation

Illus. 13-5, **Hanging Folder System in a Lateral
Three-Drawer Cabinet**

and back parts of the folders; the strips extend beyond the sides of the folders and fit over parallel rails that run on both sides of the file drawer (see Illustration 13-5). The folders are suspended over the strips. In this suspended position, folders are more easily moved and more readily accessible than are folders in standard vertical or lateral cabinets. Illustration 13-5 shows hanging folders in a lateral cabinet. This same kind of system can be used in vertical cabinets after an adaptation is made by adding parallel rods to the sides of a file drawer not originally so equipped.

Another type of hanging file equipment consists of a cabinet that has rods instead of shelves extending the full width of the cabinet. The folders have hook-like extensions on the front and the back. These extensions fit over the rods so that the folders hang from the rods. (See Illustration 13-9, page 191.)

There are many uses for hanging folder systems because (1) materials of different sizes can be held more efficiently in suspended folders than in the more stationary vertical folders; (2) hanging folder systems are flexible; folders can be easily moved, or opened, or replaced; (3) some types of hanging folders can be indexed more completely than is possible with some other types of folders and, because of this, records are more accessible in a hanging or suspended folder system.

Acme Visible Records, Inc.

Illus. 13-6, **The CENTRAC Rotary Filing System**

Rotary Equipment   The production of rotary units for holding correspondence and related materials is a developing phase of the office equipment manufacturing industry. In essence, rotary units are composed of a large outer shell within which a series of circular shelves is rotated in somewhat the manner of a lazy-susan server. On the rotating shelves, guides and folders are set and carried as spokes are carried on a wheel; or folders and guides may be set into rectangular bin sections formed as separate units on the "floor" of the rotating shelves.

The principal advantage that rotary equipment has over cabinets or shelves is that of providing greater accessibility to a larger volume of records concentrated in one general area. In some types of rotary equipment, material held in the system is much more visible than it would be if held in cabinets or shelves.

Thus, when a series of very active related records is needed in one office area and when several people must work on the same set of very active records at the same time, rotary equipment can be used to very good advantage.

The CENTRAC rotary system shown in Illustration 13-6 includes four circular sections or tiers and six work stations. Within the framework of this rotary unit, each tier moves independently; and thus each operator at a work station has access to the records being held in any part of any tier. Work stations are equipped with telephone connections enabling operators to communicate directly with persons requesting information.

The rotary system shown in Illustration 13-6 is used by a banking institution to hold depositors' records. In this system, depositors' accounts are updated daily; and the data are made available to other departments in either of two ways—by account numbers or by depositors' names. In order to do this, the spiraled compartments that can be seen in the upper tier hold computer printout sheets which show depositors' daily account balances listed by account numbers in numerical order. This listing is supplemented by an alphabetically arranged card system that is held in the remaining tiers of the rotary unit. Each card bears the name of a depositor and shows his daily account balance. These cards are filed in alphabetic order according to depositors' names. Thus, whether a request for information is made by giving an account number or by giving a depositor's name, an answer can be made in a matter of seconds.

Mechanized Filing Equipment

The process of transforming certain types of files into mechanical delivery systems is a continuing phase of progress in the field of records control. Primarily, mechanized equipment is centered around some type of mechanical system devised to locate segments of a filing system and to deliver these to a console (work station).

The use of power-driven equipment does not eliminate the need for processing papers in the customary manner before they are placed in file folders or in the tub-like containers which form a part of some electronic filing systems. However, mechanical systems do provide great accessibility to papers and documents by an operator stationed at the console of a mechanized unit. These are of definite value when the factor of equipment cost is secondary to the need for facility and speed in handling very active records.

There are two general types of mechanized filing equipment: electronic files and power-driven files.

Electronic Files. The larger and more sophisticated of the mechanized files are known as electronic files and are equipped with optical scanning devices that locate precoded folders and/or precoded tub-containers which hold folders and other types of file materials.

Illus. 13-7, **The CONSERV-A-TRIEVE—Console and Storage Sections in an Electronic File**

The CONSERV-A-TRIEVE unit shown in Illustration 13-7 consists of (1) a console (work station), which is located at the front of the unit, and (2) a large vault-like enclosure in which records are stored behind the console. The operator seated at the console is selecting a folder from a tub which has been delivered to the console by a process described below.

Illustration 13-7 shows the two sections of the CONSERV-A-TRIEVE electronic file in detail. Within the vault area there are two facing banks of metal file tubs separated by an area occupied by an electronically operated conveyor (center, rear in picture). Upon a code signal from the operator at the console, the conveyor moves to a desired tub, which is drawn onto the conveyor and then moved forward into reference position at the console. After the paper or document or folder desired has been removed or reviewed, the operator presses a button labeled "Restore"; and the tub is moved back to its original place in the vault area.

Before materials can be placed in the storage tubs of such a unit, a very definite system of identification must be made up for each item or group of items to be held in each tub. The system shown in Illustration 13-7 requires that each tub have an identification mark and that each piece of material in it be so marked. The ID (identification) mark for each tub is written on a master index list which is held at the console work station. In Illustration 13-7, notice the tub at the console is marked "LD5." This is its code number. When the operator wants a certain item, she consults a master index (not shown) which tells her that the item is held in, for example, tub LD5. She then presses out this ID number on the key control board at the console; the desired tub is located by the scanning device which is part of the retrieval column (in the center, rear of the picture). This pulls by magnetic force the desired tub and brings it forward in a matter of seconds to the console.

For complete control of records held in any of the mechanical types of equipment, there must be guiding plans, identification of filed materials, charge-out of papers or folders borrowed, and transfer of semiactive and inactive materials.

Systems like the CONSERV-A-TRIEVE shown in Illustration 13-7 have the following advantages over manually operated systems: (1) Storage space utilization is increased considerably because units can use space from floor to ceiling in a storage area. (2) Push-button speed in retrieval is far superior in relation to any other mechanical or manual method. (3) Papers and documents can be kept in security control because of the completely enclosed area in which they are held and the access by a single operator. Units of the size of that in the illustration, and larger, are being included in the construction plans of some of the newest office buildings in metropolitan areas.

Power-Driven Equipment. The basic reason for using any of the various types of power-driven equipment is to move shelves or trays of records into working positions by electronic means. In power-driven equipment, records are brought to the operator rather than having the operator move from place to place to consult records located in various sections of an office or of a building.

Power-driven equipment for correspondence and document files is made in diverse forms with varying mechanical features as well as with unique types of delivery systems.

Power-driven units such as that shown in Illustration 13-8 usually hold about 18 shelves in a vertically moving suspension system that is controlled by a push-button panel located at or near the work station in front of the cabinet area. By using this control, an operator can select any of the shelves in the unit and have it delivered to reference position by machine action. Notice that guides and folders are side-tabbed so that the operator, being in the center-front of the machine, can search at eye-level across the length of a file drawer for a needed folder.

Power-driven equipment is also produced in units smaller than that previously described and illustrated. Small units of the ferris-wheel rotary type can be selected from a variety of units which are fitted to hold cards or correspondence-type materials. Illustration 12-5, page 167, shows one of these units that are used for holding card records.

Control of Specialized Records

Types of Specialized Records. Up to this point, equipment and systems have been considered for correspondence, documents, and cards. There are, however, many other types of records that must be held under control programs because they are vital to successful operations either in an entire organization or in a department.

An example of specialized records used by one department of a company is the records kept by the purchasing department and related to vendors of the various articles that are purchased for use or for resale by an organization. The purchasing department keeps a very active record of such matters as vendors' products, prices, and terms of sale. Purchasing departments may also maintain very active catalog files and/or master records in loose-leaf form, which will serve either to supplement or to summarize data taken from vendors' catalogs.

A transportation company or a traffic department also uses many types of specialized records as transportation routings are being written or as reservations are being arranged. These records may consist of rate schedules, routing schedules, and reservation schedules. Some of these specialized records are similar in form to catalogs; others may appear in the form of master records held in book form, which are used to augment or supplement the more voluminous and detailed data given in original tables of rates, schedules of routing, and reservation regulations.

Another group of specialized records is composed of the maps, blueprints, plans, and tracings that are used in the offices of contractors, architects, surveyors, planning boards, and title insurance companies.

Duplicating service agencies and duplicating departments, as well as mail rooms, use various types of special equipment in order to house such materials as duplicator stencils, offset master plates, address plates, and such bulky items as directories and equipment catalogs.

Catalogs and Directories. Catalogs and directories are representative of a type of reference material that is used in many business, industrial, and service organizations. These records may be found in bound-book form or in loose-leaf binders, or they may be in transcribed form and written on cards that are filed in either visible or vertical card systems.

When records of the catalog type are in active use in their original form, rotary filing units are frequently used to hold and carry these bulky books because they are much easier to handle and much more accessible for simultaneous use by a number of workers than would be the case if such material were held in cabinets or on book shelves. Also, when catalog-type material is transcribed onto cards and the cards are held in large visible books, these also may be used to greatest advantage when held in rotary units.

When catalog-type material is semiactive, or when it is used occasionally by only a few workers, it may be kept in bookcases or in vertical filing cabinets. When held in these ways, catalogs may be marked and filed according to several plans: (1) by firm name—with a supplementary card index file, listing in alphabetic order the items or subjects included in each catalog, (2) by number—with an alphabetic card file of firm names and the subjects included in each catalog, (3) by subject—with an alphabetic card index listing of firm names.

Cross-references may be made in the catalog card index, just as they are made in any other card system, by listing on one card the places where related material can be found.

Bulky Materials. Many of the important records that are kept by business and industrial organizations are not written on standard size cards or sheets of paper. Because of this, special indexing and filing problems are encountered. Among these types of records are X-rays, maps, blueprints, tracings, duplicator plates and stencils, some types of forms, and computer printouts.

Many of these records are too large or too bulky to be held in standard file equipment, but most can be satisfactorily stored in hanging folders that are large enough and strong enough to hold large sheets or bulky objects. A system of this type frequently is used by hospitals in order to hold such large items as X-ray film and other related data. Illustration 13-9 shows a hanging folder system for such records. Each of

Illus. 13-9

OBLIQUE Hanging Folder System for Hospital Records

Robert P. Gillotte & Co., Inc.

the folders in this system is equipped with a vertical tab which holds a numbered insert slip to identify the folder. The numeric system of guiding is used on an open file so that hospital records will be filed by an indirect system and thus held in an impersonal manner as well as in a unit form. This requires that a master index be kept which shows personal names in alphabetic order and lists the folder numbers assigned to those persons. Such a master index is seen in the lower right corner of Illustration 13-9.

Another way to solve the problem of storing large and bulky materials it to use oversized equipment. Various manufacturers produce units of this kind. Most of these are combination types of equipment which will hold various kinds of materials in single cabinet units. The combination cabinet shown in Illustration 13-10 is an example of a multiple-use storage unit with features designed to accommodate bulky objects and large sheets, as well as standard cards and/or sheets.

Lear Siegler, Inc./Borroughs Division

Illus. 13-10

The ADAPTAFILE—Adjustable Oversized Storage Unit for Large and Bulky Materials

The ADAPTAFILE unit shown in Illustration 13-10 can be adjusted in several ways in order to hold various types of oversized materials, as desired in any particular office.

There are five *sections* in the cabinet shown at the left. Each can be fitted to hold any of the types of materials shown. The top section holds legal-size folders and guides, but it could also hold letter-size ones; or the section could be fitted to hold any of the other kinds of materials illustrated. The second section from the top shows two shelves of index card trays. Trays can be ordered for card sizes 5″ x 3″, 6″ x 4″, and 8″ x 3″.

The third section from the top is equipped to hold two shelves of disk packs; but like the other sections, it could be changed to hold other types of records. The next section is constructed to hold jumbo-size hanging folders, which can store such items as large X-ray film or large job envelopes.

The cabinet is equipped with roll-out shelves that can be extended like the one shown in the fourth-from-the-top section.

Duplicator Plates and Stencils. Departments or business enterprises that perform duplicating services require equipment and systems that will hold and identify a number of specialized materials. Among these are plates used in offset printing and stencils used in duplicating.

The most commonly used equipment for plates and stencils is closely related to the hanging equipment previously described for holding catalogs. The hangers for holding stencils and plates, however, are single units resembling ordinary coat hangers except that a series of small hooks are formed on the front face of stencil hangers; the stencils are hooked over these and hung in vertical position in a cabinet.

Guiding systems for offset plates and stencils can be developed when the hanger-type equipment is used because metal or plastic clips are made which can be used as guide tabs as in correspondence files. Typed labels can be inserted into these tabs so that any desired system of identification can be prepared for stencil and plate files.

Auxiliary and Portable Equipment and Systems for Desks and Work Stations. Two of the more important work areas which require planning and equipping for records control are the desk and work stations. In such areas as these, filing systems are limited to relatively small units but are of no less importance because of this. Frequently, difficulties are encountered in trying to control these types of filing systems because of their "personalized" nature and the rate of turnover of papers held in these systems.

Oxford Pendaflex Corporation

Illus. 13-11, **The EXECUTIVE LATERAL SYSTEM—An Auxiliary Desk-Side Filing Unit**

One major step in controlling desk and auxiliary files is to start with a carefully planned system held in suitable equipment. A second step is to maintain order in the system by continuously weeding-out unwanted papers and constantly transferring other papers to less active sections of the filing system.

Illustration 13-11 shows a type of equipment especially designed to serve as a desk-side or work-station-side unit. Notice that this one-drawer lateral unit is equipped for a hanging folder system and that folders face forward toward the operator. This system has two major advantages as a desk auxiliary file: (1) Hanging folders are easier to handle than are "fixed-position" folders; (2) all folders face the person who is referring to the file so that all parts of the guiding system are visible. Therefore filing and finding time is reduced to a minimum.

Systems for guiding desk records can be as diverse as those used for any phase of business operations. However, subject and alphabetic guiding plans are those most frequently used for the control of executive records.

Oxford Pendaflex Corporation

Illus. 13-12, **Sorter and Temporary File**

Other types of useful auxiliary units are available in portable or stationary styles. One such unit is the Pendaflex ORGANIZER, shown in Illustration 13-12. This is designed as an auxiliary unit for holding current papers at a ready position for a period of time so that the retrieval of very active papers will not require a search of the general files. Notice that hanging folders are sidecut to permit reference to letters or documents without having to remove them from the file. Papers are filed from the top of the file but are removable from the side. These features add greatly to the usability of this particular type of equipment.

QUESTIONS FOR DISCUSSION

1. What do you need to know about a filing system before you can properly plan and equip one?
2. In what kinds of equipment can correspondence be kept?
3. Are filing cabinets useful in ways other than for storage of papers? In which other ways are they used?
4. What are some of the advantages and disadvantages of shelf filing?

5. What main advantage does lateral filing have over vertical cabinet filing?
6. What are some advantages of using hanging folder equipment?
7. What is the main advantage of rotary equipment over cabinets or shelves?
8. What is the principal difference between an electronic filing unit and a power-driven filing unit?
9. What advantages and disadvantages are there in using mechanized files as compared with using manually controlled files?
10. Would you use mechanized files for semiactive papers? Explain.
11. What is the principal advantage of using power-driven units for correspondence files?
12. Why should a guiding system for a correspondence or a card file be made as customized or individualized as possible?
13. What are some of the types of specialized records for which filing systems and equipment must be provided?
14. Why are rotary cabinet units sometimes very useful for holding catalog and directory types of materials?
15. How are duplicator plates and stencils usually stored? What type of guide is usually employed in a stencil file?
16. Why are desk files difficult to control?
17. Why might there be advantage in holding very active incoming and outgoing papers for a short period of time in a sorting and temporary filing unit?

FILING PROBLEM

The best way to learn about the types of equipment used for records control is to observe them in a working situation. It is suggested that you make an appointment (through your instructor) to visit an office and there to determine the use that is made of various types of equipment.

Depending upon the variety of equipment that you find in a given office, ask questions similar to the following.

1. What types of cabinets or shelves are used for correspondence files? Were these selected for a particular reason? If so, what reason?
2. What kind of guiding system is used in the correspondence files? Was this purchased as a unit, or was it developed by those who work in the records department?
3. If any form of special equipment is used, why is it used? For which types of records is it used? (Note: Special equipment might include such items as visible card files, carousel units, wheel files, tub files; mechandized correspondence; and document files.)
4. How is expansion handled in the correspondence and card files?
5. What type of storage equipment is used? Where are transferred papers held? How often is transfer made? What kind of records system is used in connection with transferred papers?

Your instructor might request that you present a detailed report of your visit since this would be very useful to others in your class.

CHAPTER 14

DATA PROCESSING AND MICROFILMING

The volume of information that must be stored and later located for immediate use has increased dramatically. In many businesses, the need for rapid finding of certain types of information has made manual means of retrieval too slow and cumbersome. It has therefore been necessary to develop mechanical and electronic machines to help with the filing and finding tasks. In this chapter, some of the data processing, microfilming, and other related systems designed to help control this volume are described.

It is important to note that with the use of these newer systems, the tasks of coding and indexing information are still the most important part of each system because the information must be prepared accurately for machine processing. The equipment is merely a tool to speed up the processes of filing and finding. In fact, some of the cards, sheets, and films produced by electronic data processing means and by microfilming must still be stored and retrieved by the same type of manual means used to control materials held in systems like those already studied.

SECTION 1 DATA PROCESSING

The term *data processing* refers to the manipulation of information—an activity that has been carried on since people used chisels and stone tablets to keep records. As the volume and need of these records increased, inventions provided faster and more accurate ways to record the information. Pen and paper, typewriters, and adding machines are all examples of these tools.

As the need for greater speed and accuracy increased, three types of automated data processing systems developed: (1) punched card systems, (2) integrated data processing systems, and (3) electronic data processing systems. The major effect of these systems on files operators is primarily in the areas of sorting and retrieving information, both

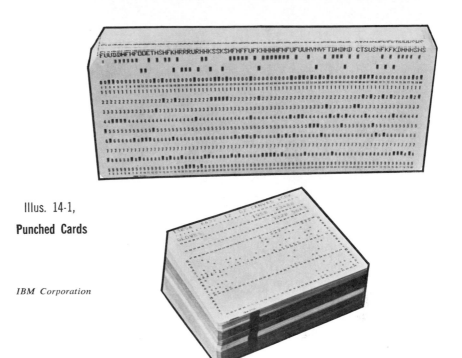

Illus. 14-1,

Punched Cards

IBM Corporation

of which are being done more and more with some form of automated equipment.

Large businesses are installing their own equipment. Smaller concerns, because of the high cost of purchasing or renting data-processing equipment, are increasingly using the services of data-processing service centers. All information pertaining to a payroll, for example, may be sent to such a center. There, for a fee, the payroll computation is completed on data processing equipment, including the preparation of the paychecks.

Punched Card Systems

The leading manufacturers of punched card machines are International Business Machines (IBM) and the Remington Rand Division of the Sperry Rand Corporation.

Both the IBM machine and the Remington Rand machine use a standard card that has 80 vertical columns. (See Illustration 14-1.) In addition, IBM has designed a 96-column card for use with its small, low-cost computer.

Each column on a card can accommodate one or more punched holes. Each column that is punched represents a single number or letter. Information is punched into the card according to a standard arrangement with certain columns on the cards reserved for the recording of specific information. For example, several columns on the card may be

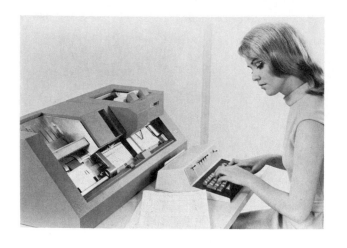

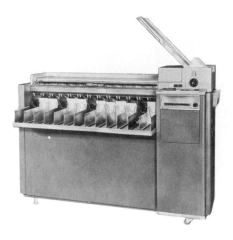

IBM Corporation

Illus. 14-2, **Keypunch**

IBM Corporation

Illus. 14-3, **Sorter**

reserved for the name of an employee; another group of columns, for his address or department number; still other columns, for pertinent information about him. Each of these groups of columns is called a field; for example, the columns containing his address would be one field.

Cardpunching. Cardpunching is the basic method of transferring original information into punched cards. The keypunch operator reads the original document and, by stroking the keys on a cardpunch keyboard, causes the machine to position the card, record the data, and eject each card automatically. (See Illustration 14-2.)

Any data that can be reduced to alphabetic or numeric code (or a combination arrangement) may be punched into cards.

Card Verifying. Verifying is the process of checking the accuracy of the keypunch operator. A different operator usually verifies the original punching. This is done by depressing the keys of a verifier while reading from the same source of information used to punch the cards. The machine compares the key depressed by the verifier with the hole already punched in the card. Any difference will cause the machine to stop, indicating a discrepancy between the two sets of punching.

Card Sorting. After the punched cards have been verified for accuracy, they may be sorted into alphabetic or numeric order according to the needed information that has been punched into them. The sorting is done by a machine called a *sorter*, which operates somewhat along the same principles as terminal digit filing, sorting from right to

IBM Corporation

Illus. 14-4, Tabulator

Illus. 14-5, →

Punched Card File

TAB Products Co.

left, only by one letter or number at a time instead of by two or three digits. (See Illustration 14-3.)

Information regarding prospective customers, for example, might be punched into a series of cards and then sorted according to the salesmen's territories or the cities and states in which the prospective customers live. Since 450 to 2,000 cards may be sorted in one minute, this operation is vastly faster than hand filing and retrieving.

Tabulating. After the cards have been sorted, they may be fed through a tabulator for listing or tabulating. The tabulator reads the holes punched into the cards and prints out the information on paper or cards. The tabulator is capable of reading all or selected information punched into the cards, depending on what information is needed. The tabulator normally performs computations of addition and subtraction. Tabulators operate at speeds ranging from 50 to 150 cards per minute, depending upon the type of machine used. Some tabulators may be attached to another machine in order to summarize punched cards instead of, or in addition to, preparing lists. (See Illustration 14-4.)

Card Filing. Tabulated cards are placed in long trays or drawers that are held in specially constructed cabinets. In Illustration 14-5, three indexing systems are suggested: (1) in the lower two rows, *numeric filing*, a system which frequently is used for parts inventory records;

(2) in the second row from the top, *alphabetic filing,* a system which could be used for such material as customer name and address cards; and (3) in the top row, *grouped card sets,* a system which could be used for such applications as sales records where individual cards are not so important as is a collection of all sales of a particular department or for a particular item.

Each tray or drawer bears a label on which is written a description or a code showing the contents. The labels are similar in use to labels on the front of file drawers in cabinets. There is a variety of specially constructed equipment for punched card filing systems, all designed to assemble systems comparable to those used for index card systems.

The desired card or cards may be located in the same manner as other material by locating the proper drawer or tray by the label card, then scanning the guides in the drawers, and finally by reading the printed coding on the top of each card until the proper card is found. When many cards are needed, or when printed coding is not placed on the top of the cards, all cards from the appropriate section of the tray or drawer may be placed in the sorter and mechanically located.

Integrated Data Processing Systems

Integrated data processing (IDP) is a system of machine control based upon the ability of certain office machines to transfer information to other machines automatically. Such a system follows this basic rule: *Do it only once.* This means that the exact information should be captured on some type of common language medium the first time the information is prepared. The next time this information is needed, it is automatically written from its common language (machine readable language) form.

Punched Paper Tape. Punched paper tape is one type of *common language* medium. The tape can be prepared automatically by a small attachment to an electric typewriter, adding machine, cash register, printing calculator, or other common business machine. As the operator types the original document, the paper tape is automatically punched. The next time the same information is needed, the tape is fed back into the device on the typewriter or other machine, and an exact duplicate copy of the original is prepared automatically.

This system is used for a number of business operations. For example, bank checks which have the name and address of the customer printed on each check are frequently prepared on punched paper tape. When the customer wants more "personalized checks," he returns a notice to the bank requesting the checks. Frequently the bank encloses the tape in a pocket of an order blank that is sent to the customer with his set of checks. The customer keeps the order blank and tape until he needs more checks. He then returns the order and the tape to the bank. The bank (or a service bureau employed by the bank) inserts the punched tape into a machine; the customer's information, identical to that on his present checks, is automatically reproduced on a new set of checks.

Another common business application of the punched paper tape is in customer billing. This uses an automatic typewriting machine, such as a *Flexowriter* *. In customer billing, the name and address and other pertinent data about a regular customer are available to the operator on prepunched tape. This prepunched information contains frequently used data and is kept in a

Friden Division,
The Singer Company

Illus. 14-6, **Model 2201 Flexowriter**

master file near the Flexowriter operator. The folders housing the tapes for regular customers are constructed with small pockets into which the prepunched tapes are inserted. The operator simply selects the necessary folder for a particular customer, removes the prepunched tape filed in the folder, and feeds it through the machine. When the information has been recorded on the document, the tape is replaced in the folder and filed until needed again. Some information needed for a bill, such as the date and order number, will vary with each bill and must be hand-typed before or after one of the tapes has been fed into the machine to activate the machine to type automatically the customer's name, address, or other permanent information.

The Flexowriter and other machines of its type produce edge-punched cards as well as paper tape. Edge-punched cards perform the same function as paper tape. In addition, when they are kept in files, the cards are more convenient to handle. Each tape must be placed in a special pocket, whereas cards are rigid and can be filed in a manner similar to that used for ordinary file cards. The tapes and cards can be fed into a cardpunching device, thereby producing punched cards automatically. These cards can then be sorted and the information printed out on a tabulator in the usual manner.

---

* A trademark of the Singer Company.

Shaw-Walker

Illus. 14-7, **Filing Punched Paper Tapes**

Punched Tape Filing. The filing and retrieval of punched paper tape are made possible by placing the tape into a special pocket of a standard file folder or of a smaller kraft card. The tape is then indexed and filed in the same manner as other file folders or cards. Edge-punched cards are labeled and filed in a manner similar to ordinary file cards.

Electronic Data Processing Systems

Electronic data processing (EDP) processes data with the speed of light by using electronic means and is the most advanced development in the field of data processing. When an integrated data processing system uses electronic means to capture information and to process and reproduce this information, it would also be an electronic data processing system. However, not all integrated data processing systems are electronic data processing systems because they do not all use electronic equipment. EDP systems have affected filing work because of the vast amounts of data that are developed and must be stored for future use and must be available immediately when needed. Data storage media for electronic data processing systems include punched cards, printout forms, magnetic tape, magnetic disks, magnetic drums, and magnetic cores.

The storage of information on magnetic tape has many similarities to the storage of information on punched paper tape. On paper tape, information is represented by holes punched through the tape and "read" by a special machine. On magnetic tape, the information is recorded on the tape as magnetized spots that create electrical impulses which can be "read" by magnetic tape reading machines (the magnetic spots cannot be seen). This tape is similar to that used in an ordinary tape recorder found in many homes and offices.

Because of the volume of data that can be stored on magnetic tapes, disks, drums, and cores and the fact that such information on these magnetic devices cannot be read without having it printed out, it is vital that the indexing and coding be carefully planned before the processing is started. The location of information is commonly called its *address* when reference is made to the magnetic storage devices. The person who prepares the set of instructions, called a *program,* for a computer is called a *programmer.* He must be thoroughly familiar with all phases of the actual business application that must be processed as well as with the capabilities of the machine.

Payroll work is one type of business activity that lends itself to EDP. All the involved steps of preparing a payroll, including the preparation of the paychecks themselves, can become highly automated under this system. As a by-product, a considerable amount of information regarding an employee may be stored on magnetic tape and supplied whenever needed. For example, if a directory or list of employees and their work locations is needed, it is easily obtained automatically from the electronic data processing equipment.

When magnetic tape is used for storage, great care must be taken to see that no dust or dirt collects on the tape. In addition, the temperature and humidity in the storage area must be carefully controlled. A visible label must be placed on each tape as it is prepared to make identification easy. This label serves the purpose of a drawer label in regular files. Many companies employ a files operator, called a *tape librarian,* whose job is to maintain control over the magnetic tapes and to see that they are stored properly and used correctly.

Magnetic tapes are filed on end in various specially designed cabinets or on specially designed shelves. Illustration 14-8 shows one such installation.

Supreme Equipment & Systems Corporation

Illus. 14-8, **Large File Showing Magnetic Tape Storage**

The security of data processing files is a vital part of the responsibility of the files operator. The theft or destruction of one reel of tape could possibly cause the company to put in many valuable hours of work into reproducing lost information. Many security devices are designed to help safeguard this information. Among these devices are lead carrying and storage cases; locks to make the use of the reel of tape impossible without the proper key or combination; security guards at the entrance to the storage area; and the preparation of duplicate tapes, called *back-up tapes,* to be safely stored in another location.

Computer printouts are placed in specially designed binders and are filed on shelves or in file drawers designed for that purpose. The binders are labeled on the outside cover, on the back, or on tabs in the same manner as correspondence folders.

It is obvious, then, that a considerable amount of hand filing of certain types of materials is completely eliminated when an EDP system is installed. Nevertheless, the machine must be told how to do everything. This requires that those who work with the machine have a knowledge of filing procedures. The main difference is *where the information is filed* and *through what means.* As long as information must be retrieved, a considerable knowledge of filing will be necessary, because filing systems for EDP tape or punched cards or paper tape must be as complete and as efficient as systems used for index cards or for correspondence.

SECTION 2 MICROFILMING

Microfilming is a process that involves taking miniature pictures of documents. The pictures are usually taken on 16 mm. (millimeter) or 35 mm. film. For special types of work, 70 mm. or 105 mm. film are used.

In the past, microfilm was used mostly for documents that had to be protected as vital records or for documents that had to be kept in storage for a long time (15 years or more) during which time reference to the documents was expected to be limited. In more recent years, however, many records are microfilmed as soon as they are created, and microfilm systems form a part of very active files.

Manufacturers have refined the cameras and developing techniques so that equipment needed for a microfilm system is compact and very dependable. The newer equipment is easy to learn and easy to use. Almost half of all businesses now use microfilm in some form, and an additional twenty percent of all businesses are planning to use microfilm.

Eastman Kodak Company

Illus. 14-9, **Reader-Viewer**

Bell & Howell

Illus. 14-10, **Reader-Printer**

Reading and Printing

After the film has been developed, it may be placed in a projector for viewing or reading. This projector is called a reader-viewer (see Illustration 14-9). If the user wants to print out a copy of the picture, he uses a reader-printer (see Illustration 14-10). After seeing which document he wants, the operator obtains a print, called a *hard copy,* by merely pressing a button or switch on the reader-printer. The term "hard copy" refers to any copy that can be read without the use of a viewer or other magnifying device. A reader-printer can reproduce the document to any one of various sizes—smaller than the original document, the same size as the original, or larger than the original. Some readers are small enough to be portable and are very inexpensive. They can be carried in a briefcase and be used whenever and wherever necessary.

Microfilm pictures may be taken on roll microfilm, similar to motion picture film, or on sheets of film. This makes it possible to retrieve the film and locate a particular document through a variety of ways. The frequency of reference necessary is generally what determines the form of the microfilm. These different forms are possible through the use of one of two kinds of cameras: (1) a rotary camera or (2) a planetary (or flat bed) camera.

Microfilm Cameras

A *rotary camera* is the most frequently used camera (see Illustration 14-11). The rotary camera can use several sized roll films, but the most popular is 16 mm. It can reduce the size of the picture of an original document from 16 to 40 times. This is called the *reduction ratio*—the higher the number, the smaller the image. A letter that is reduced to 1/25 of its original size has a reduction ratio of 25x; that

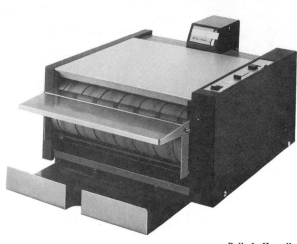

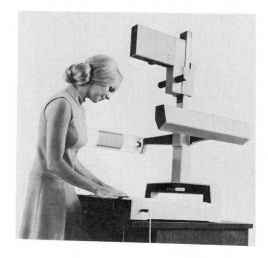

Bell & Howell   *Bell & Howell*

Illus. 14-11, **Rotary Camera**   Illus. 14-12, **Planetary Camera**

is, 25 of the smaller size would take up the space of one of the original-size documents.

A *planetary,* or *flatbed, camera* is used when the lighting has to be changed for each of the documents in order to get a good picture. It will also photograph larger documents, such as engineering drawings. Larger drawings will not fit in a rotary camera, and a rotary camera generally has only one lighting change (or a few such changes) possible. A planetary camera is not so portable as a rotary camera (see Illustration 14-12).

Aperture Cards

An *aperture card* is a card containing an aperture, or hole, cut into the card that provides a place for one or more frames, or chips, of microfilm (see Illustration 14-13). Aperture cards are generally cards that are used in a cardpunch and sorter. Through the use of a cardpunch to create punched holes to use in machine identification of the card and its microfilm image(s), aperture cards can be filed and retrieved through the use of a mechanical sorter. They may also be filed and retrieved manually. Aperture cards are used for many business purposes; engineering drawings are a frequent application. The cards can be read through a reader or a reader-printer designed to take aperture cards. Some readers will accept all types of microfilm reproductions; others are designed exclusively for one type only.

Some organizations are making use of cards with two or more apertures. Into these multiple-aperture cards can be placed two or more frames or strips of 16 mm. film. This arrangement is made possible by reducing the standard punching area, if the cards are to be

Eastman Kodak Co.

Eastman Kodak Co.

Illus. 14-13, **Aperture Card**

Illus. 14-14, **Microfiche**

used as a part of a machine data processing system. If manual retrieval is exclusively used, an even larger number of images may be placed on cards, using larger cards if it seems advisable.

A microfiche (pronounced micro fēēsh) is a transparent rectangle of film onto which from 60 to 98 small images have been photographed. Filing and other information is usually lettered across the top or bottom margins for identification of the fiche without having to use a reader-viewer. The standard size of a microfiche is 6 inches by 4 inches (see Illustration 14-14). Next to roll microfilm, microfiche is the most popular type of microfilm. It is used for storage of a series of related documents, such as a pamphlet, parts catalogs, customer mailing lists, or patients' medical histories.

Many advances have been made in microfiche. One is the development of what is called *ultrafiche*, which will hold 3600 pages on one 6- by 4-inch film. Up to 100 standard microfiche can be filed in a linear inch—a great savings of space.

Microfiche Jacket

Although not a microfiche in the strictest sense, a *microfiche jacket*, or *microcard*, is frequently used instead of the actual microfiche. The jacket is made of two panels of very thin transparent filmlike material. Lines of adhesive join the panels horizontally, dividing them into three or more strips into which microfilmed images are inserted. The images to be inserted are cut from roll microfilm and slid (either as individual images or as strips of images) into the channels of the jacket

Bell & Howell

Illus. 14-15, **Microfilm Jacket Reader-Filler**

by hand or by using a specially designed machine. Images no longer needed may be removed from the channels of the jacket and, if desired, new images inserted to update the information placed in the jacket. Microfiche jackets are usually the standard 6 by 4 inches, but other sizes are available. Jackets are frequently used instead of actual microfiche because the special "step and repeat" camera process needed for microfiche is expensive and takes up a lot of office space. The jacket process uses regular roll film and the more compact rotary camera. A jacket reader-filler is used to place strips of roll microfilm into the jackets (see Illustration 14-15). Microfiche and microcards can be viewed in a special reader or in many readers made to accept a variety of microfilms. A hard copy can be obtained by using a reader-printer.

Values of Microfilm

Microfilming techniques and forms have developed rapidly in recent years. As a result of these developments, many values are claimed. Duplicate copies can be made of rolls of film, microfiche, or aperture cards in less than one minute on small office copiers. Prints of microfilm images are made even faster and the prints can be made larger or smaller than the original document to make copies easier to read and handle.

As much as the contents of a 5-drawer file can be recorded on one 200-foot roll of film. This amounts to approximately 20,000 8½″ by 11″ documents on the roll. As many as 3,200 8½″ by 11″ documents can be placed on one 6″ by 4″ ultrafiche. Frames for about 350 microfilmed documents can be mounted in a 5-inch-high stack of aperture cards. This storage technique makes possible the saving of enormous amounts of floor space and great numbers of filing cabinets. As much as 98 percent of the space can be saved.

Although documents reduced to microfilm save considerable space, microfilm cannot be economically used for space savings alone because the cost of the microfilm equipment may be greater than the cost of the space saved. In an active file, when the original filing arrangement is accurate, microfilm simplifies and speeds up the retrieval of information by making it impossible to refile an item incorrectly. It must be remembered that microfilm captures not only the records but all of their defects as well. Records must be carefully and correctly arranged before filming.

Microfilm also offers security for valuable records in that copies are sent rather than originals. Cross-references are easily handled by photographing extra copies whenever they are desired. Microfilm is durable in that it can be kept indefinitely and when used does not show wear and tear as the original document would.

Microfilm, especially microfiche, can be mailed to other locations at a minimum cost. Microfilm systems can now be adapted to both high- and low-volume offices.

When to Microfilm

All firms face the problem of deciding when it is best to microfilm rather than continue to store original documents. *Not all records should be microfilmed.* The following guides are acceptable to many firms:

1. It is advisable to microfilm immediately when it is necessary or wise to release the original documents or when the microfilm is used for an *active technique.* Banks commonly microfilm checks before returning the checks to the depositors who drew them. Department stores commonly microfilm sales slips before they send the originals to the customers along with their monthly bills. This same procedure is followed if duplicate copies are needed for distribution in the form of rolls or aperture cards.

2. If records are to be retained three years or less, it is less costly to retain them in files than to microfilm.

3. If records are to be retained four to seven years, it is less costly to place them in storage areas than to microfilm.

4. If records are to be retained seven to fifteen years, it may be wise to microfilm, depending on the need for accessibility and the relative cost of storage space.

5. If records are to be retained longer than fifteen years, it may be best to microfilm instead of retain them in original form.

6. If records are of permanent value, or if they need particular protection, they should be microfilmed. The films or the originals should then be stored at a safe location some distance from the usual point of use.

Special Applications

Microfilming was once used exclusively as a method of protecting vital records or as a means of saving space. Today it is even more useful as a method of processing and retrieving information on an active basis.

Almost all types of businesses now use microfilm for certain types of records in their active files. The largest users include utilities (gas, electricity, water), financial institutions (banks, investment companies, savings and loan associations), insurance companies, government agencies (federal, state, local), military agencies, transportation companies, educational institutions, manufacturing firms, retail and wholesale distributors, and hospitals.

Microfilm is used for catalogs, computer printouts, account status reports, parts lists, inventory lists, statistical lists, price lists, sales bulletins, invoices, statements, engineering drawings, hospital patient records, general accounting information, customer mailing lists, and many other active business reports and papers. Businesses which must provide extensive records and data to the government for tax or other purposes can send it all inexpensively on standard microfiche.

Banks. At the end of each month, the commercial banks return to customers checks that have been charged against their accounts. Before doing so, however, banks make a microfilm copy of both the front and the back of each check.

When the film is developed, it is placed in a specially designed filing cabinet. If a customer claims an error, the film is run through a reader-viewer or a reader-printer until the check in question is found. It may then be viewed by the customer and the bank clerk, and the question of error may be settled. If it is not convenient to have the customer view the film, a full-size print (hard copy) is made and given to the staff member who will settle the problem with the customer.

Department Stores. When goods are sold in a department store, the clerk usually prepares a sales slip on which the items sold are listed together with the quantity, description, price, extension, and total. A copy is given to the customer or is sent with the order; but the original is kept for company records. At the end of the account month, the store prepares for each charge customer whose account shows any activity during the preceding month a statement on which are listed any balance due at the beginning of the month, the amount of each charge sale, the amount of each payment made, and the final balance due. Many department stores send the original copies of the sales slips, as well as the statement, to the customer. Before doing so, however, the store microfilms the sales slips and statements. The company thus avoids the problem of filing the sales slips, and the customer receives the original slips for quick reference in checking the statement. If the customer makes a complaint, the developed roll of film is run through a reader-printer. A photographic hard copy of the disputed item is prepared and sent to the customer or the staff person who is dealing with the complaint.

Mail-Order Firms. Many mail-order firms prepare their catalogs on microfiche. When they want to update the catalog, they change only those microfiche that need changing. Customer names and addresses are updated and sent to branch stores on microfiche every few weeks. Mailing is economical as copies of a microfiche cost only a few pennies each. Parts catalogs for repair parts are placed on microfilm and mailed to stores and branch offices. This saves using many heavy, hard-to-handle catalogs which take up valuable space in each office and makes it possible to keep the catalogs up to date and readily available.

Publications and Research. Many universities and publishers make complete copies of theses, books, periodicals, reference material, and special documents available in microfilm. These microfilmed reproductions may be purchased or may be viewed at libraries. Some libraries have installed reader-printers with a coin attachment. When using such a machine, a student or researcher can scan the roll of film for the precise section desired, drop a coin in a slot, press a plunger, and produce a hard copy.

Engineering Drawings. Engineering drawings have always been awkward to file and store because they are prepared on oversized sheets of paper and often rolled rather than folded. With the use of microfilm and aperture cards, however, engineering drawings and specifications can be reproduced in miniature form. In this type of work, 35 mm., 70 mm., or 105 mm. film is often used. It is now common practice to duplicate copies of a roll of film or a set of aperture cards and distribute them to various firms bidding or working on the same project. Engineers studying plans (for a bridge or a building, for example) may have a set of plans reproduced on aperture cards at their desks. When they are studying any specific part of the plans, they place the aperture card that contains a picture of that part in a reader-viewer or reader-printer. If a copy is desired, the reader-printer will produce it.

Manufacturing concerns and public utilities are heavy users of aperture cards for their engineering drawings. The use of aperture cards saves space, and the cards are readily located by using an automatic sorter.

Hospitals. Patient records are placed on microfilm, frequently microfiche. When reference is needed, small portable readers are available at convenient locations throughout the hospital and in doctors' offices. The use of microfiche makes it possible to have a copy of each patient's record reproduced for a few pennies each and, when new information is available, to prepare a new fiche or jacket to keep the record up to date.

Legal Implications

As a result of the action of the Eighty-Second Congress of the United States, in general, microfilmed documents may be presented as evidence in courts of law. Most people in business would advise filming vital documents as a means of records protection, with the original documents stored in a safe place. The originals of less important documents, however, are often destroyed after they have been microfilmed and the film has been inspected. A careful study of local, state, and federal laws governing records retention should be made before certain documents are destroyed.

As a regular practice, it is wise to have on file a certificate indicating that the film is a true copy of the original document. It is also wise to microfilm according to a predetermined and regular schedule, thus demonstrating that microfilming is a part of normal business procedure. When the film is finally destroyed, a certificate of destruction should be obtained and kept on file.

Although courts and the government have tended to be quite lenient regarding the use of microfilm, certain records relating to tax determinations, such as journals, ledgers, and cashbooks, are not always acceptable in microfilm form. The federal government also prohibits photographic reproductions of government securities, money, licenses, citizenship and naturalization papers, passports, and draft cards.

Retrieval

In general, any standard system of classification and indexing can be applied to microfilm. It is important, however, that the system used be well planned and used consistently.

Rolls of film can be rapidly scanned on a reader. Color coding can be used by color coding film magazines or boxes for each category contained on the particular roll. Motorized viewing machines enable the operator to scan a roll of film quickly by use of predetermined signals (called *targets*) and codes which serve the purpose of guides in a regular file drawer.

Aperture cards can be sorted rapidly by a mechanical sorter which "reads" the punched holes in the cards. If aperture cards are manually indexed, coded, and filed, they are retrieved just as cards are in any regular card file. Color may also be used with aperture cards by color coding the cards themselves or by color coding the guides in the same manner as ordinary card files.

Microfiche and jackets are filed in the same manner as cards using the top or bottom "header" column to record indexing information. Machine sorting is possible through magnetic marks placed invisibly on the header part of the microfiche. These magnetic markings are "read" by the automatic equipment.

Other Microfilm and Related Retrieval Systems

During the past few years a considerable advancement has been made in developing systems of rapid information transmission and retrieval that combine microfilming with electronic equipment. These systems began mostly with large installations such as the government or the military. Now, they are becoming commonplace in many business offices. A brief discussion of some of these systems may prove to be helpful.

Computer Output Microfilm (COM). One of the difficulties of computer processing of information is the volume of paperwork that is produced and must be stored. To reduce the storage space needed, this paper (output) can be microfilmed after it is printed by the computer, but such a procedure is very slow as the computer works so fast that the printer cannot keep up with it. With computer output microfilm equipment (COM), it is possible to place the computer output directly onto microfilm without having to print it on paper (hard copy) first. This is done through the use of a cathode ray tube not too different from a television picture tube, mirrors, and a microfilm camera. Indexing information is added while the picture is being taken. Roll microfilm or microfiche are used in COM. A COM recorder can record about 30,000 pages of information an hour or approximately 20,000 lines a minute! Developments are now underway to enable the computer to get its input directly from microfilm, thereby eliminating the creation of a hard copy for further processing.

Some authorities claim that COM is the first practical device that can produce original information at a lower price than it could be produced on paper. Since retrieval of information on microfilm is generally rapid, almost unlimited use of COM is claimed. It is now used for such items as legal files, accounts receivable, accounts payable, corporate reports, credit files, sales and billing records, personnel files, patent files, medical files, reference catalogs, marketing reports, and research information. Computer Output Microfilm systems are being installed so rapidly that there is expected to be ten times as many installed in 1978 as there were in 1971. There are now over 20 manufacturers of COM equipment.

Facsimile. Although not a new development, facsimile transmission (sending an exact reproduction) of information has recently become important to business offices. The sending of fingerprints and pictures over telephone or telegraph wires has been common. Now businesses are sending business information in the same way, thereby saving many days of delay. Copies of letters, financial records, purchase orders, engineering drawings, and many other records are being sent through the facsimile equipment. Information from one sheet of paper can be sent across the country in from 3 to 6 minutes. Advancements are rapidly reducing the time necessary to send the information. Facsimile units can scan microfilm images and produce a hard copy at the receiving end. For legal purposes, facsimile copies are treated in the same manner as photostatic copies.

Miracode. Miracode is an automated microfilm information filing and retrieval system developed by Eastman Kodak. Documents are microfilmed onto 16 mm. film and at the same time identified on the film by a machine-readable coding pattern. These codes become a part of the film and may contain such information as customer account numbers or terminal digit filing numbers. This coding makes it possible to automatically search up to 350 documents a second for rapid retrieval. A hard copy can be easily made of any document in the file, or regular viewing can be made as in any microfilm system. Miracode is used for customer orders, product shipment, invoicing, and accounts payable as well as other operational files.

Information Distribution System. The Mosler Safe Company has developed a system which combines a television screen (video screen) and microfilm. Information can be viewed at a remote monitor, or a hard copy can be made at a remote video printer. An image can be enlarged up to 250 times its original size, and only a small portion of the original document need be viewed or printed. The storage unit can contain from 200,000 to 11,000,000 documents for rapid retrieval by a number coding, such as a part number, customer number, patient number, or order number.

Illustration 14-16 shows an engineering drawing on an aperture card that has been placed on the video screen. Microfiche and roll microfilm are also used.

Systems by other manufacturers are equally effective and give the user retrieval times of 5 seconds and hard copies in less than 10 seconds. One such system (Videofile by Ampex Corporation) copies all documents on video tape. The top border of the tape contains space for identity numbers (alphabetic, numeric, or alphabetic and numeric) as well as cross-referencing information. These codes are also machine readable. The files are easy to expand and update. Seven reels of video tape can store the contents of the equivalent of 150 four-drawer filing cabinets. With this system, the original document never leaves the file; therefore, if it is carefully filed originally, it can always be located. The images can be available at remote locations and at more than one location at the same time.

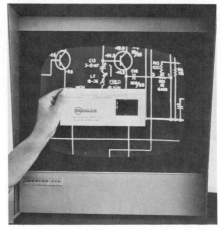

Mosler Safe Company

Illus. 14-16, **Aperture Card of Engineering Drawing on Video Screen**

QUESTIONS FOR DISCUSSION

1. Why have mechanical and electronic machines been developed to help with filing and finding tasks?
2. What are the most important parts of mechanical and electronic filing systems?
3. What is the major effect of the use of data processing systems on files operators?
4. Name three types of data processing systems currently in use.
5. When a punched card system is used, what is the function of the sorting machine?
6. How is punched paper tape stored for retrieval?
7. How is information stored in an EDP system?
8. What is the job of a tape librarian?
9. What does a reduction ratio of 25x mean?
10. What is an aperture card? How are such cards filed?
11. What is a microfiche? a microfiche jacket?
12. What are some of the values of the use of microfilm?
13. How is microfilming used in banks? in mail-order firms? in hospitals?
14. What types of documents may not be used as legal evidence in microfilmed form? What types of documents are prohibited from being photographed?
15. How are targets used in a microfilmed filing system?
16. What is COM?

CHAPTER 15

MAINTAINING AND IMPROVING RECORDS CONTROL SYSTEMS

It is not possible to know the extent to which you, as a new employee, might be given responsibility for maintaining and improving any phase of a records control program. However, after you have worked for a period of time and have some understanding of how the records system is operated, you might be given responsibility relating to the maintenance and to the improvement of the system.

With this possibility in mind, Chapter 15 has been designed to give you information that should help you to upgrade your own job by being prepared to improve the records control system, or a part of it, in your own department or for your company.

General Procedures for Gaining Control of Records

The first work that you will do in on-the-job filing and records control work probably will be to follow filing procedures that have been long established. And, if the organization for which you are working has an orderly, well-planned system, the following steps will be taken to insure the efficient functioning of the system:

1. Records control routines will be carefully planned and strictly followed. It will be recognized that even though filing might be only a part of general office work or secretarial work, a definite allotment of time must be made available for it.
2. Papers will be indexed, coded, and processed in accordance with definite rules and routines.
3. Responsibility for directing filing and records control operations will be definite. One person probably will be given this duty.
4. Only personnel assigned to perform records control work will be allowed to operate the filing system.
5. A manual of procedures (a guide) will have been prepared and will be kept up to date. The manual will include technical items such as these: (a) a general description of the records control system and its various parts or divisions, (b) a listing of indexing rules to be followed, (c) a detailing of coding practices to be used, (d) a description of charge and follow-up procedures, (e) a definition of procedures to be followed prior to and during transfer time.

Planning for Records Control

Under a well-run records control program, attention will be given to maintaining order in the files and in all procedures relating to control.

1. The files will not be overcrowded. Working space will be provided in and around the files.
2. Time for transfer will be definite, and procedures will be completely described.
3. The guiding systems for correspondence and card files will have been carefully planned.
4. The equipment and supplies used will have been selected only after careful study has been made of the needs of the department.
5. Order will be maintained in all phases of records control by using accepted practices such as the following;

    (a) Worn folders will be replaced.
    (b) Papers will be placed neatly within folders.
    (c) Torn sheets will be mended.
    (d) Pins and clips will be taken off papers in the files.
    (e) Tops of filing cabinets or shelves will be kept clear of materials.
    (f) Miscellaneous folders will be checked regularly, and individual folders will be started for active correspondents.
    (g) Individual folders will be inspected and extended when necessary.
    (h) Filing procedures and standards will be listed in a filing manual, which will be available at all times for reference purposes.

6. A plan for charging and tracing materials which have been borrowed will be in operation.

Preparing and Using a Records Control Manual

Regardless of how large or how small a records department might be, it is always advisable to have a records control manual to be used as a guide by all those who work in the department. This is especially true because of two factors common to all records control work.

First, all such work must be as closely related as possible to the unique practices and standards that are used in any particular company because each has certain routines and standards peculiar to its own type of operation. These must be made known to workers if efficient operations are to result. Also, as procedures are developed or improvements are made in departmental routines, these must be explained in permanent form; otherwise they will be lost or misunderstood or misused as time passes and personnel changes occur.

Second, a records control manual assembles in summary form a variety of technical information that is vital to a coordinated and efficient practice. Thus, many of the rules and procedures that you have studied in this textbook will be found in summary form in company manuals. But it should be understood that some of the rules and routines given in this textbook must be adapted for use in a particular company. For example, the basic rules for indexing must be used by all who keep records; but a given company might operate in a specialized field that would require an elaboration or extension of one or another of the basic rules for indexing. It is very possible that a company dealing with agencies or branch offices in foreign countries might require a more detailed statement of the basic indexing rule for processing foreign names. Such an extension of the rule would be explained in the company manual.

In summary, records control manuals, or filing manuals, are prepared for the following reasons: (1) to formalize records control procedures which are used in a given company so that all personnel will be informed and will be able to proceed in a uniform manner; (2) to record technical information in order to guide and train departmental personnel; (3) to relate general standards of performance to the specific needs of any given organization.

Specific Standards for Records Control

A critical matter which every organization must consider is the formulation of specific standards for filing practice and records control. If specific standards are not developed, filing practice will be unregulated—a condition not apt to result in the control of records.

A records control program cannot be effective unless general standards for good practice are translated into specific, usable terms by a particular company. For example, a general standard concerning the handling of miscellaneous folders requires that such folders should not be overcrowded and that individual folders should be added to a system whenever they are needed to relieve an overcrowded condition. In order to make this general standard applicable to a specific situation, it must be restated in such specific terms as these: When 5 or more pieces of correspondence to, from, or about one person or firm have accumulated in a miscellaneous folder, an individual folder must be prepared for that correspondent. Thus, a known general standard is made specific and usable in a working situation.

Specific standards are usually developed in terms of the relative activity of a filing system, that is, according to the amount of use that is made of the system. As an example of this, a very active filing system would need more guides per file drawer than would be required in a drawer of a semiactive system. Specific standards for the use of guides vary with the activity of one system as compared with the activity of another. In terms of relative activity, files are classified as (1) very active, (2) active, (3) semiactive, (4) inactive. According to this classification, a *very active file* is one in which approximately 6 percent of the total number of papers in the file are acted upon in one way or another during a working day; that is, papers are received and processed, or are requested and borrowed or returned to the files. In an *active file*, about 5 percent of the total contents are handled in a given day. In a *semiactive file*, only 2 to less than 5 percent of the materials are handled in one day. An *inactive file* has less than 2 percent activity in a given day.

General Standards for Guides and Folders

General Standards for the Use of Guides. Associations and corporations engaged in the records control field frequently make studies relating to general standards for equipment and procedures. Two of these organizations, The Oxford Pendaflex Corporation and the National Office Products Association, both suggest that an average of from 20 to 25 guides (of all types) be used per 26-inch file cabinet drawer. An average of 20 guides would be used in an active system; an average of 25 would be used in a very active system.

For shelf filing systems, the Barkley Company of Chicago suggests the use of one guide for each 6 inches of shelf space for very active systems, and one guide per foot for active systems.

General Standards for the Use of Folders. Most organizations and companies concerned with records control recommend using from 6 to 8 to 10 folders behind guides. These variable maximums are given in relation to the relative activity of a system. Less active systems can use more folders per guide and more papers in folders without impairing the efficiency of the system.

Miscellaneous folders are necessary parts of most filing systems, but they are difficult to control and are potential sources of misfiling. Because of this, some organizations using shelf filing systems have discontinued the use of miscellaneous folders and use only individual ones. This can be done only when a repetitive type of correspondence is involved, that is, when papers from more-or-less the same correspondents are always handled.

A generally applicable standard for extending an individual folder has been given by the Yawman & Erbe of Calif. Corp. to the effect that a new individual folder should be added to one already established when 30 or more papers have accumulated in the original folder during a period of one month. Or a series of dated folders should be started at this point if it is known that correspondence with this company or person will continue over a period of time.

Capacity of Folders. It is an all-too-common practice to file too many papers in one folder and thus create a potential for misfiling and losing papers. Because of this tendency, recently stated general standards for folder capacities have been adjusted to lower levels than those formerly recommended. For example, the National Office Products Association now recommends a *maximum* of 50 sheets of paper per folder in active filing systems. This would result in an *average* of about 25 sheets per folder in an entire system.

Most file folders are formed and scored at the bottom to hold about ¾″ of material. With this thickness, a folder can be made to hold at least 150 sheets of medium-weight paper. This is far too many to be held in the folders of either a very active system or an active system. One hundred sheets per folder is a maximum number frequently given for folder capacity. However, the *relative activity of a system is a more important factor to consider when determining a specific standard for folder capacity in a given system*. The 100-sheet maximum is too high for some operations and possibly is too low for a semiactive or an inactive (storage) system. In any event, folders must never be overcrowded in relation to the activity of the system.

Determining Working Space in the Filing System

One of the most important factors to consider in controlling records is to organize and operate a system in such a manner that no part of it is filled to capacity. This means making provision for free space in file drawers, on file shelves, and in folders, as well as in and around the filing area. This working space does not exist of itself; without careful planning and vigilant checking, free space will quickly disappear.

Usually the amount of free working space suggested for a 26-inch file drawer is from 3 to 4 inches. This includes the space used by a follower-block or its equivalent that is used to hold folders in an upright position within a file drawer. In order to maintain this amount of space, it is necessary to follow a plan which includes the elements of (1) estimating the future expansion of a system and ordering equipment and supplies on this basis and (2) planning for the transfer of materials from the active files to the semiactive or storage files. Transfer of relatively inactive materials is imperative because this action, in addition to the constant weeding-out of unwanted materials, provides new working space in the system.

Control of Filing Space

The most crucial element in controlling the use of filing space is that of determining the limitation to be placed upon the number of sheets and/or upon the bulk of material to be held in file folders. This is true because sheets and related materials constitute the primary source of files input and, therefore, are the greatest users of files space.

Setting limits involves determining maximum capacities for folders in terms of the relative activity of a filing system, which previously has been defined as (1) very active, (2) active, (3) semiactive, (4) inactive. Determining the degree of activity of a given system is a relatively simple matter if a tally of all work relating to handling papers is kept for a period of time, and totals from such a check are compared with an estimated total number of papers being held in the system.

Once the activity rate has been determined, the specific standards for filing operation can then be determined on a firm basis. Specific standards must be established for the following elements: (1) the number of papers to be held as a maximum amount in each folder, (2) the number of guides to be used in each drawer in a cabinet or on each shelf section, (3) the number of folders to be used behind each guide, and (4) how many cabinets or shelves will be needed for the entire system.

Calculating the Use of Space

The following analysis is that of a *very active* correspondence filing system. It shows the kind of information that is needed in order to make calculations for the control of space. This same method can be used in making calculations for active, semiactive, and inactive systems.

The Point System. The linear space used by guides and folders is given in terms of *points*. Manufacturers and dealers both use this means of designating the thickness of guides and folders. One *point* is the equivalent of .001 of an inch (one thousandth of an inch). Guides are commonly used in either 20-point or 25-point pressboard. The space used by either can be determined by multiplying points by .001; for example, 20 times .001 equals .02, or 2/100 of an inch, the linear space used by one 20-point guide.

Folders also are measured by the point system. An 11-point manila folder is one that is commonly used; its linear measure is found by this procedure: 11 x .001 equals .011. This total must be doubled because each folder has two sections, a front and a back; thus, 2 x .011 equals .022. Then, an allowance must be made for space used at the base of a folder because of the fold and the score marks. These add approximately .0155 to the linear dimension of each folder. So, .022 plus .0155 equals .0375 (this is 375/10,000 of an inch). This does not seem to be a figure that should be reckoned with, but it builds up in relation to the size of a system.

One other note on the space used by guides: those guides having eyelets at the base (see Illustration 5-4, page 50) use almost twice as much linear space as those without eyelets. Eyelets are made of metal or plastic, which projects out from surface of the guide. A long rod is run through the eyelets to prevent the guides from being pulled out of a drawer when folders are removed from the drawer. The linear space allowance for an eyelet is usually .03 (three hundredths) of an inch.

Use of Space in a Very Active System. In the material that follows, an exemplary, very active filing system is analyzed in order to show how filing space is used to best advantage.

1. The system is used for correspondence records and holds about equal amounts of substance 20# rag bond and substance 13# bond (copy paper).
2. The system is very active; 6 percent or more of the total papers being held are acted upon in some manner during one working day.
3. An *average* of 25 guides per drawer in vertical cabinets are used. This figure includes all types of guides.
4. An *average* of 6 folders per guide are used.
5. Vertical filing cabinets have 26-inch drawers (inside depth).
6. A maximum of 50 papers per folder has been established. A sample count of papers per folder has determined that the *average* number of papers held per folder is 25.
7. Four inches of free space per file drawer is maintained. This is for working space and for expansion room. The four inches include linear space used by a follower-block in each file drawer.

The following calculations are based on the space usage in the filing system described in the preceding paragraph.

1. **Guides:** 25 guides per drawer: 25-point pressboard: with metal eyelets. 25 points x .001 equals .025 of an inch per guide
   25 guides x .025 equals .625 or ⅝ inch (without eyelets)
   (Allowance for eyelets equals .03 inches per guide.) 25 guides x .03 = .75 inches
   Totals: .625 plus .75 equals 1.375, or 1⅜ inches for 25 guides

2. **Folders:** an average of six 11-point folders per guide
   6 (folders) x 25 (guides) equals 150 folders per drawer
   150 (total folders) x .0375 (linear space for each folder) equals 5.6250 inches, or 5⅝ inches total space used by 150 empty folders per drawer

3. **Free space per file drawer:** 4 inches

4. **Total space used by guides, folders, and free space:** 11 inches

5. **Available filing space per drawer:** 26 inches less 11 inches equals 15 inches

6. **Available space in terms of reams of paper:** contents of the drawer estimated at half 20# rag bond paper and half 13# bond (copy) paper:
    (a) one ream of 20# rag bond equals 2½ inches of linear space
    (b) one ream of 13# bond (copy) equals 1¾ inches of linear space
    (c) the average of (a) and (b) is 2⅛ inches
    (d) 15 inches of available filing space ÷ 2⅛ inches per ream equals 7 reams of paper, or 3,500 sheets per file drawer

If space usage in a filing system is being checked or estimated by using such standards and making such calculations as those given in the example above, adjustments must be made if there is deviation of any sort from the basic figures shown in the example.

Allowance in calculations must be made for such deviations as the following: (1) If the number of guides or folders used varies from those given above; (2) if the weight (points) of guides or folders is not the same as those given above; (3) if the length of file drawers varies from the 26-inch inside length used above; (4) if the amount of free space to be left per drawer varies from the 4 inches used above; (5) if materials being filed vary in weight or bulk from figures given in Point 6 above.

Using a Temporary Very-Active-File. One of the ways of increasing the working space and the efficiency of a filing system is to hold recent papers in a pending file for a period of approximately one month before transferring them to the regular filing system. This practice has been found effective under certain conditions because papers of recent origin are subject to call much more frequently than are the older papers in the files. Thus, a temporary very-active-file provides greater accessibility to high-demand papers, saves filing and retrieval time, and keeps high-demand papers out of the main filing system until demand has leveled out.

Day-to-Day Checking of the System. Authorities on records control frequently recommend the practice of making daily checks of a filing system in order to determine if problems exist and to make corrections and adjustments of one kind or another. This involves such action as the weeding-out of unneeded materials, checking and relieving congestion in miscellaneous folders, starting new subsections in the system, and checking the activity of the system in terms of having to extend it in order to maintain sufficient working space and expansion room. These types of work must be scheduled on a regular basis or they will be overlooked and, as a result, control of records will be impaired.

Transfer and the Retention of Papers

The transfer of filed materials and the determination of how long papers should be kept are matters of primary concern in records control work. Statements concerning these matters are usually included in the records control manual.

Most companies transfer records in accordance with one or another of the plans which are described in Chapter 7, "Transfer and Storage Controls." However, minor differences in procedure can occur as conditions relating to transfer vary from one company to another. One condition that varies considerably is the matter of determining the length of time for keeping various types of papers. The answers to such matters as how long certain types of records should be kept, and at what point in time they should be destroyed, are usually determined only after a careful study has been made and a records retention schedule has been prepared.

Records Retention Schedule

A records retention schedule (plan) is needed by any office where files are maintained because, in the absence of such a plan, many serious problem situations can arise. These could include (1) holding dead materials in storage, thereby wasting time, equipment, and space; (2) destroying papers that still have value; and (3) eliminating papers that might have current reference value.

Formulating a retention schedule can be a relatively simple action, or it can be a very complex matter. This depends upon the size of an organization and upon the types of materials being held in the filing system. Basically, however, a plan can be developed for any organization by analyzing the types of papers that are held in storage and estimating their value and their relative activity for reference purposes.

A functional retention schedule must also be planned in relation to certain federal and state statutes which define the periods of time for retaining such records as those concerning tax matters and legal conditions of one kind or another. Also, some records have permanent value and must be kept for the life of a business organization. Other records, such as correspondence, are useful only for such time as they have reference value.

Finally, all data relating to the retention of filed materials should be reviewed and evaluated by a committee on records retention or by its equivalent in a small organization. The work of such a committee should result in the establishment of a company records retention schedule.

Business Use of Indexing Rules

The indexing rules and the coding practices followed in an organization will be given in the company records control manual, and coding directions will be made known to all who mark and release papers to the filing department.

The indexing rules that you studied in Chapters 2, 3, and 4 represent standard practice and will be found in company manuals. They are not always in the exact wording of the rules in this textbook but are in closely related forms.

One important deviation from the rules given in "training form" in Chapters 2, 3, and 4 is the abbreviated and consolidated form used by most companies. Such rules are stated in the most usable terms to avoid the duplication made necessary in a training situation where rules for names of individuals and business names are given in separate sections. Thus, Rules 1 and 10 would be consolidated into one rule, as would Rules 3 and 19 and Rules 4 and 15. The meanings of rules would not be changed by combining them; only the form of presentation would be altered for the sake of brevity.

Having studied the detailed "training rules," you are in a position to use a set of combined rules comparable to those frequently used by business firms. Also, if you are preparing a series of indexing rules for your company, you can use the consolidated rules in total; or you can use as many rules as are required to control the records in your particular company.

Combined Indexing Rules for Use in Filing Manuals

The following set of indexing rules parallels the rules given in Chapters 2, 3, and 4; but it presents some of those rules in a combined form. Whenever possible, rules for indexing names of individuals and those for indexing business names have been combined. Whenever feasible, the wording of the combined rules has been summarized in order to present the concise style of writing that is preferred for business usage.

Although only a minimum number of examples are included with the combined rules, the numbers of the original rules in Chapters 2, 3, and 4 are cited so that additional examples can be more easily located.

Note 1: A company filing manual should give definitions for the following terms: *indexing, indexing unit, key unit,* and *coding.* Cross-reference practice should be defined.

Note 2: The numbers C-1, C-2, C-3, etc., are used to number the *combined rules* which follow.

RULE C-1 **Order of Indexing Units.** A business name is indexed as it appears in written form unless it contains a personal name. A personal name is indexed in this manner: The surname is the key unit; the given name or initial is the second unit; the middle name or initial is the third unit.

```
         2                2  3              2  3            4
Eastern/Airlines     James/J./Benton     C./J./Benton (&)/Co.
```

(For other examples, see Training Rules 1 and 10, pages 11 and 21.)

RULE C-2   **Minor Words in Business Names.** Such minor words as *and, the, of, by, to,* and *for* do not add meaning to a business name and are not used as indexing units. When such other words as *at, on,* or *in* appear as *meaningful first units* in names, they are used as key units.

```
             2        3                2     3          4
(The) Erie/House (of)/Tools     In/Town/Markets,/Incorporated
```

(For other examples, see Training Rule 11, page 22.)

RULE C-3   **Names of Married Women.** A married woman's legal name (when known) is used for filing purposes.

```
          2      3                         2     3
(Mrs.) Mary/Jones/Walker       (Mrs.) Mary/Anne/Walker
```

(For other examples, see Training Rule 8, page 15.)

RULE C-4   **Articles and Particles.** A foreign language article, such as *De, Del, Des, El, La, Las,* and *Los,* or a particle, such as *Den, Mc, O', Ten,* and *Von,* in a business or personal name is combined with the part of the name following it to form a single indexing unit.

```
            2                2  3                          2
La Fata/Restaurant     John/C./Mac Afee     De Lux/Products
```

(For other examples, see Training Rules 3 and 19, pages 12 and 26.)

RULE C-5   **Identical Names.** When either business names or personal names (including seniority designations) are identical, addresses are used to determine filing order. City names, street names, and house or building numbers are usually used in that order. Seniority titles in otherwise identical names can be used as a secondary means of determining filing order.

(For examples, see Training Rules 5, 6, and 20, pages 13, 14, and 26.)

RULE C-6   **Single Letters and Abbreviations.** Single letters (with or without hyphens and with or without spacing between them) in business names, and initials in personal names, are treated as separate indexing units. Abbreviations of commonly known words (*Co.* and *Inc.*) and abbreviations of personal names (*Wm., Jos., Thos.*) are considered to be written in full. Brief personal names (*Ted, Jon, Rod*) are used as they are spelled.

```
The GTO Co.:          C-R-Y Co.:              Thos. T. Grant
        2  3  4           2  3  4                2   3
(The) G/T/O/Company   C-/R-/Y/Company        Thomas/T./Grant
```

(For other examples, see Training Rules 2, 12, and 13, pages 11 and 22.)

RULE C-7   **Titles.** A title in a business name is considered to be an indexing unit. A title used with a personal name is not considered to be an indexing unit unless it is used with only one name (*Brother John*). The units in such a name are indexed in the order in which they are written.

```
Dr. Ray Pet Shop:
        2   3   4              2  3                    2
Doctor/Ray/Pet/Shop    (Dr.) C./L./Burns      Sister/Anne
```

(For other examples, see Training Rules 4 and 15, pages 13 and 24.)

RULE C-8   **Possessives.** When an "s" is added to a name in order to form a possessive (*Brown's*), the added "s" is not considered in alphabetizing.

(For examples, see Training Rule 16, page 24.)

RULE C-9   **Compound Names.** The separate parts of compound personal names (*St. John*), of compound geographic names (*New York*), and of compound business names, either coined or actual, are treated as separate indexing units. Hyphens are disregarded.

```
Paul Bentley-Adams:   Can-Am Co.:              Double-Eagle Brand:
   3        2              2  3                      2       3
Paul/Bentley-/Adams   Can-/Am/Company        Double-/Eagle/Brand
```

(For other examples, see Training Rules 7 and 14, pages 15 and 23.)

RULE C-10   **Numbers.** A number written in digit form is considered to be in written-out form and, despite its length, is used as a single indexing unit. Four-digit numbers are considered to be written out in hundreds (3060 is considered to be Thirty hundred sixty).

```
The 95-West-Club:                The 910 Building:
                   2    3                                2
(The) Ninty-five-/West-/Club     (The) Ninehundredten/Building
```

(For other examples, see Training Rule 18, page 25.)

RULE C-11   **Separated Single Words.** When a single word (*southwest*) or a word and a prefix (*nonstop*) is separated into two or more parts in a business name (*south west; non stop*), the parts are considered to be a single unit. Hyphens in such names are disregarded.

$$\overset{2}{\text{(The) }\underline{\text{Sand-man}}\text{/Motel}} \quad \overset{2}{\underline{\text{North East}}}\text{/}\overset{3}{\text{Toy}}\text{/Shop} \quad \underline{\text{Re-Education}}\text{,/}\overset{2}{\text{Inc.}}$$

(For other examples, see Training Rule 17, page 25.)

RULE C-12   **Unusual and Obscure Names.** Unusual and obscure business names are indexed as written. The last unit in the as-written form of an unusual personal name is used as the key unit.

$$\text{James/}\overset{2}{\underline{\text{Henry}}} \qquad \underline{\text{Mohamed}}\text{/}\overset{2}{\text{Ayoob}}\text{/}\overset{3}{\text{Cía.}} \qquad \underline{\text{Tapia}}\text{/}\overset{2}{\text{Zamora,}}\text{/}\overset{3}{\text{S.}}\text{/}\overset{4}{\text{A.}}$$

> Note 1: The abbreviation "Cía." stands for "Compañía" and means "Company."
> Note 2: The letters "S. A." are the abbreviation of "Sociedad Anónima" and mean "Incorporated." If the files operator does not know the meaning of the abbreviation, the individual letters "S." and "A." would be considered to be separate units.

(For other examples, see Training Rules 9 and 21, pages 16 and 27.)

RULE C-13   **Selective Indexing for Names of Organizations, Institutions, and Agencies.** Certain names of organizations, institutions, and agencies can be correctly indexed according to either of two methods: (1) the "descriptive" method or (2) the "as-written" method. When indexed by the descriptive method, the most definitive part of a name is taken as the key unit. When indexed by the as-written method, a name is taken unit by unit as it appears in written form.

> Note: Company policy should dictate that only one of these methods should be used in a given organization.

Descriptive Method	**As-Written Method**
$\overset{2}{\text{Association (of)/}}\underline{\text{Accountants}}$	$\underline{\text{Association}}\text{ (of)/}\overset{2}{\text{Accountants}}$
$\text{Lincoln/}\overset{2}{\text{National}}\text{/}\overset{3}{\text{Bank,}}\text{/}\overset{4}{\underline{\text{Omaha}}}$	$\underline{\text{Lincoln}}\text{/}\overset{2}{\text{National}}\text{/}\overset{3}{\text{Bank,}}\text{/}\overset{4}{\text{Omaha}}$
$\text{Evangelical/}\overset{3}{\underline{\text{Methodist}}}\text{/}\overset{2}{\text{Church}}$	$\underline{\text{Evangelical}}\text{/}\overset{2}{\text{Methodist}}\text{/}\overset{3}{\text{Church}}$
$\text{Western/}\overset{2}{\text{High}}\text{/}\overset{3}{\text{School,}}\text{/}\overset{4}{\underline{\text{Tulsa}}}$	$\underline{\text{Western}}\text{/}\overset{2}{\text{High}}\text{/}\overset{3}{\text{School,}}\text{/}\overset{4}{\text{Tulsa}}$
$\text{John/}\overset{3}{\text{Adams}}\text{/}\overset{2}{\text{High}}\text{/}\overset{4}{\text{School,}}\text{/}\overset{5}{\underline{\text{Ogden}}}$	$\text{John/}\overset{2}{\underline{\text{Adams}}}\text{/}\overset{3}{\text{High}}\text{/}\overset{4}{\text{School,}}\text{/}\overset{5}{\text{Ogden}}$
$\overset{2}{\text{University/(of)/}}\underline{\text{Vermont}}$	$\underline{\text{University}}\text{ (of)/}\overset{2}{\text{Vermont}}$
$\text{Hotel/}\overset{3}{\underline{\text{New}}}\text{/}\overset{2}{\text{Yorker}}$	$\underline{\text{Hotel}}\text{/}\overset{2}{\text{New}}\text{/}\overset{3}{\text{Yorker}}$
$\overset{3}{\text{W}}\text{/}\overset{4}{\text{C}}\text{/}\overset{5}{\text{K}}\text{/}\overset{6}{\text{Y}}\text{/}\underline{\text{Radio}}\text{/}\overset{2}{\text{Station}}$	$\overset{2}{\text{W}}\text{/}\overset{3}{\text{C}}\text{/}\overset{4}{\text{K}}\text{/}\overset{5}{\text{Y}}\text{/}\overset{6}{\text{Radio}}\text{/Station}$
$\text{North-Western/}\overset{2}{\text{News}}\text{ (}\overset{3}{\underline{\text{Chicago}}}\text{)}$	$\underline{\text{North-Western}}\text{/}\overset{2}{\text{News}}\text{ (}\overset{3}{\text{Chicago}}\text{)}$

(For other examples, see Training Rules 22 to 28, pages 35 to 39.)

RULE C-14   **Government Names.** The name of a foreign or domestic government agency is indexed by (1) the name of the government unit—United

States, Virginia, San Diego; (2) the principal words in the name of the department; (3) the principal words in the name of the bureau, division, or agency. The various units are considered in the descending order of importance, from highest to lowest.

```
             2         3                    2
United/States/Government          State (of)/Indiana
     4          5                     3          4
Commerce/Department               Purchasing/Department
     6       7
Census/Bureau
```

(For other examples, see Training Rules 29, 30, and 31, pages 39 and 40.)

Modifications in the Rules

Because of the great diversity in business operations, many organizations have specialized indexing problems requiring the extension of one or another of the basic rules for alphabetic indexing. All such extensions and other modifications should be fully explained in the company records control manual. Conversely, some organizations will not need to use all the basic rules which are listed here. These companies will be able to select from the list only those rules required in order to process their records adequately.

Improving Records Control Systems

Determining how a records control system can be improved is a phase of work not usually within the range of a new employee. However, after a period of time involved in filing and control work, a person familiar with the system in his company should be qualified to upgrade the system if he knows the procedures to be followed in such an operation. As a first step, he must make an evaluation of the existing system before trying to estimate future needs. In doing this, he must consider the following matters: (1) What types of materials are being filed? (2) What volume of each type of material is being processed during a given period of time? (3) How are materials requested from the files? (4) Which systems of filing are being used for each type of material being filed? (5) Are the procedures and methods indicated by results of investigations relating to points (3) and (4) adequate and efficient? (6) Are charge-out and follow-up procedures operating in an effective manner? (7) What types of equipment and kinds of supplies are being used, and are these adequate and efficient? (8) Is the system of transfer being operated in an efficient manner and is it adequate? With such questions as these answered as completely as possible, there is a basis for determining needs and suggesting required changes in a records control system.

When a study similar to that indicated above has been made, a basis is formed for estimating the future needs and the type of control required to keep the system in a state of efficient operation and controlled growth.

**QUESTIONS
FOR
DISCUSSION**

1. What are some of the steps that must be taken in order to have a well-planned and orderly program of records control?

2. Name and describe some of the specific things that must be given attention so that order will be maintained in the files.

3. Why is it considered necessary to have a manual of operations in a records control department?

4. A general standard in filing practice is that a miscellaneous folder should not be overcrowded with papers. What can be done to apply this standard to a particular filing system?

5. Why is it necessary to consider the relative activity of a filing system when determining specific standards for it?

6. What are some of the standards for filing practice that relate to the use of guides in a system?

7. What are some of the standards for filing practice that relate to the use of file folders?

8. Why is it advisable to allow a certain amount of free space in the drawers or on the shelves of a filing system?

9. Why do you think that it is necessary to prepare a records retention schedule for each of the various types of records that might be held in a filing system?

10. Why do you think that indexing rules given in company records control manuals are written in concise terms?

11. What are some of the points to be considered before trying to estimate the future requirements of an existing records system?

INDEX

A

Abbreviations, cross-referencing of, 29; in business names, 22, 226; in personal names, 11, 226

Accession book or register, 130

Active file, 219; contents of, 85

ADAPTAFILE, 192

Addresses, with identical business names, 26; with identical personal names, 14

Agencies, names of, indexing, 228

Alpha Code System, 101, 106

Alpha-numeric subject filing, 150

Alphabetic card file, illustration of, 7; in a geographic file, 119; in a subject file, 148

Alphabetic card filing, 4; uses of, 4, 5

Alphabetic card guides, 5; captions, 6; tab cuts, 6; tabs, 5

Alphabetic correspondence file, arrangement of guides and folders, 53; cabinets and shelves, 51; drawer label, 51; drawer of an, 55; elements of an, 52; equipment and supplies, 48; expansion in an, 56, 150; file section with special name guide, 55; file section with subject guide and folder, 55; filing of related materials, 48; folders in an, 48, 53; guides in an, 50, 53; gummed labels in, 50; illustration of drawer in, 55; master guiding plan, 53; organization of, 48; special date sections, 55; special geographic sections, 58; special name sections, 58; special subject sections, 55, 150

Alphabetic correspondence filing, geographic filing in, 120, 121

Alphabetic correspondence filing procedure, coding, 62, 64; cross-referencing, 64; general information about, 47, 48; inspection, 60; making key title decisions, 60; placing correspondence in folders, 68; placing processed papers in file, 68; processing of papers before transmission to filing department, 59; processing of papers in filing department, 60; reading, 60; release mark, 59; sorting, 67; time stamp, 59

Alphabetic file, miscellaneous, in a numeric file, 129

Alphabetic filing systems, approaches to installing, 98; color in, 103; commercial, 99; geographic filing in, 120; types of, 99

Alphabetizing, 10; business names, 21; personal names, 10

Aperture card, on video screen, 215

Aperture cards, 206; retrieval of, 212; sorting of, 212

Apostrophe s ('s), 24, 227

Applications, coding of correspondence pertaining to, 41; handling of, in an alphabetic file, 55, 56; handling of, in a numeric file, 127

Armed Forces decimal filing, 153

Articles (English), disregarded in indexing, 22, 226

Articles (foreign), indexing of, 12, 26, 226

As-written method of indexing, 33, 34

Associations, indexing names of, 35

Automated data processing systems. 196

Auxiliary card guides, 6

Auxiliary correspondence guides, in an alphabetic file, 54, 55

B

Banks, indexing names of, 35; use of microfilm by, 210

Branch correspondence, handling, 118

Brief forms of given names, 12, 227

Broadcasting stations, indexing names of, 38

Bulky materials, filing of, 191

Business names, businesses known by more than one name, 43; minor words in, 22, 226; order of indexing units, 21; personal names in, 21

C

Cabinets, drawer labels, 51; in vertical card files, 166; lateral, 182; types of, 51, 52, 180; vertical, 180

Captioned and dated follow-up folder, 82

Captions, alphabetic, 49; card guide, 6; combination of letters and numbers in, 6, 54, 55; double-closed notations, 102; folder, 49; gummed labels for, 49; how to type for folders, 49; multiple-closed notations, 102; single-letter notations, 101; single-unit notations, 102

Card files, alphabetic system for, 161, 162; color as a signalling device in, 165; cross-referencing in, 17, 18, 28, 29, 41; encyclopedic subject method of arranging, 162, 163; guides in alphabetic, 5; illustration of, 7, 159; in geographic filing system, 119; loose-leaf visible, 173; organization of, 6; signals for, 170; vertical, See Vertical card files; visible, See Visible card files

Card filing, in data processing. 199

Card guides, 5; auxiliary, 6; captions on, 6; combination of letters and numbers in captions, 6; cuts of, 6; illustration of, 5; number required in an active file, 7; number of cards filed behind, 7; primary, 6; purpose of, 5; secondary, 6; special auxiliary, 6; tabs on, 5

Card index, control file in numeric filing, 129; in geographic file, 119; in numeric file, 129; in subject file, 148

Card record systems, equipment for, 160; nature of, 160

Card records, geographic systems for controlling, 164; subject systems for, 162

Card records and systems, importance of, 159

Card sorting, in data processing, 198

Card tickler file, 78

Card verifying, in data processing, 198

Cardpunching, in data processing, 198

Cards (index), follow-up, 81; how to type, 16; illustration of, 16; ruling on, 5; sizes of, in alphabetic card file, 5

Cards, storage record, 93

Carrier folder, 76

Catalogs, filing of, 190

CENTRAC rotary filing system, 186, 187

Charge methods, canceling charges, 76; carrier folder, 76; in storage operations, 95; lined and printed out guide, 75; out card with printed lines, 72, 73; out card with requisition slip, 72, 73; out folder with printed sections, 74; out folder with requisition slip, 74; out guide with requisition slip, 75; out sheet, 73

Charge-out system, 70; phases in, 70; requests for entire folder, 74; requests for selected papers, 72; requisition sheet, 71; requisition slip, 71

Churches, indexing names of, 36

Closed method (subject file), 144

Closed notations, 102

Clubs, indexing names of, 35

Coding, definition, 10; example of, in alphabetic filing, 10; example of, in as-written method, 33; example of, in descriptive method. 33; example of, in geographic filing, 117; example of, in subject filing, 149; in an alphabetic correspondence file, 62, 64; in a geographic file, 116, 117; in a numeric file, 130; in a subject file, 147, 149; preliminary name coding in a numeric file, 130; random filing of card records, 177

Coined compound business names, 23

Colleges, indexing names of, 37

Color, as signalling device in card files, 165, 166; in alphabetic systems, 103; in numeric filing, 135

Colorscan System, 99, 103

Commercial filing systems, 99

Common language medium, 200

Compound names, business, 23; indexing, 227; personal, 15

Computer output microfilm (COM), 213

Conjunctions, disregarded in indexing, 22

CONSERV-A-TRIEVE, 188

Copy of outgoing letter coded and marked for cross-reference, 65

Correspondence coding. See Coding

Correspondence guides, alphabetic, 50; arrangement of, in file drawer, 53, 54, 55; auxiliary, 54; description of, 50; in an alphabetic system, 53, 55; in a geographic file, 112, 114; in a subject file, 142; label inserts, 50; number needed, 57, 221, 222; out, 74, 113, 128, 144, 184; primary, 53, 57; secondary, 54; special, 54, 56; standards for use of 219; tabs of, 50; use as signalling

devices, 165; visible cross-reference, 66
Correspondence sorter, 67
Cross-reference, on folder tab in geographic file, 118
Cross-reference cards in card files, 18, 28, 29, 42
Cross-reference sheet, for an alphabetic file, 65; for a geographic file, 117; for a subject file, 148, 149
Cross-references in numeric file, 131, 132
Cross-referencing, abbreviations and single letters in a business name, 29; businesses known by more than one name, 43; combined surname and coined name in a firm name, 29; combined surnames in a firm name, 28; compound business names, 24; facsimile copy in, 66; foreign language names and governmental agency names, 43; importance in filing systems, 64; in alphabetic correspondence, 64, 66; in card files, 16; names of married women, 17; names of newspapers, 42; names of periodicals, 42; similar names, 43; unusual personal names, 18
Cuts, of card guides, 6; of folder tabs, 49

D

Daily secondary guides, in a tickler file, 78
Data processing, 196; electronic, 202; integrated, 200; types of, 196
Dated follow-up folders, 81, 82
Decimal filing (subject), 152
Degrees, with personal names, 13
Department stores, use of microfilm by, 210
Descriptive method of indexing, 33, 34
Destruction file, 96
Dewey Decimal System, 152
Dictionary method (subject file), 142
Direct subject filing, 140
Directories, filing of, 190
Disposal of business papers, 84
"Dr.," 13, 24
Double-closed notations, 102
Drawer, labels, 51; number of guides needed in a, 219
Due dates of borrowed materials, 76, 77
Duplex-alphabetic system, 154
Duplex-numeric system, 154
Duplicator plates, filing of, 193

E

Educational institutions, indexing names of, 36
ELECTROFILE, 176
Electronic data processing, 202
Electronic files, 187
Encyclopedic method in subject filing, 144
Encyclopedic subject method, card file based on, 162, 163
End guides, 162, 165
Engineering drawings, use of microfilming with, 211
Equipment, auxiliary and portable, 193; evaluating, 184; for correspondence and document filing, 179; hanging folders, 184; in records control, 178; lateral filing, 182; mechanized filing, 187; power-driven, 189;

rotary, 186; shelf-filing, 181, 182
EXECUTIVE LATERAL SYSTEM, 193
Expansion, in an alphabetic correspondence filing system, 56; in a geographic correspondence filing system, 120

F

Facsimile copies, in a geographic file, 116; in microfilming, 214; use of, to avoid follow-up on borrowed materials, 79; uses in cross-referencing, 66
Federal government names, indexing of, 39
File cards, 5; cross-referencing, 17, 18, 28, 29, 41, 42, 43; number filed behind one guide, 7; series typed in index form, 17; typing, 16
Files, active, 85, 219; as the "memory" of the business, 2; inactive, 219; mechanized, 187; semiactive, 219; temporary, 194; very active, 219
Files operators, 2; capacities of, 2; qualifications of, 3
Filing, definition, 2; holding or disposing of papers, 84; purposes of, 2, 70; random, 176; rank in office activities, 1; records stored at home, 1; scope of, 3; types of records filed, 1, 3; why study, 1
Filing cabinets, See Cabinets
Filing control, cycle of work areas, 7
Filing rules, need for, 8
Filing space, control of, 220
Filing system, basic equipment for starting a, 56; day-to-day checking of, 223; definition of, 52; expansion of a, 56; organization of a, 48
Financial organizations, indexing names of, 35
Fine sorting, 68
Firm names, indexing of, 21
"I (First)," in indexing, 13
Flexowriter, 201
Folders, arrangement in a file drawer, 53; arrangement of materials in, 68; capacity of, 220; captioned and dated follow-up, 82; captions of, 49; carrier, 76; cut of, 48, 49; dated follow-up, 81, 82; follow-up with movable signals, 82; gummed labels for captions, 49; hanging, 184; in an alphabetic correspondence file, 48; individual, 53, 57; miscellaneous, 53; number per file drawer, 219; number put behind one guide, 219; out, 74; placing correspondence in, 68; point system, 221; removing from the file, 74; special, 54; standards for use of, 219; tabs of, 49; transfer, 87
Follow-up card, 81
Follow-up file, 78
Follow-up methods, 76; master control sheet, 77; scanning the files, 77; system for, 77; time of return of papers, 77
Follow-up procedure for future-order items, 80; dated follow-up folders, 81; microfilming in, 79, 80; on-call cards, 81
Follow-up procedures, 78; exact copies in, 79
Foreign article or particle, 12, 26, 226
Foreign government names, indexing of, 40, 41

Foreign language names, cross-referencing of, 43
"IV (Fourth)," in indexing, 13
Future-order items, follow-up procedures for, 80

G

Geographic files, arrangement of, 112; lettered guide plan, 112, 113; location name guide plan, 114, 115
Geographic filing, definition, 111; in an alphabetic system, 120, 121
Geographic filing procedure, coding, 116, 118, 119; cross-referencing, 116, 117, 118; inspection, 116; placing materials in folders, 118; sorting, 118
Geographic filing systems, basis of, 111; businesses that use, 111; card index file, 119; expansion in, 120; nature and uses of, 111; subject filing in, 122; supplementary card index, 119
Geographic names, order of indexing units, 21
Geographic systems for controlling card records, 164
Government names, foreign, 40, 41; indexing of, 228
Group method (subject file), 144
Guides, card, See Card guides; correspondence, See Correspondence guides
Gummed labels for folder captions, 49

H

Hanging folder system in a lateral three-drawer cabinet, 185
Hanging folder systems and equipment, 184
Hanging folders, 184
Hard copy, 205
Hospitals, use of microfilm, 211
Hotels, indexing names of, 39
House numbers, 14
Hyphenated business names, 23, 226
Hyphenated personal names, indexing of, 15
Hyphens, disregarded in business names, 23

I

Identical names, 226; addresses in, 14; business, 26; personal, 13; seniority titles in, 13
Inactive file, 219
Incoming interoffice communication form coded, time-stamped, and released for filing, 63
Incoming letter coded, time-stamped, and released for filing, 61
Index cards, See Cards (index)
Indexing, as-written method, 33, 34; descriptive method, 33, 34; dividing names into units, 10; key unit, 10; selective, 33
Indexing rules, 9; business and geographic names, 21; business use of, 225; combined, 225; modification of, 229; names of organizations, government agencies, and subjects, 33; personal names, 9
Indexing units, in business and geographic names, 21; in personal names, 11; order of, 225

Individual folders, illustration of, with dates, 55; in an alphabetic file, 53, 55, 57; in a geographic file, 112, 114, 115; in a numeric file, 132; opening, 57; placing correspondence in, 68
Information distribution system, 214
Initials, in a personal name, 11, 226
Insert label for a guide tab, 50
Inspection of correspondence, 60
Institutions, names of, indexing, 228
Integrated data processing, 200
Interoffice communication coded, time-stamped, and released for filing, 63

J

Job qualifications, 2
"Junior," in indexing, 13

K

Key titles, rules for selecting, 60; subjects as, 62
Key unit, 10
Keypunch, 198

L

Labels, drawer, 51; folder, 49; transfer box, 93
Lateral cabinets with pull-out shelves, 51, 52
Lateral filing equipment, 182
Lettered guide plan, 112, 113, 118
Lined and printed out guide, 75
Location name guide plan, 114, 115, 119
Loose-leaf visible books, 168
Loose-leaf visible systems, 173

M

"M," as the code of material filed in a miscellaneous folder in a geographic file, 120, 121; as the code of inactive correspondence in a numeric file, 131, 132, 133
Magnetic tape, 202
Mail-order firms, use of microfilm by, 211
Manual, records control, 217, 218
Married women, cross-referencing names of, 17; indexing names of, 15, 226
Master control in storage areas, 94
Master control sheet for follow-up, 77
Maximum-minimum period transfer method, 90
Mechanized filing equipment, 187
Microcard, 207
Microfiche, 207; jacket, 207
Microfilming, aperture cards, 206; definition of, 204; hard copy, 205; legal implications, 212; microfiche jacket, 207; reader-printer, 205; reader-viewer, 205; reduction ratio, 205; retrieval, 212; special applications, 209; use in follow-up, 80; use of, 204; value of, 208; when to microfilm, 209
Middle digit filing, 134, 135
Minor words, in business names, 22, 226
Miracode, 214
Miscellaneous alphabetic file, in a numeric file, 127, 129
Miscellaneous folders, captions on, 53; in an alphabetic file, 53, 55; in a geographic file, 112, 113, 114, 115; in a small system, 57; in a subject file, 142; overcrowding in, 57; placing correspondence in, 68; relieving congestion in, 57
Monthly primary guides, 78
Motels, indexing names of, 39
"Mr.," 13, 24
"Mrs.," 13, 15, 24
"Ms.," 13, 24
Multiple-closed notations, 102

N

Name coding, preliminary, in a numeric file, 130
Newspapers, cross-referencing names of, 42; indexing names of, 38
Numbers, as indexing units, 25, 227; assigning of, in numeric file, 131; in business names, 25; on captions, 54, 55; use of, in subject file notations, 150
Numeric coding, 131
Numeric file, accession book or register, 130; advantages of a, 127; application folders in a, 127; arrangement of a, 129; captions in a, 129; color in a, 135; cross-references in a, 127; disadvantages in a, 128; folders in a, 129, 132; guides in a, 129; illustration of a, 128; index card control file, 129; main file, 127; miscellaneous alphabetic file, 129; nature and uses, 126; numbered captions in, 129; organization of a, 127; parts of a, 127
Numeric filing procedures, adding individual folders, 132; alphabetic sorting, 130; assigning numbers to correspondents and subjects, 131; cross-references, 131; inspection, 130; numeric coding, 131; placing material in folders, 132; preliminary name coding, 130; sorting for numeric filing, 132
Numeric-Name System, 136

O

Obscure domestic names, indexing, 27, 228
Obscure foreign names, indexing, 27, 228
On-call cards, 81
One-period transfer method, 89
One versus two units, 25
Open-shelf files, 181
Organizations, indexing names of, 228
ORGANIZER, 194
Out card, with printed lines, 72; with requisition slip, 72
Out folder, with printed sections, 74; with requisition slip, 74
Out guides, 184; lined and printed, 75; with requisition slip, 75
Out sheet, 73
Outgoing materials, filing copies of, 48
Overcrowding in miscellaneous folders, 57

P

Paper tape, 202
Papers, holding or disposing of, 84; values of various, 84
Parentheses, 13, 15, 22

Particles, foreign, 12, 26, 226
Periodic transfer method, 88
Periodicals, cross-referencing names of, 42; indexing names of, 38
Perpetual transfer method, 88
Personal correspondence, coding of, 62
Personal names, in business names, 21
Planetary camera, 206
Point system in calcualting space, 221
Political subdivisions, indexing names of, 40
Possessives, in indexing, 24, 227
Power-driven equipment, 189; advantages of, 168; for card files, 166; for correspondence files, 189
Power-driven visible card unit, 172
Prefix, 12, 26
Preliminary name coding, in numeric file, 130
Prepositions, disregarded in indexing, 22; rule for filing names when first name is a preposition, 22
Primary card guides, 5
Primary correspondence guides, 53
Professional titles, 13
Program in electronic data processing systems, 202
Programmer in electronic data processing systems, 202
Publications, indexing names of, 38; use of microfilm in, 211
Punched card systems, 197
Punched paper tape, 200
Punched tape filing, 202
Push-button control panel for a power-driven card file unit, 167

Q

Qualifications for the filing job, 3

R

Radio stations, indexing names of, 38
Random filing of card records, 176
Reader-printer, 205
Reader-viewer, 205
Reading correspondence, 60
Records, business, that should be filed, 3, 4, 5; controlling, 216; disposing of, 95, 96; information about, needed for developing control plan, 179; that should be filed, transferred, or discarded, 84; types of specialized, 190
Records control, cycle of, 96; equipment in, 178; planning for, 179; problems to be solved before ordering equipment and supplies, 179
Records control clerks, 2
Records control manual, 217
Records control systems, control of, 216; improving, 229
Records-retention schedule, 91, 224
Reduction ratio, in microfilming, 205
Release mark, 59
Religious institutions, indexing names of, 36
Religious titles, 13
Requisition sheet, 71
Requisition slip, 71
Research, use of microfilming in, 211

Retrieval control file, 94, 95
Rotary camera, 205, 206
Rotary equipment, 186
Rough sorting, 68

S

s apostrophe (s'), 24, 227
"Saint," foreign equivalents of, 15; rules for indexing names beginning wtih, 15
"Sainte," "San," "Santa," "Santo," "São," 15
Schools, indexing names of, 36, 37
"II (Second)," in indexing, 13
Secondary card guides, 6
Secondary correspondence guides, 54
Selective indexing, 33
Semiactive file, 219
"Senior," in indexing, 13
Seniority titles, 13
Separated single words, indexing, 25, 227
Service organizations, indexing names of, 35
Shelf-filing equipment, 181, 182
Shelf-filing unit, 51, 52
Shelves, in vertical card files, 166
Signals, for vertical card files, 165, 166; for visible records, 170, 171; types of, for vertical-visible files, 174
Similar names, cross-referencing of, 43
Single-letter notations, 101
Single letters, cross-referencing, 29; in business names, 22, 226
Single-unit notations, 102
Sorters, for aperture cards, 212; for correspondence, 194; in data processing, 198
Sorter and temporary file, 194
Sorting, alphabetic, in a numeric file, 130; fine, 68; in alphabetic correspondence filing, 67; in a geographic file, 118; in a numeric file, 132; in a subject file, 148; rough, 68
Soundex System, 136
Space, calculating the use of, 221; control of filing, 220; use of, in a very active system, 222
Special auxiliary card guides, 6
Special folders, 54; in an alphabetic correspondence file, 55, 56, 57; placing correspondence in, 68
Special geographic sections in an alphabetic correspondence file, 58
Special name sections in an alphabetic correspondence file, 58
Special subject section in an alphabetic correspondence file, 55, 56
Specialized records, control of, 190

Stencils, filing of, 193
Storage, equipment and supplies used in, 85; records required to maintain order and record statistics in, 94
Storage areas, 92
Storage record cards, 93
Street names, numbered, 14
Subdivisions, indexing names of political, 40
Subject decimal filing, 152
Subject file, arrangement of a, 142; direct alphabetic, 142, 143; encyclopedic, 142, 144, 145; folders in, 142; guides in, 142; illustration of a, 143, 145; illustration of alphabetic list of subjects in a, 140, 141, 144, 146; index to a, 148; master record of subject captions in a, 147; organizations having a, 141; out card, 146; subdivisions in a, 141; subject divisions in a, 140; types of, 142
Subject filing, comparison of various notations used in, 154; decimals in, 152; direct, 140; direct decimal, 152; in a centralized file, 142; in a geographic system, 122; index to, 148; nature of, 142; numeric file, 150; use of numbers and letters in notations, 150; uses of, 141
Subject filing procedure, coding, 147, 149; cross-references, 148, 149; inspection, 147; placing materials in folders, 148; sorting, 148
Subject guiding plan in a vertical card fiilng system, 163
Subject sections in alphabetic filing systems, 150
Subjects, as primary titles, indexing of, 41
Super-Ideal System, 100, 106
Supplementary card index, in a geographic file, 119; in a numeric file, 127, 129
Synagogues, indexing names of, 36

T

Tabs, cuts of, on card guides, 6; definition of, 5; folder, 49
Tabulating, in data processing, 199
Targets, 212
Television stations, indexing names of, 38
Temporary file, 194
Temporary very-active-file, 223
Terminal digit filing, 133, 135
"The," indexing names beginning with, 22
"III (Third)," in indexing, 13
Tickler file, 78; for destruction dates, 95
Time stamp, 59

Titles, in business names, 24, 227; in personal names, 13, 227; religious, 13
Transfer, control procedures for transferred records, 92; equipment and supplies used in, 85; purposes of, 85
Transfer boxes, 86, 92
Transfer cases, 87, 92
Transfer files, 85
Transfer folders, 87
Transfer methods, 88
Transfer policies, 91
Triple Check Automatic System, 136, 137
Two-period transfer method, 89

U

Ultrafiche, 207
United States Government, federal departments, rules for filing, 39
Universities, indexing names of, 37
Unusual names, cross-referencing, 18; indexing, 16, 228

V

Variadex System, 99, 105
Vertical cabinets, 51, 52, 180; ways to use, 181
Vertical card files, 161; equipment for, 166; guiding plans for, 161; signals for, 165, 166; subject guiding plan in, 163
Vertical-visible card file, illustration of, 174
Vertical-visible files, 168, 169; description of, 173; signals for, 174
Very active file, 219
Visible card files, 168; systems for, 169
Visible card unit, power-driven, 172
Visible cross-reference guide, 66; for a geographic file, 116
Visible panels for reference records, 172, 173
Visible records, signals for, 170, 171
Visible systems, types of, 168; and equipment, 168
VIS-U-TRIEVER, 172

W

Wheel files, 174, 175
Words disregarded in indexing, 22
Working space in a filing system, determining, 220

X

X, to indicate cross-reference in coding, 65, 66